D1160830

THE GREEK FATHERS

ADRIAN FORTESCUE

THE GREEK FATHERS
THEIR LIVES AND WRITINGS

*Isti in generationibus gentis suæ gloriam adepti sunt
et in diebus suis habentur in laudibus.*
—*SIRACH 44:7*

"These were famous among their own people
and praised in their own time."

IGNATIUS PRESS   SAN FRANCISCO

Original edition © 1908 by the Catholic Truth Society, London
and co-published with B. Herder, St. Louis, Missouri, in 1908
Published with ecclesiastical approval
Used by permission of The Catholic Truth Society

Cover art: *Saint Athanasius* (Mosaic)
S. Marco, Venice, Italy
Photo credit: Scala/Art Resource, N.Y.

Cover design by Riz Boncan Marsella

Published in 2006 Ignatius Press, San Francisco
ISBN 978-1-58617-013-4
Library of Congress Control Number 2006924089
Printed in the United States of America ⊗

ΝΙΚΟΛΑΩΙ ΤΩΙ ΟΡΘΟΔΟΞΩΙ

ΑΔΡΙΑΝΟΣ Ο ΚΑΘΟΛΙΚΟΣ

ΑΜΦΟΙΝ ΤΩΝ ΠΑΤΕΠΩΝ

ΤΟΥΣ ΒΙΟΥΣ

CONTENTS

FOREWORD

As ever when approaching one of Adrian Fortescue's works, prepare yourself for a treat. For in these pages we will travel extensively throughout the ancient Christian East, from Alexandria to Caesarea, from Constantinople to Jerusalem, to Alexandria again and thence to Damascus, "the real eternal city" in Fortescue's estimation.

We will be introduced as if in person to the great Greek Fathers of the fourth, fifth and eighth centuries of the Church's history: to the great Father of the Christological debates, Saint Athanasius; to Saint Basil, "one of the greatest of that younger generation of Catholic bishops who carried on the fight that Athanasius had fought and finally stamped out the Arian heresy". We will meet Saint Basil's dear friend, Saint Gregory Nazianzen, "the patron saint of people who do not want to be bishops", and Saint John Chrysostom, the "great model and patron of preachers". There are also two Saints Cyril to encounter: the first, of Jerusalem, who spent sixteen of the thirty-five years of his episcopate in banishment, and the second, of Alexandria, the champion of the Mother of God against the Nestorian heresy. Finally we will meet the eighth-century Saint John of Damascus, the first of the Christian Aristotelians who lived his entire life under Muslim rule.

Through Fortescue's introductions we will learn Catholic theology by reliving the gritty events in which it was originally hammered out. We will see its champions suffer and at times take questionable paths. Yet we will also witness their fortitude and perseverance and glimpse in their struggles a tangible sanctity from which any age—not least our own—can learn very much indeed.

For Adrian Fortescue (1874–1923), a true polyglot, while an utterly English Roman-rite priest, possessed the heart of an Eastern Catholic. He travelled extensively in the East and wrote prolifically about their churches, doing much to raise the awareness of many Westerners in respect of the life and traditions of our Eastern brethren. So Eastern were Fortescue's sensibilities that in 1908 he seriously considered giving his priestly services to Cyril VIII, the Melkite Catholic Patriarch of Damascus (1902–1916), with whom he had stayed for the greater part of December 1906. The Patriarch was prepared to go personally to Pope Saint Pius X in order to gain Fortescue's release from England to work in Damascus.

In fact, it was with this prospect uppermost in his mind that Fortescue wrote *The Greek Fathers*. For in the same letter (February 16, 1908) in which he confided his Damascene aspirations to a close friend, he reported:

> Now I am tearing through John Chrysostom (nice person) and making purple patches about the great and God-beloved city of Antioch. He ought to be done on Wednesday; then Gregory of Nazianzum (I can't stand him), two Cyrils & John Damascene (meek person who loved Damascus—like me in many ways). They ought to all be done in a fortnight.

But Fortescue remained in England. Later that year he wrote (November 30, 1908) that Cyril VIII was angry with him because "I am shut up in a distant grey island under cloudy skies; but my soul is back in the land of Syria sleeping under the apricot trees, where the waters of Barada splash in the fountains under the hot sky and the camels growl by the shady vaults of the gates." Under those grey skies he continued faithfully to pastor his small new parish of Saint Hugh, Letchworth, to write his "purple patches" on the Christian East and to love the Church Catholic, East and West.

Fortescue's love for the East, combined with his refined intelligence and wide experience of the East, is why he is such a reliable guide. And it is one reason why, a century later, one ought to read this book. Certainly, much has been written about these Fathers in the intervening years, but his passion for the people, events and churches that this work encompasses retains its value.

Fear not his style. As the above excerpt from his correspondence illustrates, he frequently says what he thinks. And his ecclesiology is stark, as stark as that of the subjects of these biographies, indeed, perhaps too much so for some contemporary ears. Yet his straight-speaking comes from his conviction that a man must speak the truth, and if his writing thus helps us to examine our own tendency to obfuscate it, perhaps he has done us good service thereby.

Not unnaturally Adrian Fortescue's considerable gifts led him to dream of becoming the bishop's secretary, of eventually himself donning the bishop's purple and even a cardinal's hat. That was not to be. As well as contemplating becoming a priest of an Eastern Catholic Church, in 1909 he sought admission to the Benedictine Abbey of Melk in Austria. This, too, never came to pass. In God's Providence his lot remained that of the founding rector of a small rural parish. He considered himself "not really very good" at parish work, yet he boasted to friends that his little church was "the only church worth looking at west of Constantinople". After his early death from cancer in 1923 it became apparent just how fine a pastor he in fact had been, and indeed how fine a church he had built.

Indeed, Fortescue "scribbled" day and night in order to make ends meet. Nothing but the best would suffice for the parish of Saint Hugh. His writings were an exercise of his scholarship, yes, but they were above all an oblation ordered to the greater glory of Almighty God. They were also ordered to the edification of the Church. For as retiring and sensitive as Fortescue was by nature, he could not allow an opportunity to pass wherein he was able to introduce others to aspects of Catholic tradition of which they were unaware—he was a natural and gifted teacher. Hence this volume's thoroughly enjoyable, profound introduction to our Greek Fathers.

When we have travelled the East with Fortescue these Fathers will no longer be mere figures of early Church history. Yes, we shall have enjoyed Fortescue's style and yes, we shall have grown in wisdom and knowledge from his erudition. But we shall also have gained some new friends, the great Fathers of the early Eastern Church, to whom in this life, as we strive faithfully to live and hand on the faith that was theirs, we can turn in the communion of saints for the benefit of their example and the assistance of their intercession, especially on their liturgical feasts, and with whom we hope to enjoy the next. Please God our guide, also, is in a position to assist us today not only through his writing of a century ago, but also with his prayers.

Alcuin Reid
March 27, 2007

EDITOR'S NOTE

Father Adrian Fortescue ended each chapter of his original edition of this book with a bibliography. These bibliographies contained many foreign language sources that are long out of print. The present edition omits these no longer helpful lists.

Father Fortescue's preference for spelling, especially of Greek names, has generally been retained. A few names have been updated to reflect the now universally standard spelling. Occasional obsolete words have been replaced by their synonyms. Also, asterisked or bracketed notes have been inserted by the editor to give post–Vatican II feast dates for saints or to indicate material that may now be obsolete. We hope that these minor changes will prove helpful to the reader.

PREFACE

What is a *Father?* The word is used in various senses. Bishops are our Fathers in God, and the Chief Bishop is called, as by a special title, the Holy Father. The name Father is also given correctly to priests. The members of a general Council are the "Fathers" of Nicæa, of Ephesus, of Trent. And then by common consent rather than by any formal rule we speak of certain famous Christian writers as the *Fathers of the Church*.

For anyone to be called a Father of the Church these four conditions must be met. First, he must be an *author*, whose works are still extant. The Fathers are important because they are quoted as authorities in theology. Obviously, then, they are all people who wrote works that we can quote. Saint Antony the Hermit, Saint Lawrence, Saint Sebastian are not Church Fathers because they have left no writings. Secondly, he must be a *Catholic*, who lived in the communion of the Church, whose writings are correct and orthodox. Otherwise the writer's authority is of no value as a witness of the Catholic faith. Apollinaris of Laodicea (d. ca. 390) and Tertullian (d. 240) were learned and prolific authors; but they are not Fathers because they were heretics. Thirdly, a Father is a person of eminent *sanctity* as well as learning. The title is an honourable one given only to saints, or rather it includes and involves the title of saint.[1]

---

[1] The legal process of canonization is a late development. Pope Alexander III in 1170 made the first rule about it. The present law dates from Pope Urban VIII in 1634. None of the Fathers was ever formally canonized. The

So Clement of Alexandria (d. ca. 217) and Origen (d. 254) are not strictly Fathers, because they are not saints. As a matter of fact, the root of the matter in this case, too, is the want of orthodoxy that prevents them from being either saints or Fathers. The fourth criterion is *antiquity*. This is the most difficult one to determine exactly. Antiquity of some kind is always supposed. The Fathers are the great authorities for ancient tradition; they are witnesses of the faith in earlier times. The age of the Fathers begins at once after that of the apostles; it is not so easy to say when it ends. No one calls Saint Thomas Aquinas (d. 1274) or Saint Francis de Sales (d. 1622) a Father, because of their late dates. The Fathers end when the middle ages begin; and there is no clear line of division here. Practically, there is a chain of great Catholic writers, whom we call the Fathers, in east and west; then after a time of comparative stagnation begins another line—that of the Schoolmen. It is in the case of a few saints who come in the intermediate time that one may doubt whether they are to be called the last Fathers or the first mediæval writers. In the east, the connected line ends with Saint Cyril of Alexandria (d. 444), in the west with Saint Gregory I (d. 604). After a long break come Saint John Damascene (d. ca. 754) in the east and Saint Bernard of Clairvaux (d. 1153) in the west. These two are generally called the last of the Fathers, though Saint Bernard, at any rate, certainly belongs to the middle ages. By taking the eighth century as the limit, and by allowing Saint Bernard as the one later exception (since by common use he is called a Father), we shall fix our period as it is generally accepted. Any saint, therefore, who wrote in defence

title *saint* (much less of a technical term in Latin or Greek) was given originally by general consent, vaguely controlled by the local bishops.

of the Catholic faith between the first and the eighth centuries and whose works are still extant is a Father of the Church.[2] The Fathers are then further divided into these five classes: (1) The *apostolic Fathers*, first in order of time and first in importance in every way. They are the immediate disciples of the apostles, whose age ends at latest by the year 150. All wrote in Greek. (2) The *apologists*, who lived during the persecutions and wrote apologies of the Christian faith against Jews and pagans, nearly all in Greek. Their age ends when Constantine became emperor (323). The *great Fathers*,[3] who wrote against the heresies of the fourth and fifth centuries, and so on till the beginning of the middle ages, namely, (3) the *Greek Fathers*, (4) the *Latin Fathers*, and (5) the *eastern Fathers*, chiefly Syrian, with whom may be classed any who wrote in Coptic, Armenian or other eastern language.[4]

This little book contains outlines of the lives of the great Greek Fathers,[5] from Athanasius to John Damascene, with

[2] At the beginning we must of course mark off those writers of the New Testament who belong to a still higher class. No one counts St Paul as one of the Fathers. The title of *Doctor of the Church* (now given by an act of Papal authority) on the other hand involves no idea of antiquity. All the Fathers whose lives follow have been declared Doctors too; but the line of Doctors goes on till modern times. The last Doctor of the Church is St Alphonsus Liguori (d. 1787). [The author was writing this sentence in 1908.—ED.] The title is a general recognition of eminent service as a theologian.

[3] They are called *great* because their works are so much more voluminous. All the apostolic Fathers together make up a smaller book than the New Testament, whereas St Augustine alone, for instance, fills sixteen volumes of Migne.

[4] It is proposed to make other little books like this one, as soon as possible, that shall in the same manner treat of each of these other groups of Fathers.

[5] The spelling of the Greek names in this book is not consistent. It cannot be so unless one spells them all in Greek or all in Latin. Neither course seems possible. I wish one could spell all in Greek. But Athanasios, Basileios, Kyrillos would look pedantic and absurd. Still less would I make all Greek names into very bad Latin. That some such forms have made their way into English is no good reason for increasing the evil by making more. So I have

lists of their chief works.[6] No one will expect to find anything new in what does not profess to be more than a series
of popular sketches. The only object of the book is to give
in a small space, and in English, a general account of what
is commonly known about these Fathers. I have described
their lives and adventures rather than their systems of theology. It is true that most Fathers owe their importance
chiefly to their works and to the theology contained therein.
But to understand discussions about their schools and principles requires at least some training in technical theology;
and this little book is meant for laymen. My object has
been less ambitious than a scientific investigation of the
growth of theology. All these Fathers have another side too.
Apart from their writings they stand out as great figures in
the Church history of their time. They are mighty patriarchs
or famous bishops, they lead councils, resist Cæsar and suffer

---

used such Latin forms as seem too well known to be avoided; and have left
all the others in Greek. Once one accepts this rule it is a matter of detail
how many names fall into either class. I have reduced the Latinized ones and
spelt in Greek as far as I dared. No doubt some people would put many in
sham-Latin that I have left Greek. Certainly by using mixed principles one
lays oneself open to an obvious objection of inconsistency: If one writes
Athanasius, why not *Eusebius?* We could go further and ask, if *Basil*, why not
Euseb; if *Antony*, why not *Euseby*; if *Antioch*, why not *Heracl?* I think the
answer is that we all treat names in this way in every language. When a form
is well known we use it, as *Rome, Milan, Naples, Vienna*; but in the case of
smaller and less known names we leave them in their own language—*Rocca
di Papa, San Michele, Heilig-Kreuz*. In English we all say *Florence*; but we all
say *Fiesole*. I have done just in the same way in the case of these Greek
names, except perhaps that I have admitted as few as possible to the well-
known and therefore mutilated class.

[6] I have quoted the works in Latin too, as they are very often referred to
under Latin titles, and it may be easier to find them by the Latin names. I
have also in each case given an exact reference to the volume and page where
they will be found in Migne's *Patrologia Græca*. Migne is very far from being
the ideal edition, but it is the one still commonly used and best known.

persecution. It is in this light that I have tried to present them. It is easier to understand and appreciate this side of their lives than to follow the development of Origenism. And it will be something gained if people who are not prepared to study a treatise of technical dogmatics have at least an idea of who these Fathers were and what they did. For one does not need to be a Greek scholar nor a theologian to honour the memory of the Greek Fathers. They lived a long way off, a long time ago and spoke a strange tongue. But they are joined to us in a closer bond than any tie of race or language, for they, like us, were citizens of that great Kingdom of God on earth that stretches over land and sea and knows no division of nations. These Greek Fathers were Catholics as we are. They belonged to the great united and visible Church in communion with the holy Roman See, where sat the bishop whom they, too, obeyed as the successor of the Prince of the Apostles. What they defended was the Catholic faith that we profess. We, who are the heirs of so great a tradition, ought to know at least something about the story of the long chain that joins us back to the first Whitsunday. And if we are to know anything at all about Church history we must not forget the Greeks. Athanasius, Basil, Chrysostom should be something more than mere names to us. They were great and mighty men who stand out very clearly in the long and changing line that stretches now over twenty centuries. It would be a gross ingratitude to forget that they are just as important, did just as much for our cause as our own Latin Fathers.

Letchworth, May 2, 1908
Athanasii episc. conf. et doct. *duplex*.
Ἡ ἀνακομιδὴ τοῦ λειψάνου Ἀθανασίου τοῦ μεγάλου.
κατάλυσις οἴνου καὶ ἐλάιου.

CHAPTER ONE

SAINT ATHANASIUS (293–373)

Athanasius, some time Patriarch of Alexandria, is the first and, without question, the greatest of the Greek Fathers. The apostolic Fathers and apologists had written in Greek, but they form classes of their own. When we speak of the Greek Fathers, we mean the great saints who in the eastern part of the empire wrote defences of the faith in various forms after the age of persecution was over, during the time of the great heresies, that is, in the fourth and fifth centuries. Of these Greek Fathers, Saint Athanasius is the first in order of time. Against each of the heresies, the Church had some one great champion, one leader who stood for the Catholic side against the heretics as the chief defender of the faith, who was the acknowledged guide of the others. The first heresy after the persecution was Arianism; it was also the most disastrous and far-reaching in its effects. And Saint Athanasius was the defender of the faith against the Arians. There were others too, Saint Hilary in the west, Saint Basil and the Gregories. Every Father of this time has something to say against the Arians, but they all acknowledged Athanasius as their leader. From the beginning, he had been the chief opponent of Arius, so much so that "Athanasian" was often used as the name of the Catholic party, as opposed to "Arian". To tell the story of his life is practically to tell that of the Arian troubles. He lived through the whole movement. As a young deacon he saw it begin, and for nearly fifty years he fought it from his throne by the Nile. His name was always the watchword for either side. Every Arian synod declared its policy to be "away with Athanasius"; every Catholic synod took up his defence. Under five emperors and five popes, he was the one tower of strength and rallying point to all Catholics in that hopeless confusion of synods and anti-synods, banishments and usurpations. Five times he himself was driven into exile for the faith, and when at last he died in his own home, the most famous bishop of his time, he had won his fight; Arianism was practically dead too. And he left a name whose glory no length of time can ever make us forget.

1. The Beginning of Arianism

When Constantine (306–337) proclaimed the Edict of Milan (313), the Christians thought that the end of their troubles had come. The persecution was all over at last; no longer would anyone be banished or burnt or thrown to the beasts for the name of Christ. What could they foresee but that the Church should now settle down in peace, spread her boundaries on every side and reign united and triumphant till her Lord came again in power and glory, to found his thousand years of earthly paradise? Naturally they thought so; and yet never were people more mistaken. The great heresies were coming as successors to the great persecutions, and the Church was to be more troubled and to suffer greater evils from her own children than she had from the sword of the Roman magistrates. The first heresy was already brewing while the happy bishops were reading the new edict and thanking God for having sent his servant Constantine. During the very lifetime of the heroes who could show the glorious wounds they had received under Diocletian, the Christian Church was tossed by a raging storm that nearly wrecked her. Bishops fell on every side, intruders and counter-intruders filled every see, Anathemas and counter-Anathemas thundered across the empire from Tyre to Milan, so that the wretched layman who wanted to serve God in peace may well have wondered whether the old cry of *Christianos ad leones* were not on the whole pleasanter than the shouts of *Homoüsios* and *Homoiüsios*, of which he understood nothing except that, whichever he said, someone was sure to excommunicate him.

In the beginning of the fourth century, Bishop Alexander reigned at Alexandria. He too, no doubt counted on peace for his old age since Diocletian was gone, and he certainly did not foresee how great a storm would grow out of a little cloud that rose in his own city. For among his priests was one Arius, a Libyan from the south. Few men have left so unsavoury a memory as this Arius (Ἄρειος).[1] He had been a well-meaning and zealous person once and had narrowly escaped in the Diocletian persecution. If the Roman governor of Egypt had been a little more zealous we should, perhaps, now honour Saint Arius as a holy martyr, instead of shuddering when we hear his ill-omened name. He had then joined sides with Meletios of Lykopolis. This Meletios (quite a different person from Meletios of Antioch, who made a more famous schism sixty years later) had got into trouble with his patriarch,[2] apparently for ordaining people outside his diocese, and had made a small schism in 306. But Arius soon left his Meletian friends and was

---

[1] If we call him by the Latin form of his name, we must accentuate the *i* (Arīus) according to the Latin accent rule, because the *i* is long. In Greek, Ἄρειος is pro-paroxytone.

[2] Lykopolis is in Egypt.

ordained priest by Achillas of Alexandria, Alexander's predecessor, in 311. Under Alexander, we find him a parish
priest with a church in the city called the Baukalis (ἡ
Βαύκαλις). Epiphanios says that he was a tall, thin, ascetic-
looking man, well-educated, popular with his parishioners,
especially with pious women.[3] He explained the Scriptures,[4] and in this explanation the poison appears, for what
he taught was Subordinationism.

It will be well to explain at once what all the trouble was
about, by drawing up the points in which Arius and his
followers were heretics. In the first place, Arianism did not
spring full-grown and fully armed at one moment from the
mind of one man. We know now that no heresy ever really
began like that. It is never the case that one man out of
sheer wickedness suddenly invents a false doctrine. We can
always trace germs and tendencies, that afterward develop
into the heresy, back to many years before the father of the
sect was born. A movement begins, often very rightly, by
insisting on one aspect of the faith; very often at first it is
a vigorous and extreme opposition to some patently false
teaching. Then this way of looking at things crystallizes and
hardens; it is taken up enthusiastically by some school, it
becomes a point of honour with a certain party to insist
upon it, it is the national teaching of some country. At last,
someone gets hold of the theory, oversteps every limit in
his defence of it, and is eagerly supported by the rest of the
party. And then he finds himself condemned by the Church,
and his name goes down to history as that of a heresiarch.

It was just so with Arius. Centuries before he was
born, learned and most pious persons naturally had been

---

[3] Epiphanios, *Hær.* lxix, 3 and 9.
[4] Theodoret, *Hist. Eccl.* i, 2.

concerned as to how we are to conceive the relation between
the Persons of the holy Trinity. It was especially the relation between God the Father and God the Son that was in
question—one hears less about the procession of the Holy
Spirit at this time. Christians declared their belief in one
God. But they were everlastingly accused by Jews and pagans
of having at least two. Did they adore the God of Israel?
Certainly. Then if Jesus is a God as well, there are two
Gods, or is he the God of Israel, and if so who is the Father
to whom they pray through him? A certain Sabellius, who
had lived in Rome under Pope Zephyrinos (202–218) had
tried to solve this difficulty by explaining that God the
Father and God the Son were merely two names for exactly
the same Person. There is only one God. To the Jews,
he had revealed himself as the Father, and then he had been
pleased to become man and be called the Son and the Word
of God. Whenever he in the Gospels seems to distinguish
between himself and the Father it is only a manner of
speaking. Father and Son are only two modes of existence
of the same Person. That is the *Sabellian* heresy:
we hear of it also as *Modalism* and *Patripassianism* (*"Pater
passus"*, the Father suffered, meaning that God the Father
became man and was crucified). Against this, the right teaching insisted on the real difference between God the Father
and God the Son. Some people in opposing Sabellius went
too far. The great Origen (d. 254) was one. If the Sabellians quoted the text, "I and the Father are one" (Jn 10:30),
he and his school answered with the other text, "The
Father is greater than I" (Jn 14:28). These extreme
anti-Sabellians maintained that not only is God
the Son really a different Person from the Father, he is even
less than the Father. They knew him to be the Son of
God, but is not a son necessarily in some way less than his

father? So there arose the school of those who, while still calling our Lord God, thought that in some vague way he is not quite so much God as God the Father. These people are the *Subordinationists*—they subordinate the Son to the Father. And Arianism is nothing but an extreme form of Subordinationism.

There were many Subordinationists before Arius. Paul of Samosata (Patriarch of Antioch, 260–269) taught something of the kind, further complicated by a distinction of person between the Logos and the man Jesus Christ,[5] and Lucian (d. 311), a priest of Antioch and martyr at Nicomedia under Diocletian, taught Subordinationism at the Antiochene school. It is very significant that Arius had been his pupil. From this master, then, the heretic had learned what he taught at the Baukalis church at Alexandria. He further developed the theory and at last it took this form. The root of the heresy is that God the Son is not equal to God the Father. In its perfect form, Arianism may be summed up in these six points: (1) The Son did not exist from eternity. If he is the Son, he must have been born at some moment; so before his birth he did not exist. "There was a time when he was not"[6] was the favourite Arian formula. (2) He is not begotten of the essence of the Father—God's essence cannot be divided—but he was created by the Father out of nothing. (3) He is therefore a creature (ποίημα, κτίσμα). (4) He is the first and most exalted creature, through whom God created all the others. This is the Neo-platonic idea that God would be defiled by touching matter, so he creates and rules the world through an intermediary, a

---

[5] So this Paul had the unique distinction of being the remote ancestor of two famous heresies—Arianism and Nestorianism.

[6] Ἦν ποτε ὅτε οὐκ ἦν.

Demiurg (Δημιουργός). (5) He may be called God, but only
in an extended and analogical sense; the Father made him
a sort of God by his grace. (6) His will is created and fal-
lible. He could commit sin. That is the teaching of which
Arius at Alexandria maintained at any rate the germ.

In 318, the Patriarch Alexander heard of the trouble;
he was told that Arius had fallen foul of other priests
because of his Subordinationism. So he sent for him and
reprimanded him. But Arius was obstinate and went on
forming a party that included even many nuns. So in 321
Alexander summoned a synod to examine the matter. It
should be noted as a sign of the great power and extent of
the patriarchate of Saint Mark that no less than one hundred suffragan bishops of Alexandria attended this synod.
They condemned and excommunicated Arius with all his
followers, who included already two Egyptian bishops, Secundus of Ptolemais and Theonas of Marmarica. And while
Alexander presided, by his side as his counsellor and secretary sat a young deacon, Athanasius.

2. Saint Athanasius' Early Life

The saint who from this point becomes the chief opponent
of Arius was then just twenty-eight years old. Various state-
ments made by people who lived at the time make it practically certain that he was born in the year 293.[7] His parents
were probably Christians; they were certainly Greeks of Alexandria, members of the great Greek colony that filled that
city to the exclusion of native Egyptians (Copts) since the

---

[7] The chief witness is a Coptic panegyric (edited by O. V. Lemm in the
Mémoires de l'académie imp. des sciences de St. Pétersbourg, série vii, vol. 36, n. 11
[Petersburg, 1888]), which says that when he became patriarch in 326 he was
thirty-three years old.

Ptolemies had reigned there (B.C. 323–B.C. 30). Apart from the fact that Athanasius never spoke or wrote any language but Greek and Latin, his name[8] shows that he was one of that great multitude of people, either born Greeks or completely Hellenized, who filled the towns of the Levant since Alexander (336–323 B.C.). One must remember that at this time all the cities in eastern Europe, Syria and Egypt were Greek. Peasants went on speaking the old languages of their countries, but everyone who had any claim to culture, all townsmen, philosophers, governors and bishops used what was the common tongue of the east, the late form of Greek that we call Hellenic. Latin in the west and Greek in the east were the two languages of the civilized world.

Of Saint Athanasius' early years we know little but what we can conclude from his later writings; and there is one legend that we should not take seriously. He certainly had what we should call a liberal education. His city, Alexandria, was at that time the chief centre of learning in the empire, and its schools were the most famous in the world. That he attended these schools and there read the Greek classics whose study formed scholarship in his days is plain from the allusions he makes to them throughout his life. Homer was the fountain of culture to Greeks always, and Athanasius knew Homer very well (cf., e.g., *Orationes* IV *contra arianos*, 29). He knew Plato too and could discuss Platonic and Neo-platonic theories (*Oratio contra gentes*, 40). His language is always that of a late Greek philosopher; he writes naturally of archetypes and universals and categories and immanent ideas. Sulpicius Severus (ii, 36) says he had studied Roman law. When he was accused at the Council of Tyre (335) he was able to expose flaws in the technical

---

[8] Athanasios (Ἀθανάσιος) is Greek for *Immortal*.

legality of the case against him.[9] And, lastly, he most certainly had studied the Bible. Few of the Fathers refer to it so constantly as he does; he quotes from every book and has a special ease in quoting every kind of text that suits his purpose. In reading his writings, one has the impression that he almost knows the Bible by heart—so ready is he always with a passage, often with one that seems quite out of the way, to prove his point. So Saint Gregory of Nazianzos only confirms what we should in any case have found out from his works by telling us that he was very learned in both the Christian faith and profane letters.[10] For the rest he is not eloquent nor brilliant. He never rises to the splendid style of Saint Basil, nor does he scatter flowers of rhetoric over his work like Saint John Chrysostom. He is dignified, very determined, short and categorical in his assertions, clear and uncompromising rather than persuasive. In his manner he has something of the Latin.

The legend about his childhood is one of the famous stories that are told of great saints. One day when Alexander the Patriarch was looking out of the window of his house he saw some children playing at church. Among them was Athanasius, who was taking the leading part as bishop. He was baptizing the other boys. Alexander was so impressed by what he saw that he foretold great things of this boy's future, and from that moment took him under his special care. He further asked very exactly how Athanasius had performed the rite of baptism in his play and, finding that everything had been done quite rightly, he recognized the baptisms as valid and would not allow these other boys to be baptized again. The story is told by Rufinus (*Hist. Eccl.* i, 14)

[9] Sokrates, *Hist. Eccl.* i, 31.
[10] Gregory of Nazianzos, *Oratio pan.* xxi, 6.

and repeated by Sokrates (*Hist. Eccl.* i, 15). The dates make it very unlikely. Alexander began to reign in 313, so Athanasius was then already seventeen years old. And boys of seventeen do not play at church—Greek boys in the fourth century still less than western boys now. Moreover it is less edifying than it at first seems. That Athanasius did all the rites correctly is very well—but what about his intention? Rufinus and Sokrates did not think of that. But boys playing at baptizing have not anything like the intention that is required for sacraments. So any theologian would say at once that these baptism-games were invalid from want of intention, as well as exceedingly naughty.

To come back to what are real facts. Athanasius was ordained Lector (ἀναγνώστης, *lector*) either by Alexander or by his predecessor Achillas; and he served as Lector six years.[11] Then he was made deacon and became a kind of secretary to Alexander, who was a very old man. During this first period, before the Arian troubles began, he had already written two theological works—*A Treatise against the Heathen* and *On the Incarnation* (see p. 39 below). It was also during this time that he made friends with the first monks, the hermits who had fled from the world to the great desert south of Egypt. His admiration for and friendship with these holy men lasted through his life. He knew Saint Antony (whose life he afterward wrote, p. 40) and Pachomios well. He had stayed with them in their huts and had waited on them as a young man. So close were his relations and so often had he shared their life, that after he had become patriarch his bishops describe him as having been "one of the monks".[12] It was as an already

---

[11] Coptic panegyric, in Lemm, *Mémoires*, p. 30.
[12] Athanasius, *Apol. contra arianos*, 6.

well-known man and as the confidential friend of the patriarch that he attended the first synod against Arius. And
when Alexander, four years later, went to expose his case
against this new heretic to the great council at Nicæa, he
naturally took Athanasius with him as his theologian.

3. The First General Council (Nicæa I, 325)

Arius then was condemned and excommunicated by his patriarch, and by the whole Church of Egypt. But it did not occur
to him to submit and retract his views. We have seen that
he had large ideas about the independence of clergy from
their superiors, and that he had shown them in the affair of
Meletios of Lykopolis. Now he found that he could not do
much in Egypt—Alexander was too strong for him; so he
fortified his party, arranged an alliance with his old friends
the schismatical Meletians (they all eventually became Arians), told his followers to be true to the Subordinationist
faith and await his return and set off across the sea to Syria.

Arrived here he persuaded a number of bishops to join
him and wandered about Syria and Asia Minor making converts. He explained his ideas speciously enough, declared
that of course he taught the Divinity of Christ—in a wider
sense, that he had not had a fair hearing, and so on; his
opponents, who called him a Subordinationist, were themselves Sabellians. So in a short time he had an even greater
following in Syria than in Egypt. His chief convert was Eusebeios, Bishop of Nicomedia, an important person and distant relation of Constantine himself, who became a leader
of the extreme wing of strict Arians, and eventually lived
to baptize the emperor. From Syria, Arius wrote a meekly
complaining letter to Alexander, and here he also composed a curious work containing discussions of theological

questions, half in prose and half in verse, which he called the *Thaleia* (θάλεια, festival).[13] He also wrote songs for sailors, travellers, millers, etc.[14] His ideas by this time were known to everyone, and even the heathen began to make jokes on the stage about these disputes among Christians. Alexander had written encyclicals to other bishops warning them against Arius and showing that his teaching was simply a revival of that of Paul of Samosata and Lucian of Antioch. Then Arius in about 323 came back to Alexandria and defied the patriarch in his own city. Some bishops, notably Eusebeios of Cæsarea (the future father of Church history, d. 340), tried to arrange a compromise and to suggest explanations that both Catholics and Arians could accept. These compromisers are the beginning of the great semi-Arian party. But then, as always, the Catholic Church would have no compromise and no shuffling formulas. Arius was utterly and completely wrong, and his teaching must be utterly condemned. You must be either a Catholic or an Arian.

Constantine came to Nicomedia in 323, after he had defeated Licinius, and there the Bishop Eusebeios told him all about this new quarrel. The emperor was immeasurably annoyed. He neither understood nor cared anything at all about the nature of God the Son. He was not a Christian, though it suited him to protect Christians. But above all he wanted union and concord. He had at last succeeded in joining the whole empire together under himself, and he wanted no more disturbance. He was braving the anger of the immortal gods by being friendly to these Christians,

[13] The *Thaleia* has disappeared, but fragments of it are quoted in St Athanasius' works.

[14] Philostorgios, *Hist. Eccl.* ii, 1.

and now he found that the Christians had two parties and, whichever he defended, he would have the other for an enemy. So he thought that he could patch it all up before the trouble went any further. He sent Hosius, Bishop of Cordova, with letters to both Alexander and Arius at Alexandria. He told both that the whole question does not matter in the very least—what is the good of quarrelling over words? Arius ought not to have begun, and Alexander ought not to have stopped him when he did begin. Now they must both be quiet and say whatever they like, only not annoy each other. Constantine was a person with a modern mind. Obviously his letters did no good. Arius had the courage of his convictions as much as the Catholics, and of course, quite rightly, neither side would consent to tolerate the other. So then Constantine proposed his second plan: let all the bishops come to discuss the matter at Nicæa in Bithynia. He provided carriages and horses, and offered them hospitality while the council lasted.

From every part of the Levant, the bishops came, venerable fathers who had seen the days of persecution, many of whom still bore the marks of torture suffered for Christ, some famous as workers of miracles, others renowned for their learning. From Egypt they hurried across Syria, Potamon of Herakleia, Paphnutios of the Thebais, from far Nisibis came James, Nicholas from Myra, Leontios from Cæsarea in Cappadocia, Spiridion across the sea from Cyprus, Eustathios from the great and God-beloved city of Antioch, Makarios from the Holy Place where the tomb of Christ still lay hidden. From Africa came Cæcilian of Carthage, Mark of Calabria from Italy, Nicasius from distant Gaul, and Hosius from the Gates of the West by the Pillars of Hercules. And old Alexander, the great Lord of Christian Egypt, came with his deacon. Three hundred and eighteen fathers met at the city to whose name they were to give undying honour, so that even now the Christian traveller in Asia Minor braves the difficult journey to an unsavoury Turkish village, that at *Isnik* he may stand by the shattered palace wall and dream of the meeting of the fathers at the first and most famous of all œcumenical synods.[15] It is not necessary to tell again the story of that great synod. Arius appeared, was heard and condemned. He and his followers were solemnly excommunicated; and the emperor added a sentence of banishment. The council settled other questions too, the Meletian trouble in Egypt, the keeping of Easter and the validity of doubtful baptisms. It sat through the summer, and when all was finished, Constantine entertained the fathers at a great banquet and sent them home again. He had sat in the place of honour and had opened the proceedings with a speech. But Hosius of Cordova signed the acts first, "In the name of the Church of Rome, the Churches of Italy, Spain and all the West"; and with him sign two Roman priests, Vitus and Vincent.[16] So although the first of the patriarchs was not present, he was represented by his legates. And still Sunday after Sunday we sing at Mass the creed drawn up by this council. It is not a general profession containing the whole Catholic faith, but a definite opposition to Arius' heresy. So the memory of this first great heresy and of the venerable assembly at Nicæa

[15] The first Council of Nicæa (325) is so much the most famous of all, that when we say simply the "Council of Nicæa" or "Nicene synod", this one is always meant. There was, however, a second Council of Nicæa (the seventh general Council, in 787) against the Iconoclasts. All the eastern Churches still keep a feast in memory of "the 318 holy and God-inspired Nicene Fathers" (the Orthodox and Melkites on the Sunday in the Octave of the Ascension).

[16] Mansi, ii, 692, etc.; 882, 927.

hovers round our altars as we, too, declare our faith in the absolute equality of God the Son and God the Father; it is the voice of the 318 "holy and divinely inspired fathers" that sounds through our churches still after seventeen centuries, as we declare against the Arians that we believe in one Lord Jesus Christ "ex Patre natum ante omnia sæcula. Deum de Deo, lumen de lumine, Deum verum de Deo vero. Genitum non factum, consubstantialem Patri, per quem omnia facta sunt." [17] And throughout the council already the chief defender of the Catholics—their chief spokesman against Arius, Eusebeios of Nicomedia and the other heretics—was Alexander's deacon, Athanasius.

4. Athanasius, Patriarch (328)

Three years after Alexander came home from Nicæa, he died (April 17, 328). It is said that he had already strongly recommended his clergy to elect Athanasius as his successor (Sozomenos, *Hist. Eccl.* ii, 17). But in any case that was a foregone conclusion. Very grave and troublesome times had already begun in Egypt, and no Catholic could have doubted for a moment that there was only one man fit to take up the burden left by the dead bishop. By an overwhelming majority, Athanasius was elected Patriarch of Alexandria (*Apol. contra arianos*, vi). He was consecrated by his suffragans; and from now till his death, for forty-five years

[17] The council drew up twenty canons about points of discipline, Anathemas against the Arians and especially the Nicene creed, which, however, ends with the words: "and in the Holy Spirit". The rest of the creed we now say was added later, probably by the next general Council (Constantinople I, 381; but see Mgr Duchesne, *Églises séparées* [Paris, 1905], p. 79). The original Nicene creed is in *Denzinger*, nos. 17, 18. There were about twenty bishops present who favoured Arius, but most of them retracted. The history of the council is given by Karl J. von Hefele, *Conziliengeschichte*, 2nd ed., I, 252ff.

(328–373) he filled the succession of Saint Mark in the second see of Christendom, of which his name has become
the chief glory.

The title *patriarch* in the fourth century was still used
loosely for any specially venerable bishop; it did not become
the technical name of a definite rank in the hierarchy till
gradually in the fifth and sixth centuries. But in the time
of Athanasius there was no doubt as to the fact that high
above all other bishops, metropolitans and primates stood
three great Princes of the Church at Rome, Alexandria
and Antioch. He did not live to see the slowly climbing
ambition of Constantinople, and though the Nicene synod
had given special honour to Jerusalem, it had refused it
any place even among the metropolitan sees (can. 7). That
synod had recognized the "ancient custom" that gave the
first places to the three old sees only (can. 6); so during
Saint Athanasius' life no one disputed that Alexandria
was the first throne in the east, the second (after Rome)
in the whole Christian world. He ruled all Egypt and the
lands to the south, Ethiopia[18] and part of Nubia that were
converted from Egypt. And whether he sat on his throne
by the great harbour in the richest and most famous centre of the Hellenic world, or wandered in exile in the
west, or the desert, every Catholic looked up to Athanasius as the Lord of the East, who brought to their cause
not only his learning and virtues, but the honour of so
great a see. And yet, great as was the place he filled, there
was little cause to envy him. When the bishops left Nicæa,
they must have thought that the trouble was all over. The
Church had spoken. For the first time since the apostles

---

[18] In the second year of his reign (329), Athanasius ordained St Frumen-
tius Bishop of Axuma and sent him to convert the Ethiopians.

had settled the question of the old law at Jerusalem (Acts 15:6–29), she had solemnly declared her faith by a general assembly of her rulers. Here was a plain case to which to apply the text: "Who hears you hears me, and who despises you despises me" (Lk 10:16). And Cæsar had spoken too, so that whoever was not moved by excommunication would be by banishment. And yet the Arian troubles had really only just begun. The council that should have ended the whole question only closed the first and shortest period of its history. From that point till the end of the century, the storm became steadily worse and worse. The beginning of the reaction against the council was when Constantine, who had hitherto been the stern enemy of the Arians, suddenly veered round and began to be their friend. His sister Constantia, widow of Licinius, was an Arian. She died in 328, and on her death-bed she implored the emperor to have pity on Arius and his banished friends. We have seen that Constantine had never really understood the question at issue. He had no convictions of his own, and so he was easily moved to change his policy. From then till his death he became a favourer and protector of the heretics, and under his sons, too, they had the court on their side as long as the movement lasted. First the banished Arian bishops were recalled; then they did all they could to force Athanasius to restore Arius at Alexandria. When they saw how utterly hopeless were all such attempts, and that in any case they would never be able to make Athanasius even temporize, they began the long career of calumny against him, and of persecution, that lasted nearly till his death. At this point there also began that endless series of Arian and semi-Arian synods that fill up the history of this heresy. Before we come to them we may here give an outline of the different parties into which the Arian body broke up after the Council of Nicæa.

5. The Arians and Semi-Arians

The Nicene synod had declared that our Lord is *consubstantial* with God the Father. That is a Latin word meaning "of the same nature". The Father and Son have the same identical divine nature; they are different persons in the same nature or substance. So obviously they are absolutely equal. Comparisons are made according to the natures of the things compared, and they have, not equal natures, but the very same nature. That is the Catholic faith that we have all learned in our catechisms. "Consubstantial" is Latin. We have it from the Latin translation of the Nicene creed. The original Greek word is *Homooüsios*[19] (ὁμοούσιος). This word became the test-word of the Catholics. Whoever said our Lord is "Homooüsios" to the Father was a Catholic and no Arian. *Homooüsians* were Athanasians, Athanasians were Nicenes, and Nicenes were Catholics. So we have a plain test for one side. The other side was, as heretics usually are, divided against itself. They all agreed in denying Homooüsios—the negative agreement one always finds; whatever they may think, they do not think what the Church has defined. Out of very complicated ramifications we can distinguish three chief parties of anti-Nicenes, though the boundaries between them were vague and changeable. First there were the strict and uncompromising Arians. Their words were *Anomoios* (ἀνόμοιος, "unlike") or *Heteromousios* (ἑτερομούσιος "of another nature").

---

[19] Whoever wishes to pronounce Greek properly must never sound the letter H in it. *Consubstantialis Patri* (in the creed) in Greek is ὁμοούσιος τῷ πατρί.

They said that our Lord is simply unlike, of a quite different nature from God the Father. Of these was Arius himself as long as he lived, Eunomios of Kyzikos[20] and Aetios, a deacon of Antioch. They are called *strict Arians*, *Anomoeans* and *Eunomians*. Then there were the people who hoped for a compromise between Athanasius and Arius, the people who thought both went too far and that a *via media* could be arranged by taking what is good from both. We know them in all controversies, the people who tell us that no doubt there is a great deal to be said on both sides. In this controversy that attitude was represented by the *semi-Arians*, and, as usual, they satisfied no one. Their word was *Homoioüsios* (ὁμοιούσιος, "of a similar nature"). They thought our Lord was neither of quite the same nor of a quite different nature. His nature was similar, very like, almost the same as that of the Father. The semi-Arians formed for a time a very large party of their own. Their leaders were Basil of Ankyra,[21] George of Laodicea, Theodore of Herakleia and, in the west, Auxentius of Milan.[22] Then, lastly, between the utter Arians and the compromisers, there were the compromisers of a compromise, people between the Arians and the semi-Arians, three-quarter Arians. Their word was *Homoios* (ὅμοιος, "similar"). They thought Christ to be like the Father, but not of a like nature, and preferred not to talk about his nature at all. Their leaders were Akakios of Cæsarea (in Palestine),

---

[20] He was a Cappadocian (d. 395) and a pupil of Aetios. As Bishop of Kyzikos on the Hellespont, he became so great a leader of this party that they are generally called *Eunomians* after him.

[21] Ankyra in Galatia, now Turkish Engkür, Angora, where Angora cats come from. The branch of the Baghdad railway from Eskijehr ends here [in 1908], and you must go on six days' ride to Cæsarea in Cappadocia.

[22] St Ambrose's predecessor.

Eudoxios of Antioch,[23] Uranios of Tyre. They are called *Homoians*. Eventually the situation was simplified; the semi-Arians ended by falling in with the Catholics and the Homoians fell back to the strict Arians.

Since Gibbon,[24] these discussions about one letter have been a favourite object of humour. What, it is asked, can the difference between Homooüsios and Homoioüsios matter? Was it worthwhile to rend the whole Church for the sake of an iota? Undoubtedly to a person who cares nothing for any dogmatic belief, to whom the Christian faith means either nothing at all or a vague humanitarianism, the discussion will seem absurd; so will any theological controversy. But to people who take historic Christianity seriously one may point out that the question at issue was the vital one of all. It was that of the Divinity of Christ. Are we to believe him to be God, or only some sort of superior creature having rather more likeness to God than we have? That is what is involved in the issue between Homooüsios and Homoioüsios. And that the two words look so much alike is due to an accident of Greek grammar and to the fact that the semi-Arians chose their word deliberately, because it looked like ours. These passwords were technical forms that stood for very real differences.[25]

---

[23] He succeeded Eusebeios at Antioch and was then Bishop of Byzantion from 360–369.

[24] *Decline and Fall*, chap. xxi (ed. Bury, vol. 11 [1897], pp. 351–53).

[25] The Russian arms look very like those of Austria, and are, as a matter of fact, a rather bad copy of them. But in the case of a war between these countries an Austrian soldier would not waver in his allegiance because of that. It is very obvious that the change of one letter in a word may completely alter its meaning. Cardinal Newman somewhere quotes the example of *Personage* and *Parsonage*. Scores of instances in any language will occur at once to anyone.

6. The First Attacks against Athanasius (335–339)

As soon as the Arians felt their own position safe through Constantine's change of policy they moved heaven and earth to have their great opponent degraded and banished. In 330 they had succeeded in deposing Eustathios, the Catholic Patriarch of Antioch, in a synod held in that city. Then they flew at higher game. In 335 they called together a synod at Tyre to try Athanasius. He came to it with forty-eight Catholic bishops of his patriarchate; against him were sixty Arian bishops. He was accused of these crimes: (1) He had sent a certain Makarios to persecute a pious priest named Ischyras. Makarios, acting under Athanasius' orders, had forced his way to Ischyras' altar, had broken the chalice and burnt the holy books. (2) Athanasius had murdered a bishop, Arsenios of Hypsele, had cut off the dead man's hand and used it for working magic.[26] The Arians even produced the hand. (3) He had committed sin with a certain woman. The dramatic and triumphant defence of Athanasius has been the joy of every Catholic ever since. He proved that Ischyras was not a priest at all; Arsenios came and showed himself, very much alive with two hands, and the lady did not even know him by sight when she saw him. But the Arians were not prepared to accept even that defence. They could not help Arsenios and the lady; but they promptly ordained Ischyras bishop, to make up for his not having been a priest before; they declared Athanasius contumacious, deposed him and forbade him to go back to Alexandria. Then they all went to Jerusalem, consecrated the new Anastasis church with great pomp and began their arrangements for deposing another Catholic

---

[26] The bloody hand of a murdered man as a weapon of magic is a very old superstition. We know it in the "Hand of glory" in the Ingoldsby Legends.

bishop, Markellos of Ankyra. Meanwhile Athanasius went
to Constantinople to ask Constantine to see fair play. So far
Constantine, in spite of his Arian leanings, had had a great
respect for the saint and had refused to countenance the
attempts of his enemies. Now he sent for the leaders of the
Arians at Tyre and asked them to explain themselves. Eusebeios of Nicomedia and others came, and they entirely
changed the ground of their complaint. The former accusations, although certainly striking in themselves, suffered
from a deplorable want of evidence. Arsenios was still going
about with both his hands, and they were not sure that the
lady would recognize the patriarch even this time. Also the
date of Ischyras' ordination promised to be a difficulty. Moreover, Constantine would not trouble much about a broken
chalice, and his own career had shown that he had no very
strong feeling against either murder or rape. So on the way
to Constantinople they thought of a far better case. They
said nothing more about these misdemeanours; Athanasius
had done something much worse—he had stopped the corn
from Egypt! Egypt paid her taxes in corn, and the whole
empire depended on the yearly export from Alexandria. This
corn was by far the most valuable asset of all the taxes to
the government. So Constantine had no hesitation when
he heard that. Athanasius had stopped the corn—Very well,
he shall be banished to as distant a land as possible, where
there is no corn. The emperor would hear no defence, and
Athanasius was sent to Trier on the Mosel. This is the *first
exile* (335–338); it lasted till after Constantine's death. In
the same year (335), the Arians carried out their plan of
deposing Markellos of Ankyra in a synod at Constantinople, and Pope Sylvester I died (314–335). The next year,
336, saw what Catholics have always remembered as one of
the most striking judgements of God in history. The Arians

had triumphed on every side now. Only one thing was still wanting, the restitution of their founder, Arius, himself. In the capital of the empire, he was to be solemnly received and restored. The emperor ordered the Bishop of Constantinople, Alexander, to receive him back into communion. Arius hurried to the city from Alexandria; an enormous crowd of his friends came with him. The Catholics of Constantinople shut themselves up in despair. The Nicene synod had been held to no avail, and the Nicene faith was to be openly denied in the very heart of the empire. And the Arians made the most of their victory. The court was to receive the heretic with every possible honour; they arranged a gorgeous procession to pass through the city, to flaunt the triumph of their side before the whole world. The procession began, they sang out their hymns, and there was the famous Arius himself marching in the place of honour. Suddenly he felt unwell and retired to a private place. The procession waited, the hymns died out, and then gradually the news was whispered among the crowd. Arius was dead. In the midst of his triumph, he had died like Judas. In a shameful place, his body had burst open, and his entrails were scattered over the floor. *Crepuit medio*, and as his friends stole away silently to lay aside their finery, the amazed Catholics learned that sometimes in this world too the strong arm of God is stretched out and that his awful vengeance had fallen at the very moment when he was being defied.[27] And then in the next year Constantine died, too. On his death-bed at last he made up his mind to be a Christian, and he was baptized by his Arian cousin,

---

[27] For Arius' death, see Athanasius, *De morte Arii*, chap. 2; Ep. *ad Ep. Aegypti*, chap. 19; Sokrates, *Hist. Eccl.* i, 37; Sozomenos, *Hist. Eccl.* ii, 29; Theodoret, *Hist. Eccl.* i, 24.

Eusebeios of Nicomedia. He died at Nicomedia on Whitsunday, May 22, 337. His body was robed in the Imperial
purple, placed in a coffin of gold and brought to the city
he had founded. There he lay in the church of the holy
Apostles, first of the long line of Roman emperors who
were buried around him, till in 1463 the Turk cleared
away the burial-place of the Cæsars to make room for the
mosque of Mohammed the Conqueror. The Orthodox
Church has canonized him, as well as his mother, and
on May 21 they keep the feast of "the holy, glorious, mighty,
God-crowned, equal-to-the-Apostles sovereigns, Constantine and Helen". The Catholic Church, more difficult in
her standards of sanctity, honours Helen only as a saint.[28]
Nevertheless, a certain halo will always surround the figure of that mighty prince who joined together the
whole empire under his rule, founded New Rome, summoned the Nicene fathers, and is remembered as the first
Christian emperor. And Athanasius, among the Germans
in distant Trier, heard the news of the awful death of his
old enemy, Arius, and then of the tardy baptism and death
of his old friend the emperor. The exiled patriarch had been
received at Trier with great honour by the bishop Maxi-
minus. He had with him some of his Egyptian clergy, and
he could write letters to his flock at home. It was during
this time that he wrote his first Paschal letter (see p. 41
below). And Constantine, although he had banished the
lawful patriarch, had not allowed any intruder to be set up
at Alexandria.

---

[28] Constantine was, in any case, only a catechumen till his death-bed, and
then an Arian. He persecuted the Catholic bishops and had a weakness for
murdering his near relations. None of these things can be held up as examples of heroic sanctity.

7. Appeal to Rome; The Second Exile (340–345)

After Constantine's death, his three sons divided the empire between them. *Constantius* had the east (*Præfectura Orientis*), *Constantine II* Gaul and *Constans* Illyricum and Italy. But this arrangement only led to fighting between them. In 340, Constans defeated and slew Constantine II at Aquileia. Ten years later, in 350, a usurper named Magnentius defeated and slew Constans, and after three more years, in 353, Constantius defeated and slew Magnentius. So again the Roman world had only one lord, Constantius (353–361). He reigned, of course, at Constantinople, began to persecute the pagans and was himself, without any sort of compromise, a declared Arian. So the government and the court were now even more enemies of the Nicene faith than in Constantine's later years. However, as soon as Constantine was dead, Saint Athanasius was able to go back to his own city. The three sons began their reigns by proclaiming a general amnesty and restoring all exiled bishops. In 338, Athanasius entered Alexandria again, to the great joy of all faithful Catholics. But his enemies did not mean to leave him long in peace. The next year they set up an Arian anti-bishop, a certain Pistos, at Alexandria and sent a long complaint against Athanasius to the three emperors and to the Pope, to persuade them to recognize Pistos. Athanasius then did what every Catholic bishop would do. He, too, formally appealed to the Pope. He "sought refuge in Rome as in a most safe harbour of his communion".[29] But in 340, Constantius, having refused to allow Athanasius to defend himself, let the Arians in a synod at Antioch again declare him deposed. Then he banished him and set up, instead of Pistos, one

[29] St Jerome, Ep. 127, n. 5.

Gregory, a Cappadocian, as rival bishop. Gregory, of course
an Arian, seized the churches at Alexandria with the help
of the Imperial prefect of Egypt and began a fierce persecution of the Catholics. And Saint Athanasius set out on
his *second exile*. The Pope, to whom he had appealed, had
not forgotten him. Julius I (337–352) had succeeded Sylvester I. As soon as the complaint of the Arians and Athanasius' appeal reached him, he summoned both sides to Rome.
Athanasius went at once, even before Gregory the usurper
had arrived at Alexandria. But the Arians, denying the Pope's
jurisdiction, like all heretics, did not appear.[30] Pope Julius
then, in 341, held a synod at Rome, attended by fifty bishops, in which he declared Athanasius to be innocent of all
crimes of which his enemies had accused him and to be
the only lawful bishop of Alexandria. The story of Saint
Athanasius' appeal to the Pope and of the Pope's judgement is one of the many famous cases of *appeals to Rome* in
the early Church. Here, again, we see the greatest bishop
in the east, the mighty patriarch who held the second see

---

[30] Their language sounds curiously like what we hear in this country
[England]. They said they could not allow the Pope to discuss the matter,
because it had been settled by councils. So it had, by a dozen councils; and
every council had settled it in a different way. To appeal to councils is a
splendid argument, when you are quite sure which councils are the right
ones to appeal to. At that time there was a council of some kind every year
somewhere, and some councils were Homoüsian, some Homoiüsian, some
Homoian, and they all deposed somebody and set up somebody else, and
they all anathematized everything done by all the others.

These Arians also told the Pope that he had no more authority than any
other bishop; no doubt his see was a very important and venerable one, but
he had no jurisdiction over them. (Protestantism is an older movement than
people suppose.) For this impudent Arian letter to the Pope, see Athanasius,
Hist. arian, chap. 11; Ep. *Jul. ad Ant.* (quoted in Athanasius, *Apol. contra arianos*, chap. 21–35); Sokrates, *Hist. Eccl.* ii, 15, 17; Sozomenos, *Hist. Eccl.* iii,
7, 8, 10.

of Christendom, the leader of the Catholics against Arians, and the greatest of eastern Fathers solemnly appealing to the Bishop of Rome as his over-lord to judge his case. It was no question of Roman patriarchal jurisdiction. Egypt had nothing to do with the Roman patriarchate. The only claim the Pope could have to interfere in a quarrel at Alexandria was his claim to universal jurisdiction over the whole Church of Christ. And Saint Athanasius showed plainly enough what he thought of that claim. He had always steadfastly refused to admit the emperor's right to judge in ecclesiastical affairs,[31] but when he was in really great trouble he appealed to the Pope. This is Theodoret's account of the matter: "The Eusebians, having got together calumnies against Athanasius, had denounced him to Bishop Julius, who then ruled the Roman church. And Julius, following the rule of the Church, ordered them to come to Rome, and he also summoned Athanasius to explain his case. Athanasius, obeying the summons, started at once on the journey. But they who had made up the fable would not come to Rome, because they knew that their lie would be found out."[32] And Julius wrote a stern letter to these Eusebians, saying: "Do you not know that this is the custom, that you should first write to us and that what is right should be settled here."[33] So Saint Athanasius passed his second exile at Rome under the protection of the Pope. Meanwhile the bewildering succession of synods and anti-synods was going on

[31] For instance, he says triumphantly of this very Roman synod in 341: "No Imperial governor was there, no soldiers stood before the doors, the affairs of the synod were determined by no laws of the government" (*Hist. arian.*, chap. 11). Indeed, throughout his life he never ceased protesting against the interference of the state in these theological questions.

[32] Theodoret, *Hist. Eccl.* ii, 3 (*PG* 82:996).

[33] Ep. 3 *Julii ad Eus.*, 22 (in Athanasius: *Apol. contra arianos*, 21–36).

all over the empire. In the same year as the Roman one
(341), there was a great Arian synod at Antioch, when the
bishops met to dedicate Constantine's Golden church.[34] In
343, the Catholics met at Sardica (now Sophia in Bulgaria),
defended Athanasius and confirmed the right of appeal to
the Pope that every accused bishop has,[35] and at the same
time the Arians met at Philippopolis and again declared Athanasius deposed. But while he lived Constans was Athanasius' friend, and he at last persuaded his brother, Constantius,
to allow the patriarch's return. In February 345, Gregory,
the Arian usurper at Alexandria, who had ruthlessly persecuted the faithful subjects of Athanasius, went too far,
and they rose up and murdered him. Then Constantius
invited the lawful bishop back. He wrote him a very friendly
letter and offered him the use of the government's convey-
ances. So in 345, Athanasius made a second triumphal entry
into his city. This return was the most famous of all. He
had passed through Adrianople, Antioch and Laodicea (where
another council met and declared him innocent), and when
he came to Alexandria, "like another Nile",[36] the people
streamed out to meet him. They spread their carpets in the
streets for him to walk upon and cut down palm-branches
to carry before him. "Who", he said himself, "that beheld
such peace in our church did not wonder at the sight? Who
did not praise God for the joy of the people?" [37] And Pope
Julius wrote a letter full of praise of the saint and of joy at
his return. "If precious metals are tried by fire, what shall
we say of so great a man who has overcome so many trials?

---

[34] This is the synod *in encæniis* (ἐν ἐγκαινίοις, "at the dedication").

[35] Canons 3, 4 and 5 of Sardica are the most famous instance of an eastern
synod solemnly recognizing this right of appeal to Rome.

[36] Gregory of Nazianzos, *Oratio* xxi, 27.

[37] Athanasius, *Hist. arian.*, 27.

... Receive, therefore, my dear brethren, your bishop Athanasius, with joy and with thanks to God."[38] To this day the eastern churches keep a feast in memory of the end of Gregory's tyranny and Athanasius' happy return.[39] For ten years he now reigned in peace at Alexandria, restoring order in his patriarchate and writing one treatise after another against the Arian heresy.[40] Meanwhile the synods went on. In 344, the Arians at Antioch drew up another formula, which was rejected by the Catholics at Milan in 345. In 351, the Arian Synod of Sirmium[41] proposed yet another form, carefully avoiding the word *Homooüsios*; in 353, at Arles, they deposed and banished Saint Paulinus of Trier. And in 355, they met again at Milan.

8. Third Exile, in the Desert (356–362)

This Arian Synod of Milan professed to depose Pope Liberius (352–366), who had succeeded Julius. He and Lucifer of Calaris in Sicily then had to go into exile. It also deposed Athanasius for the third time. Constantius had again changed his mind. He was always an Arian, and he quite rightly looked upon the great patriarch as the most powerful and uncompromising enemy of his belief. This time he tried to have him murdered. On February 9, 356, while Athanasius was keeping the night hours in the church of Theonas at Alexandria, it was surrounded by the emperor's soldiers, who shot their arrows into the church. At last the Catholics

[38] Athanasius, *Apologia*, 52.

[39] In the Byzantine Church on Jan. 18.

[40] Throughout his life he was always occupied in writing defences of the faith. We shall come to these in the list of his works (pp. 38–42 below).

[41] *Sirmium* was in Lower Pannonia near the river Sava. Now it is in Slavonia, north-west of Belgrade.

succeeded in breaking through with their patriarch, and he fled for refuge to the fathers of the Libyan desert.[42] This is the *third exile* among the monks (356–362). Saint Athanasius had always had a very great admiration for the monks who lived away from the world in the great Egyptian desert. We have seen that even before he was patriarch he had known and served them (p. 10 above). It is said that he was one of the founders of western monasticism while he was at Rome, and he had made many journeys to their settlements in his patriarchate. So it was natural that, now that he was fleeing for his life, he should go to these monks, where he could hide from the emperor's soldiers in the desert and where he would have the comfort of their company. For six years, he wandered about the different settlements of these fathers south of the Thebais where the great tawny lions crouch behind the burning rocks. Meanwhile, in Alexandria, his Catholics were fiercely persecuted. The soldiers hunted for the patriarch throughout Egypt. As they could not find him, they broke open and burnt down houses, scourged his clergy (Eutychios, a subdeacon, died under their rods), violated nuns and took away all the churches to give them to the Arians. Indeed, all over the empire there was now a furious persecution of the "Athanasians". For a second time, the government set up an intruder in Saint Athanasius' see, this time George, another Cappadocian. This George was a quite horrible person, an Arian, of course. Sozomenos says that he was a notorious drunkard and a man of evil life, stupid, coarse and brutal (*Hist. Eccl.* iii, 7). He meant to make money out of his place, so he secured

[42] Before he could get away, he lay hidden in Alexandria while the soldiers hunted for him in his friends' houses. Eudaimonis, a nun, was tortured to make her say where he was; but she kept the secret. Another lady hid him in her house for days while the pursuit was hottest.

monopolies for salt, paper and nitre and did a thriving trade in coffins on his own account by refusing Christian burial to anyone who was not brought in one made at his own factory. Catholic bishops were deposed and imprisoned, Catholic monasteries burnt down, and every meeting of Catholics interrupted by soldiers, who scourged all the people they found, sometimes even to death. But Athanasius, from his hiding-place, still cared for his desolate church and wrote constantly to encourage his faithful subjects. "Our churches", he says, "are taken from us and given to the Arians; they have our places, but we have the faith. They cannot rob us of that." Many strange and romantic stories are told of the saint's adventures while hiding in the desert. The loyal hermits watched for the coming of soldiers and sent him on from place to place, bearing themselves the brunt of the soldiers' rage when they missed him. One story is famous. The soldiers actually met him once face to face, but they did not know him by sight. "Where is Athanasius?" they asked. And he answered, "He is not far off." So they hurried on, and he escaped. This story is often told as an example of a mental restriction. It was one of a very innocent kind. During this third exile, he wrote many of his most famous works, including the *Apology of His Flight* (p. 39 below). While he was there Saint Antony, the father of monks, died and left his cloak of palm-leaves as a legacy to the exiled patriarch.[43] Throughout the Church, the hopeless confusion of synods went on. In 357, the Arians met again at Sirmium and drew up an even more uncompromisingly Anomoian formula than that of the first Synod of Sirmium (in 351); the semi-Arians held a synod at Ankyra in the same year. In 358 came the famous

---

[43] Athanasius, *Vita Antonii*, 91.

third Synod of Sirmium, with its semi-Arian formula that
Pope Liberius is said to have signed; in 359, the fourth Synod
of Sirmium, and the great Synod of Ariminium[44] that Constantius forced to accept the fourth Sirmian formula. The
trouble and confusion were now at their height. There were
at least twelve different creeds[45] that claimed the allegiance of the pious Christian layman; every shade of Arianism and semi-Arianism clamoured for his acceptance; only
the faith of Nicæa and Athanasius was forbidden and persecuted. It is of this time, just before Constantius died in
362, that Saint Jerome wrote: "The whole world groaned
and wondered to find itself Arian."[46] But the simple people kept the faith through all this clash of quarrelling
bishops,[47] and they looked out toward the hot Libyan
desert where the column of the faith lay hidden till God
should bring him back. Saint Athanasius' return after his
third exile was brought about in just the same way as his
former one. Julian (361–363) declared himself emperor,
and Constantius died on his way to fight him (362).
Julian began his reign by recalling all banished bishops, and
George the intruder at Alexandria, who had made himself even more hated than his predecessor, Gregory, of
unhappy memory, was murdered by the people. Only this
time it was the pagans who murdered him, thereby earning
the gentlest of reproofs from Julian, who thought that this
time the zeal of his fellow-Hellenes had exceeded the bounds

[44] Rimini in Romagna on the coast between Ravenna and Ancona.

[45] Five of Antioch, four of Sirmium, one of Constantinople, one of Akakios of Kyzikos and the Nicene creed.

[46] *Ingemuit totus orbis et arianum se esse miratus est* (Jerome, *Contra Luciferianos*, 19).

[47] St Hilary (d. 366) says that the ears of the people were holier than the
lips of the preachers (*Ad Constantium*, 4).

of moderation. So Saint Athanasius came back again to his city (362).

9. The Fourth and Fifth Exiles (362–363, 365–366)

From this time, the tide of Arianism turned back, and the whole movement gradually disappeared. But Athanasius had to go into exile twice again before he died. He was by now without comparison the most famous man in the Christian Church and the acknowledged leader of the Catholics. At Alexandria, he converted so many pagans that the pagan priests complained to Julian that if he stayed there, there would soon be no more gods at all in Egypt. So Julian again banished the saint as being "an enemy of the immortal gods", and he again went to the monks in the Thebais. This is the *fourth exile* (362–363). It did not last long. Poor Julian was killed fighting the Persians in 363, and his successor, Jovian (363–364), as usual, began his reign by proclaiming an amnesty and the return of all exiles. So Athanasius entered his city again. But Jovian died after eight months, and Valentinian I (364–375) appointed his brother, Valens, to be regent of the east. Valens was a declared Arian, and he immediately ordered that all Homooüsian bishops who had been banished by Constantius and restored by Julian should again leave their sees (May 5, 365). Athanasius had to go, too, and fled to his father's tomb by the Nile.[48] But there was so great a tumult among his people at this continued persecution of their patriarch that the emperor had to give in and recall him after four months. So this *fifth and last exile* (365–366) was a short one. Once more, and for the last time, the old patriarch

[48] Sokrates, *Hist. Eccl.* iv, 13; Sozomenos, *Hist. Eccl.* vi, 12.

entered his city in triumph, and from then till his death he lived there in peace.

10. Athanasius' Last Years and Death

The saint's last seven years were spent in finishing the work of his life, the destruction of Arianism. And now, after all his troubles, he was able to see the storm calmed before he died. Arianism was disappearing as fast as it had arisen. In spite of Valens, the Arian Cæsar, everywhere the Nicene faith was being restored. Catholic bishops were coming out of their hiding-places, and a new and younger band of defenders of the faith was routing the heresy in east and west. Saint Basil (d. 379), Saint Gregory of Nyssa (d. ca. 395) and Saint Gregory of Nazianzos (d. 390) on the one side, Saint Ambrose (d. 397), Saint Jerome (d. 420) and Saint Damasus the Pope (d. 384) on the other, finally destroyed the evil that had threatened to swallow up the whole Church. And at last—but this was after Athanasius' death—the great Catholic emperor, Theodosius I (379–395), ruled over a united Catholic empire, and Arianism became only an episode of history and a memory of the most fearful storm that has ever raged in the Church of Christ.[49] And all these younger Fathers looked up with unbounded reverence to the old patriarch who had borne the burden of the fight before they were born, whom they recognized while he lived as their leader and champion, whom they remembered after his death as the great standard-bearer of the Nicene faith. After so great a storm he tasted this peace during those last seven years. From every side came news of the reconciliation of Arian churches and the conversion

[49] Arianism went on outside the empire for a long time still as the religion of the Teutonic peoples. The Goths were Arians.

of Arian bishops In his own city, he ordered everything peaceably for the firm establishment of the Catholic faith, and he saw the last poor remnants of paganism and heresy gradually die out dishonoured and unnoticed. Naturally from every side people appealed to him in their difficulties. Saint Basil wrote to him from Cæsarea asking for sympathy and help in his own difficulties, and when a new heresy began—that of Apollinaris—once more people turned to Alexandria and begged the old patriarch to refute this, as he had so often refuted the Arians. His treatise *Against Apollinaris* was almost his last work. And then, after all his troubles, after he had been hunted down, had fled for his life so many times, after he had spent those long years of exile hiding among the rocks of the desert, or wandering in the distant western lands, after all he died at home in the city that had been his since his birth, that had become more famous because of him than it had been in the old days of Alexander and the Ptolemies. On May 2, 373, the old patriarch, who had fought his good fight, finished his course and kept the faith, went to receive the crown of righteousness that the Lord gave him at that day. We are not surprised that the whole Catholic world from end to end united to honour his glorious memory. He was buried at Alexandria with great honour by the people who had been faithful to him through all the persecution. The whole city formed a great pomp to follow his relics to their rest. Gregory of Nazianzos preached a glowing panegyric[50] of him. "To praise Athanasius is to praise all virtues. To name him is to name a gathering of all that is admirable in one man." He was the "Pillar of the Church, rich in doctrine, edification and comfort, a

---

[50] *Oratio* xxi (*PG* 35:1082–128), probably in 380.

triumph of truth and right". Every one of these later Fathers, Greek or Latin, has something to say of the great hero. To Saint John Damascene (d. ca. 754) in far Damascus he is the "Foundation-stone of the Church of God", and to Vincent of Lerins in still further Gaul, he is the "most faithful of confessors, most enlightened of teachers". Naturally, he is, first of all, the great national saint of Egypt. Ask any Egyptian Christian who is the greatest saint of his country, and he will answer at once "Athanasius the Great". The four patriarchs who now dispute the succession of Saint Mark[51] all claim him as their most glorious predecessor. And, beyond the boundaries of Egypt, east and west keep the memory of the champion of the faith against the greatest and worst of heresies. Orthodox and Catholics remember him every year on May 2, the day of his death. The Orthodox pray to him: "Speaker for God, Athanasius, who overcame endless dangers and trials, now you have become worthy of the delights of paradise. You followed God's commands, conqueror of justice, now you are crowned with the crown of the heavenly kingdom, glorious in your eternal triumph." And the Roman Church that he honoured and obeyed[52] honours him, and throughout the world her priests read on May 2 of the great saint who "for six and forty years during the greatest changes of times with very great holiness ruled the Church of Alexandria"; and we pray that God may hear the prayers that we say on the feast of the blessed Confessor Athanasius, and that he may forgive us all our

[51] There are four Patriarchs of Alexandria, an Orthodox, a Monophysite Copt, a Uniate Copt and a Melkite. The Latin titular patriarch at Rome has no pretence of succession from the old line and need not be counted. [Written in 1908.—Ed.]

[52] Above, pp. 25–27.

sins through the merits of the saint who served him so
worthily.[53]

II. Table of Dates

293 *Birth of Athanasius.*

306–337 Constantine the Great, sole emperor from 323.

311 Arius ordained priest.

313–328 Alexander of Alexandria patriarch.

314–335 Saint Sylvester I Pope.

ca. 319 Athanasius ordained deacon.

321 Synod of Alexandria against Arius.

325 FIRST GENERAL COUNCIL AT NICÆA IN BITHYNIA.

328 *Athanasius Patriarch.*

335 Arian synod at Tyre.

335–337 *First exile at Trier.*

335 Saint Sylvester I dies.

336 Arius dies.

337 Constantine dies.

337–362 Constantius emperor; he reigns alone from 340.

337–352 Saint Julius I Pope.

338 Athanasius restored at Alexandria.

340 Arian synod at Antioch against Athanasius.

340–345 *Second exile at Rome.* Gregory of Cappadocia
        intruded at Alexandria.

341 Synod at Rome defends Athanasius.

341 Arian synod "in encæniis" at Antioch.

343 Catholic synod at Sardica. Right of appeal to Rome.

344 Arian synod at Antioch.

345 Gregory of Cappadocia murdered. Athanasius restored.
    Feast of his restoration.

---

[53] Roman brev., 2 Maii, lect. vi and collect. [These were the reading and
prayer in use when Adrian Fortescue wrote this book.—ED.]

345 Catholic synod at Milan.

351 First Arian synod at Sirmium.

353 Arian synod at Aries. Saint Paulinus of Trier banished.

355 Arian synod at Milan. Pope Liberius (352–366) and Athanasius banished.

356–362 *Third exile in the desert.* George of Cappadocia intruded at Alexandria.

357 Second Arian synod at Sirmium.

357 Semi-Arian synod at Ankyra.

358 Third semi-Arian synod at Sirmium. Liberius signs its formula.

359 Fourth Arian synod at Sirmium.

359 Synod of Arminium.

361–363 Julian emperor, alone from 362.

362 George of Cappadocia murdered; Athanasius restored.

362–363 *Fourth exile in the Thebais.*

363–364 Jovian emperor.

364–375 Valentian I emperor; Valens Cæsar in the east.

365–366 *Fifth exile by his father's tomb.*

373 (May 2) *Athanasius* dies.

12. Works

Throughout his whole life, Saint Athanasius was engaged in writing, chiefly against the Arians, but we have treatises of exegesis and history, letters, sermons and apologies by him as well. His works were first collected and printed in Greek in 1600 at Heidelberg; the Benedictines of Saint Maur published what is still the best edition of them at Paris in 1698,[54] and they fill four volumes of Migne's *Patrologia Græca.*[55] This is a list of the chief works only.

[54] Three vols, edited by J. Lopin and B. de Montfaucon.
[55] *PG* 25–28 (Paris, 1857).

APOLOGETIC WRITINGS. While he was still only a deacon, before Arius had begun his heresy, he wrote *A Treatise against the Heathen* (λόγος καθ' ἑλλήνων, *Oratio contra gentes*,[56] PG 25:3–96) and a *Treatise on the Incarnation of the Word* (λόγος περὶ τῆς ἐνανθρωπήσεως τοῦ λόγου, *Oratio de humana natura a Verbo assumpta*, PG 25:95–198).

DOGMA AND POLEMICS AGAINST THE ARIANS. His chief polemical work is the *Four Treatises against the Arians* (κατ ἀρειανῶν λόγοι δ', *Orationes IV contra arianos*, PG 26:11–526). Also *Of the Appearance in the Flesh of the Word of God and against the Arians* (περὶ της ἐν σάρκου ἐπιφανείας τοῦ θεοῦ λόγου καὶ κατ' ἀρειανῶν, *De apparitione Verbi Dei in carne et contra arianos*, PG 26:983–1028), *Exposition of the Faith* (ἔκθεσις πίστεως, *Expositio fidei*, PG 25:199–208). *Two Books against Apollinaris* (κατ' Ἀπολλιναρίου λόγοι β', *Contra Apollinarium libri II*, PG 26:1093–1166) were written at the end of his life.

HISTORICAL WORKS. Three apologies are specially valuable as telling the history of his own time, the *Apology against the Arians* (ἀπολογητικὸς κατ' ἀρειανῶν, *Apologia contra arianos*, PG 25:247–410), written in 350, the *Apology to the Emperor Constantius* (πρὸς τὸν βασιλέα Κωνστάντιον ἀπολογία, *Apologia ad imperatorem Constantium*, PG 25:595–642) in 356, and the *Apology of His Flight* (ἀπολογία περὶ τῆς φυγῆς αὐτοῦ, *Apologia de fuga*, PG 25:643–80)[57] in 357. He wrote a *History of the Arians Addressed to the Monks* (ἱστορία τῶν ἀρειανῶν πρὸς τοὺς μονάχους, *Historia arianorum ad monachos*, PG 25:691–796) between 335 and 337.

---

[56] The Latin titles are useful for reference to Migne. For the same reason I give the volumes and pages in *PG*.

[57] The lessons of the third nocturn on his feast in the Roman breviary are taken from this work.

EXEGESIS. Of Athanasius' many interpretations of holy Scripture, only fragments remain that have been preserved in Catenas.[58] Of these the largest fragment is that of his *Commentary on the Psalms* (PG 27:55–590). There are also parts of his expositions of *Job* (PG 27:1343–47), the *Song of Songs* (PG 27:1348–50), *St Matthew* (PG 27:1363–90), *St Luke* (PG 27:1391–1404) and *1 Cor.* (PG 27:1404).

ASCETIC WORKS. His *Life of Saint Antony* (βίος καὶ πολιτεία τοῦ ὁσίου πατρὸς ἡμῶν Ἀντωνίου, *Vita S. P. N. Antonii*, PG 26:835–976) is one of the great standard books on the spiritual life. It was done into Latin almost at once, and this version was one of the chief causes of Saint Augustine's conversion. He had heard a certain Pontitianus speak of Saint Antony's life and describes how he had found this book with his friends in a monastery while they were out for a walk; "and one of them began to read it and to wonder and be greatly moved, and while reading it to think about leading such a life himself and leaving the army to serve God" (Aug., *Confess.* VIII, 6). A number of Saint Athanasius' letters addressed to monks belong to this class too.

LETTERS. It is, perhaps, from these letters that one knows the saint best. He wrote a great number to all sorts of people, and in them he discusses every kind of subject; sometimes he tells the story of some synod or other event, often he again exposes the Nicene faith and argues against Arianism, or he writes exhortations and counsel for the devout

[58] A *Catena* is a collection of interpretations from the Fathers arranged together under each text of Scripture in a "chain". It was a favourite and very convenient way of making commentaries on each book in the middle ages, the commentary consisting of a mosaic of quotations. St Thomas Aquinas' (d. 1274) *Catena aurea* is a well-known example.

life. The most important are the *Paschal Letters* (ἐπιστολαὶ ἑορταστικάι,[59] *Litteræ festivales*, *PG* 26:1431–44). It was the custom for the Patriarch of Alexandria soon after the Epiphany to write an encyclical to his suffragans announcing on what day Easter would fall in that year, and he used the opportunity to discuss any other important question of the time.[60] Besides the fragments of Athanasius' Paschal letters extant in the original Greek, a Syriac version of fifteen of them has been discovered.[61] These were written between 329 and 348, many while he was in exile, and they contain most important passages about his own life and his theology. His letters to various monks, to Abbot *Drakontios* (*PG* 25:523–34), two to Abbot *Orsisios* (*PG* 26:977–80), one to a monk *Amunis* (*PG* 26:1169–76), one addressed to the Egyptian monks in general (*PG* 26:1185–88) are about the rules of monastic life and asceticism. His letters to *Epiktetos*, Bishop of Corinth[62] (*PG* 26:1049–70), to Bishop *Adelphios* (*PG* 26:1071–84) and to a philosopher named *Maximos* (*PG* 26:1085–90) explain the Catholic faith against the Arians. They were written at the end of his life, about 371. Two encyclical letters, one to all bishops (ἐπιστολὴ ἐγκύκλιος, *Ep. encyclica*, *PG* 25:221–40) in 341, and one to the *Bishops of Egypt and Libya* (*PG* 25:537–94) in 356, tell the history of the Arian attacks against him. An encyclical about the *Decrees of Nicæa* and one about the *Teaching of Denis of Alexandria* (*PG* 25:479–522) were written between 350 and 354. He

[59] The phrase ἡ ἑορτή in Greek always means Easter.

[60] These Paschal letters then were like the Lenten pastorals that our bishops now write.

[61] In 1847 in a monastery in the desert. Cureton edited them in 1848, and a Latin version of them is given in *PG* 26:1351–1444.

[62] This letter is specially famous; Epiphanios quotes it at full length in his work *Against Heresies* (*Hær.* 77).

wrote two Latin letters to *Lucifer*, Bishop of Calaris[63] (*PG* 26:1181–86) in 360, one to Bishop *Serapion* (*PG* 25:685–90) at about the same time, one to the *Antiochene Bishops* (*PG* 26:795–810), and one to *Rufinianus* (*PG* 26:1179–82) in about 362. There are also a number of other letters that can be found in Migne's Greek series among his works. Lastly, it is hardly necessary to say that Saint Athanasius had nothing to do with the so-called *Athanasian Creed*. The clauses in this against the Nestorians and Monophysites alone are enough to show that it was written after those heresies (after the fifth century). As a matter of fact, we now know that it was composed in Latin in the west (in southern Gaul or Spain) and that it was not introduced into the divine office (at Prime) till the ninth century.[64]

As a specimen of the great veneration with which the Fathers received Saint Athanasius' works we may quote what Abbot Cosmas in the eighth century says: "If you find a book by Athanasius and have no paper on which to copy it, write it on your clothes."

---

[63] Cagliari in Sicily. This is the Lucifer who afterward made the Luciferan schism in Italy.

[64] Dom. G. Morin, *Les origines du symbole Quicunque* (La Science Catholique, 1891), pp. 673ff.

CHAPTER TWO

SAINT BASIL (330–379)

Saint Basil, Metropolitan of Cæsarea in Cappadocia, is the chief of the three Cappadocians[1] who defended the faith of Nicæa in the next generation after Saint Athanasius. Like all the Fathers of that time, he wrote against the Arians; and he wrote a famous work about the Holy Spirit. But he is not known chiefly because of his polemical works. He is remembered rather as a great Catholic bishop in a troubled time, as a man of very ascetic life and as the father of organized eastern monasticism. The Byzantine Church ascribes the older of her two liturgies to him; we know him, through his letters especially, as a very charming and sympathetic person, as, perhaps, personally the most attractive of the Greek Fathers.

1. His Family, Birth and Early Years (330–ca. 345)

Basil[2] came of a distinguished family of Pontus in Asia Minor. His forbears had filled important places in the government. At that time there was no sort of hereditary nobility in the empire, but certain families succeeded in getting high places

---

[1] The other two are his brother St Gregory of Nyssa and his friend Saint Gregory of Nazianzos.

[2] Βασίλειος (*Basilius*) means *Royal*. The Greek form is pro-paroxytone, the Latin pro-perispomenon.

for their children and relations as each generation grew up, and so they gradually gathered together much wealth and large properties. Saint Basil's family was of this kind. For a long time his relations had been persons of consideration because of the offices they held; they had lands in Pontus and Cappadocia; and they all had the natural instincts of people of a certain social position. They showed a sense of distinction in style when they wrote; they nearly all became orators, and they were very keen hunters. Saint Basil's grandfather had been a great man, whose table groaned under the weight of the game he offered to his guests. He was also a Christian; he had fled to the mountains of Pontus with his wife Makrine during Diocletian's persecution. Here he lay hidden for a time, but he comforted himself by shooting birds with his bow.[3] The saint's father, also named Basil, was an orator at Cæsarea, the capital of Cappadocia; although he was a fervent Christian, he did not despise the old Greek classics. Later his successors in the school that thought it quite possible to join the Christian faith with humanism note this as a point in his favour.[4] The elder Basil married a certain Emmelia, the mother of our Saint Basil, and a lady who seems to have brought to her husband every grace and every good quality that a bride could have. She was very rich and very beautiful, but everyone especially praised her wisdom, sense and piety. Saint Basil owed his training to these ladies, Makrine, his grandmother, and his mother Emmelia; he, his brothers and all his friends constantly speak with unbounded admiration of both. Of this marriage of Basil the orator and Emmelia, ten children were born, five boys and five girls. The eldest of all was a girl, called Makrine

[3] St Gregory of Nazianzos, *Oratio* xliii, 5–8.
[4] Ibid., 11.

after her grandmother. This Makrine became a nun and a saint, as we shall see (pp. 54, 73, 81). Then came our saint, Basil, the eldest son. He was born at Cæsarea in 330.[5] His younger brothers were Naukratios, who became a monk and died young in 357; then Gregory (later Saint Gregory of Nyssa, a bishop and one of the Greek Fathers like his eldest brother); Peter, who became Bishop of Sebaste in Armenia; and another who died quite young. The names of the other daughters are not known. It was then an eminently religious family; Basil, the father, gave to the Church three bishops, a monk and a nun, and three of his children are canonized saints.[6] The father was known as a pious Christian, but it was especially the two ladies, old Makrine and Emmelia, who brought up the children in the fear of God. Saint Basil never tired of repeating that he owed everything to his mother and grandmother. "I shall never forget", he says, "the deep impressions made on me as a boy by the words and example of these venerable women." He was delicate from the first; all through his life he refers to his ill-health. The first years were spent at Cæsarea and then chiefly in Pontus, where the family had an estate near Neocæsarea. Here the father taught the boys the elements of secular knowledge, and the mother and grandmother told them stories about the old days of persecution and the sufferings of martyrs and confessors in the bad times that had just passed. Old Makrine had known Saint Gregory Thaumaturgos (d. 270), the apostle of Pontus and Bishop of Neocæsarea; and from her they learned to honour the memory of the great Christian bishop in whose footsteps three

<hr />

[5] There is some doubt about the date. It is sometimes given as 329 or 331.

[6] St Basil, St Gregory and St Makrine.

of them were to walk.[7] The boys then spent these first years on their land in Pontus in a great house full of slaves, where they had every comfort that a rich establishment in the fourth century could offer. We picture them hunting, fishing, riding through the forests along the slopes of the mountains that stretch down toward the Black Sea, then learning the first mysteries of Greek grammar, logic and rhetoric with their father or sitting round old Makrine and listening to her stories of the dreadful days when to confess the name of Christ meant torture and death. After this we shall lose sight of the others to follow our two saints, Basil and Gregory.

2. Studies (345–357)

Basil the father did not mean to keep his sons at home all their lives. He naturally foresaw for them distinguished careers as government officials or orators, and the first condition of such a career was to have studied at one of the great centres of Greek learning under some famous professor. There were then several cities that had great schools, places that corresponded to our universities. There was Cæsarea, where he himself had practised as an orator, the capital of Cappadocia and chief town of all central Asia Minor; there was the capital of the whole empire, Constantinople, still glowing with the first whiteness of new marble,[8] where Cæsar reigned

---

[7] St Gregory of Nyssa afterward wrote his life (p. 81 below). There is a pretty story about this St Gregory the Wonder-worker. As he lay dying at Neocæsarea (a large and important town), he asked how many pagans were left in it. They told him seventeen. "Thank God", he said; "when I came here there were just seventeen Christians." This Gregory was said to have literally carried out our Lord's words and by faith to have moved a mountain. His name (θαυματουργός, Wonder-worker) shows that he had a special reputation for working miracles.

[8] Constantine the Great dedicated his new city in 330.

with his court and all the world came to stand before him.
And there was Athens, dangerous, perhaps, as one of the
last strongholds of the old gods, but most attractive of all,
since here the pure Greek culture still reigned and the old
city, mother of all Hellenism, still gathered under her Acropolis the first teachers and philosophers of the world. So to
these three cities Basil sent his sons. It was the custom then
for students to go from one centre to another, learning what
they could from each and then going on to hear some other
famous teacher elsewhere. In the fourth century, the love
of Greek letters was so little dead that it was still the chief
moving force to hundreds of thousands of eager scholars.
They had never forgotten the glories of the old Greek classics. The one thing that gave a man a position and a title to
be honoured was a knowledge of Homer, the tragedians,
the history-writers and especially the philosophers. Homer
and Plato were the greatest of all names to civilised people
in the east, who still spoke their language and gloried in
being the successors and descendants of the citizens of the
old Greek states. So great a power were the Greek classics
that the love of them among all civilised people was the
one thing on which the emperor Julian (361–363) could
count in his war against Christianity. His argument was always
that this new religion would mean the death of Hellenism;
Christians were the enemies of the Greek gods, therefore
they were the enemies of Greek culture; they were barbarians, worshipping a Jew, using barbarous Jewish Scriptures
in a bad Greek version instead of the pure glory of Homer
and Plato. And his most subtle form of persecution was to
forbid Christian teachers to explain the classics. Let them
explain their Septuagint, and let all who loved Hellas and
beauty leave them to grovel in their debased superstition
and come back to the worship of the immortal gods and

the use of the optative mood. Christians, of course, indignantly denied that there was any necessary opposition between their faith and the love of what was beautiful in the old classics; Christian students flocked to the great teachers of Greek letters just as much as their pagan fellow-citizens. These students travelled enormous journeys and suffered great hardships, dangers[9] and discomfort for the sake of the austere joy of scholarship; and they continued their studies for a much longer time than the modern university student. Some of them at the age of thirty were still sitting round a professor and learning from him.[10] Basil and Gregory, then, went first to Cæsarea in Cappadocia. Here there was no danger for their faith; the city was almost entirely Christian,[11] but the schools were not the best that could be found. At that time, Cappadocians had a reputation for being rustic, rather stupid and coarse.[12] It was here that the brothers first met a fellow-countryman, also named Gregory, who remained, but for one rather bitter quarrel, their very intimate friend and comrade through life. This is Saint Gregory of Nazianzos.[13] The two brothers and the friend form the company of three great Cappadocians who by their learning and eloquence, as much as by their virtues, have redeemed the character of their fatherland, so that we now remember that province with honour as their birthplace. Gregory of Nazianzos says that already at Cæsarea

[9] St Gregory of Nazianzos was shipwrecked and nearly drowned once while travelling to Athens to hear Himerios lecture (*Carmen de se ipso*, xi, 130ff.).

[10] So Gregory of Nazianzos (ibid., xi, 239).

[11] The town council had already ordered the two great temples of Zeus and Apollo to be broken up (Sozomenos, *Hist. Eccl.* v, 4).

[12] Even in Latin "Cappadox" was almost a term of abuse, meaning "boor", "oaf".

[13] He was the son of the Bishop of Nazianzos (Diocæsarea) in Cappadocia.

Basil was the most distinguished student in the city, even then surpassing his professors.[14] From Cæsarea the brothers went on to Constantinople, the other Gregory to Palestine and Alexandria. Then they met again at Athens. The city of Pallas Athene, crowned with violets, was still ancient Athens. That wonderful vision of gleaming marble and stately orders of columns, the glowing colours of the Parthenon, the shining golden helmet of the virgin goddess, the cool arcades, crowded theatre and the glorious Propyleia—all the splendours that we now try to recall among the piteous ruins of the Acropolis—were then real things. Where we look up from the bay of Salamis and see only broken columns and the split gable of the great temple—even now incomparable in its ruin—there the sailor of the fourth century saw the Parthenon radiant with colour and the mighty statue of Athene lifting her gleaming spear over the wine-dark sea. Athens was still the heart of that rich and subtle combination of philosophy, letters and perfect aesthetic taste that make up *Hellenism*. Here were the temples and statues that formed the standard of beauty for the rest of the world; in the Dionysiac theatre under the Acropolis the chorus still sang Aeschylus' strophes; the olive-groves at Kolonos still sheltered the discussions of philosophers. And Athens was still the heart of the old pagan faith. The dying gods found a last refuge in the city where they had grown; so every Christian knew that, beautiful and fascinating as Athens was, priceless as was the erudition, the pure Greek, the perfect style that could be learned only there, still there was grave danger to the faith of young students in the plausible discourse of the Athenian philosophers. Basil took this risk, but took also every precaution while he was exposed to

[14] *Oratio* xliii, 13.

it.[15] He and Gregory of Nazianzos, now the closest of friends, divided their time between their studies and prayers. Gregory says that they only knew two roads, that road to the lecture-room and the one to the church. They kept away from the company of pagan students and succeeded in the centre of pagan philosophy in leading an almost monastic life. "We were advanced in the fear of God by the learning of the heathen, since we knew how to ascend from the imperfect to the perfect, and to find a support for our faith in the weakness of their reason." They gloried in one thing only, "in that great name of Christian".[16] We know the names of the two most famous professors whom they heard; the religions of these teachers are a sign of that time of transition. For Himerios was a pagan and Prohairesios a Christian. A hundred years before, no Christian would have been allowed to teach; a hundred years later, there were practically no pagans left. Basil and Gregory studied grammar,[17] rhetoric, logic, philosophy, astronomy, geometry and mathematics, also a little medicine. Among their fellow-students was the emperor's nephew, Julian.[18] This meeting between the future champions of the Christian faith and its future enemy is historical. Julian had not yet declared himself, so he passed for a Christian too at that time. But Gregory says afterward that even then they foresaw what Julian would become. He describes him as a young man "uncertain in manner, shifty in look and inconsistent in speech"

[15] It is uncertain whether his brother Gregory of Nyssa went to Athens with him or not. We know little about this Gregory till he became a monk (p. 70 below).

[16] Gregory of Nazianzos, *Oratio* xliii, 21.

[17] Grammar then included many things, such as the art of poetry, and even history.

[18] Afterward emperor, 361–363.

and adds that he said at the time, "See what a scourge the empire here prepares for itself." [19] Then in 355, while Gregory stayed to continue his studies at Athens, Basil went back home to the family estate by Neocæsarea in Pontus.

When he arrived home he found his grandmother and father dead. Four of his sisters were married; the eldest, Makrine, had been engaged to a young man who died before the wedding. She kept his memory sacred, gave up all thought of ever marrying anyone else and lived at home helping to bring up her youngest brother Peter. Gregory (of Nyssa) was then an orator, and by no means specially pious;[20] Naukratios after a brilliant career as an orator at Neocæsarea had retired to the mountains as a kind of hermit and had there founded an almshouse for old men. He died soon after. Peter, the youngest, the future Bishop of Sebaste, was being taught by Makrine, who was "not only his sister, but father, mother, guardian and tutor all in one".[21] Basil, after a short visit at home, set up as a teacher of rhetoric at Cæsarea. He was already a famous man. The news of his brilliant career as a student at Athens had reached his own country, so that the people of Neocæsarea tried in vain to persuade him to come and teach in their town. He preferred to stay at Cæsarea, and here for two years he was the chief and most popular master in Cappadocia.

3. Baptism and Journey to the Monks (357–358)

The great turning-point in Basil's life was his baptism in 357. He had never been wicked in any way, so that one

---

[19] *Oratio* v, 23, 24.

[20] He could not stand the long family prayers (Gregory of Nyssa *Oratio* ii *In xl martyres*).

[21] Gregory of Nyssa, *De vita S. Macrinæ*.

cannot properly call it a conversion. It was rather the natural piety he had inherited from his parents that made him at last determine to leave the world and live only for God. And his sister Makrine used her influence over him to persuade him to do so. She had always had great faith in him and had always hoped that he would become something better than a professor of rhetoric. So after two years of public life, he was persuaded to give it all up and become a monk. The first step was that he should be baptized. According to the custom of that time, although he was so pious, although he had always gloried in the name of Christian, he was not really one yet at all. Like most people, he had put off his baptism to a mature age. Afterward he and both the Gregories wrote strongly against this dangerous custom.[22] In 357, at the age of twenty-seven years, he was baptized by the Bishop of Cæsarea, Dianeios. He then at once began to make ready to lead the life of a monk. There were at that time no organized monasteries with fixed rules anywhere; it is our saint who is looked upon as the founder of organized monasticism in the east as much as Saint Benedict (d. 543) in the west. But there were many monks. Great numbers of men left their families and the cares of the world to go out into some lonely place, build themselves a hut, live by tilling the ground and spend all the time they were not digging in praying, meditating and singing psalms. These were the *ascetes* (ἀσκητής, a wrestler, warrior), *hermits* (ἐρημίτης, dweller in the desert) or *monks* (μοναχός, solitary man).[23] Some sort of organization had begun before Saint

[22] Basil, Hom. xiii; Gregory of Nyssa, *Adv. eos qui differunt baptismum*; Gregory of Nazianzos, *Oratio* xl, 16, 17.

[23] As far as its original meaning goes the word *monk* is therefore more applicable to these first solitary hermits than to members of the organized communities that we know. Μόνος means alone, *single;* and so the root idea

Basil's time. Naturally the hermits tended to form colonies, they would then look up to the oldest and most venerable among them as their leader, and young men when they first arrived would put themselves under the guidance of the older ones. So we have already the germ of a community with abbot, monks and novices. Then they would read not only the Scriptures but the lives of specially famous fathers of the desert, and they would form their lives on these models; what Saint Antony, for instance, did was a right and safe thing for any monk to do;[24] then the advice and example of old and wise hermits became accepted as a kind of law. So we have the beginning of a monastic rule. But there was as yet no legal establishment, no legal admittance to a religious order. Monasticism was still simply a manner of life, not a disciplined body. To be a monk, a man had to flee the world and go away to some quiet place to serve God. He was then quite as much a monk as anyone else. It should be specially noted that monks were never priests. The hierarchy of the Church consisted of bishops, priests and deacons; these persons administered sacraments, said Mass and had the care of souls. One did not say "secular priests" because there were no others. For with all this the monks had nothing at all to do. If a monk wanted to receive a sacrament (it was not a very common occurrence), he came out of his solitude and went to the nearest priest. Occasionally a monk is made a priest or bishop; but then the situation was quite simple—by that very fact he ceased being a monk and went back to the world. The

---

of all the words *monk, monastic, monastery* is solitude. Their secondary meaning is, of course, quite a correct one now.

[24] St Athanasius' *Life of St Antony* was a recognized model for monks to follow.

greatest and most famous colonies of monks were in Palestine, Syria, Mesopotamia and especially in the great Libyan desert south of Egypt. So when Saint Basil made up his mind to be a monk himself he first undertook a long journey to visit these places and to learn from the holy men there how to follow in their footsteps. He spent the two years after his baptism (357–358) in travelling "to Alexandria, throughout Egypt, in Palestine, Hollow Syria (Coele-Syria], and in Mesopotamia".[25] Here he lived with the ascetes, and, sharing their life, was filled with admiration for "their fasting, their courage in their work, exactness in long vigils of night-prayer, the high and noble spirit that made them scorn hunger, thirst and cold, as if they were free from the body and already citizens of heaven".[26] Then he came back to Pontus to copy this life at home.

4. Life as a Monk (358–364)

He found quite a large community waiting to lead the monastic life under his guidance. His young brother, Peter, was now grown up; there were no more duties to be done in the house at Neocæsarea. So his mother, Emmelia, his sister Makrine, Peter himself, nearly all their servants and some friends had agreed to go out from the world and spend the rest of their lives in the service of God. Basil chose a place called *Annesos* not far from Neocæsarea, in the diocese of Ibora. He had a strong sense of natural beauty,[27]

[25] Ep. 223.

[26] Ibid.

[27] In an amusing letter to Gregory of Nazianzos, he criticizes the scenery of Gregory's town, says it is full of mud, bears and wolves, and that he cannot bear ugly country (Ep. 14). Throughout his letters, we notice this sense of beauty or ugliness in scenery.

and here, on the border of the little river Iris, he found a retreat among such beautiful surroundings as would make up for the splendour of the city he had left.

There is a high mountain, not easy to reach, covered with woods; its green slopes lead down to the clear river; banks of wild flowers cluster around the roots of the trees; birds sing all day in their branches, and the river is full of fish. "No place", he wrote afterward, "ever gave me such peace. No sound from the city ever reached us; we were far away from the high road, and only rarely some hunters came to disturb our life." [28] Emmelia, Makrine, and the women lived on one side of the river, Basil, Peter, and the men on the other. As soon as he had settled here, he tried to persuade Gregory of Nazianzos to leave his mud, bears and wolves and to come and join him by the Iris. Gregory would not come at first, because, he said, his old father wanted him. However he came eventually and lived some time as a monk under Basil's guidance. Other people came, too, drawn by the fame of these men, so there was soon a large colony of monks. Everyone acknowledged Basil as their chief. He was the *hegumenos* of the laura. They worked hard to till the ground, carried wood, dug, planted, watered. Gregory was very proud of a fine birch tree he had planted himself.[29] But sometimes the rocks nearly fell on their heads, and the river was occasionally inclined to be foggy.[30] They had a hard life; often Emmelia from the other side had to send across bread because they had none themselves. Saint Basil in a long letter (written to Gregory of Nazianzos after he had left the community) describes their life

[28] Ep. 14.
[29] Gregory of Nazianzos, Ep. 6.
[30] Ep. 4.

very exactly.[31] They got up at sunrise and praised God with psalms and hymns. Then they went out to work, and while they dug and planted they still sang psalms. During the day, hours were set apart for reading the Bible; they read with it Origen's (d. 254) commentaries. Then there were meetings for prayer and the singing of psalms; once a day they ate bread and greens; they drank only water. They went to bed at sunset and got up again at midnight to sing. They dressed in one tunic and a cloak, and slept on the bare ground. It will be seen that this way of living only needs to be codified to make it a monastic rule. The singing of psalms is the divine office; abstinence from flesh-meat is always a fundamental rule for eastern monks; the handwork in the fields was for centuries the normal occupation of all monks; and the tunic and cloak are the "angelic dress". During these years at Annesos, Saint Basil did codify it. He drew up a list of a monk's duties, arranged the division of the day and so organized the ascetic life in a system. This is the first monastic rule. It is the one still followed by very nearly all eastern monks, and because of it, Saint Basil is looked upon as the founder of organized monasticism in the east, as is Saint Benedict in the west.[32] He prefers greatly that monks should no longer live entirely separated from one another, but should group themselves into communities under a leader (ἡγούμενος, *leader*, is still the Greek title corresponding to

[31] Basil, Ep. 2.

[32] The eastern monks resent being called after any founder; as they have no distinction of various religious orders it is not necessary to use any special name for them. A monk is a monk, a "good old man" (καλόγερος), and that is enough. But Latins, who are used to speak of Benedictines, Cistercians and so on, generally call eastern monks *Basilians*, and Melkite monks accept the name. If they are to have a special name, this is certainly the right one. There is a second edition of St Basil's rule, made by him later (cf. p. 77 below).

our word *abbot*), living in huts arranged as a kind of village and coming together for public prayers.[33] And the new members are to be subject to strict discipline and tried before they are admitted as regular members. The public prayer is to take place at midnight, at dawn, and then four times during the day, at the third, sixth, ninth hours and at sunset. This is the divine office of the Byzantine Church. The psalms to be sung are fixed, and every monk must leave his work to attend. Celibacy is, of course, a strict law. There are long hours of silence; when speech is allowed, it must be grave and edifying. Saint Basil led this life and ruled his monastery for five years, from 358 to 364. Then he had to leave his quiet retreat and go out into the world to defend the faith against the Arians.

5. His Priesthood (364–370)

During those years that Basil spent at Annesos, the Church was passing through very terrible times. The Arian troubles were at their height. The emperor Constantius was fiercely persecuting Catholics; many otherwise excellent bishops had not the strength to resist, but gave in for a time and signed one of the endless Arian or semi-Arian formulas that the government sent round, with the alternative of banishment. Dianeios of Cæsarea, who had baptized Basil, was such a one. Basil had always loved and reverenced him; then he heard that his old friend had signed the Arian formula of Ariminium.[34] So at once he refused to have any communion with him. But poor Dianeios had only given way

[33] St Benedict begins his rule by expressing the same preference for "coenobitarum genus, hoc est monasteriale militans sub regula vel abbate" (*Reg. Ben.*, chap. 1).

[34] The Council of Ariminium (359) was Catholic, but Constantius forced the bishops who held it to accept an Arian formula.

in a moment of weakness. On his death-bed he sent for
Basil and solemnly assured him that he had never really meant
to deny the faith of Nicæa. "God is my witness", he said,
"that I signed in the simplicity of my heart. I never meant
to renounce the faith taught by the fathers at Nicæa. Now
I ask for only one thing, not to be separated from the 318
holy bishops." [35] So the saint came back into communion
with the dying bishop. In 362, after Dianeios' death, Eusebeios was chosen to succeed him as Metropolitan of Cæsarea
by a stormy and irregular election. The same year saw the
last attempt to enliven the dying embers of paganism by
the emperor Julian (361–363). He was specially angry with
Cæsarea because it was a very Christian town and because
its citizens had destroyed two great temples (p. 48, n. 11
above). So he seized on the pretext of this irregular election to impose a heavy fine, confiscate all Church property,
take away all privileges, even the right to be a city, and
make all the clergy policemen. He did not try to hide his
scorn and hatred of its citizens. "I cannot find a single Hellene", he writes (meaning a worshipper of the gods[36]),
"among those Cappadocians." [37] Between the Arians and
the pagan emperor, the Catholics were in great straits. Julian
further proceeded to punish everyone connected with the
destruction of the temples (which had taken place quite
legally under a former government) with death or exile.
And the bishop, Eusebeios, though a Catholic, was weak
and uncertain. Under these circumstances, urged by Gregory of Nazianzos, Basil left his monastery, came to the city
and was ordained deacon and priest by Eusebeios, in 364.

---

[35] He means the 318 fathers of Nicæa I (Basil, Ep. 51).
[36] *Hellene* always means pagan at this time and for many centuries afterward.
[37] Julian, Ep. 4.

He was by far the most important person in the Church of
Cæsarea: he was known as an unswerving defender of the
Nicene faith; all the monks in the diocese were on his
side; he had much more influence than Eusebeios himself.
Eusebeios was jealous of his popularity and did not like
to see himself eclipsed by one of his own priests. So there
was friction, and there would have been grave trouble had
not Basil avoided it by going back to Annesos. But he
did not stay there long. Gregory of Nazianzos wrote to
him again, imploring him not to forsake the Church of
Cæsarea at a time when it was in so great danger from
its enemies, the Arians. Eusebeios meant well, but no
bishop ever had greater need of support; nowhere was
the presence of an uncompromising Homooüsian more necessary than at Cæsarea. "Go back since there is so much
need of you. The heretics are all at work, some already
troubling the faithful with their arguments; we hear that
others will arrive soon. Truth is in danger." [38] Saint Basil
could not resist this appeal, so he went back to Cæsarea,
made friends with Eusebeios again and stayed with him for
five years, till the bishop's death in 370. During these
years, he, with Eusebeios' consent, managed most of the
affairs of the diocese. His place corresponded to that of
a Vicar-General. And he used his power very zealously to
strengthen the position of the Catholics, to improve whatever was lacking in the services of the Church and to
help the poor. Valens, the brother of the emperor Valentinian I (364–375) and Regent of the east under him, was a
strict Arian and a bitter enemy of Catholics. He came
to Cæsarea in 365 with a train of Arian bishops. Gregory of Nazianzos says that Basil then was the soul of the

[38] Gregory of Nazianzos, Ep. 19.

resistance against him. It was Basil who encouraged waver-
ers, restrained the excessive eagerness of others and strength-
ened all to withstand Valens' persecution.[39] At this time, he
reformed the church services at Cæsarea. He shortened
the prayers of the Liturgy and office that were too long,
borrowed from Antioch the custom that two choirs should
sing the verses of psalms alternately—as we and the Orthodox still do—and arranged the various duties of each order
of clerics. This reform of Saint Basil was gradually adopted
by all churches that used Greek as their liturgical language. His influence on the Byzantine rite was as great as
that of Saint Gregory the Great (590–604) on ours. The
older liturgy of the Orthodox Church[40] bears his name,
though really he arranged and modified it rather than
actually composed it all.[41] In 367 and 368, a dreadful
famine spread over Cappadocia. Bad weather ruined two
successions of crops, and people were dying of hunger.
In this trouble, while the governor and magistrates did
nothing, Basil alone came to the rescue. He sold all
that was left of his property to buy corn for the starving
people and persuaded merchants, who wanted to sell what
they had kept in their barns at an enormous price, to
sacrifice such iniquitous profit. He opened subscriptions,
organized distribution, founded public kitchens, to
which we are told that Jews were admitted as much as

[39] *Oratio* xliii, 32ff.

[40] And of the Melkites, of course, too.

[41] The *Liturgy of St Basil* is used on the Sundays in Lent (except Palm
Sunday), Maundy Thursday, Holy Saturday, the eves of Christmas, the Epiphany and on his own feast. On other days, they use the *Liturgy of St John
Chrysostom*, a shortened form of St Basil's. And St Basil's Liturgy itself is a
modified form of the old Antiochene rite. His relation to the service that
bears his name is much the same as that of St Gregory I to the "Gregorian
chant" in the west.

Christians,[42] and encouraged the people by his sermons.[43] So we are not surprised that everyone at Cæsarea looked on him not only as the foremost churchman of the city, but as the saviour of the people, nor that when Eusebeios died in 370, everyone, the people, clergy of the town and suffragan bishops of Cappadocia, with one voice elected Basil as his successor.

6. Basil, Metropolitan of Cæsarea (370–379)

We have seen our saint as a student, scholar and monk. We now come to the last phase, in which he is a great Prince of the Church, one of the greatest of that younger generation of Catholic bishops who carried on the fight that Athanasius had fought and who finally stamped out the Arian heresy. Cæsarea in Cappadocia, his birthplace of which he now became bishop, was one of the greatest metropolitan sees, after the three patriarchates. Before Constantinople and Jerusalem became patriarchal sees, after Antioch came Ephesus, Cæsarea and Herakleia. The bishops of these places were more than metropolitans: they had metropolitans under them. They are sometimes called *exarchs*, and no doubt all three would have kept that intermediate rank between patriarchs and ordinary metropolitans[44] had not the unhappy ambition

[42] Gregory of Nyssa, *In laudem Basilii*; Gregory of Nazianzos, *Oratio* xliii, 34–36.

[43] A number of St Basil's homilies were preached at this time, as their titles show, Hom. viii, *At the Time of Drought and Famine*; Hom. vi, *On the Words: I Will Destroy Their Barns and Build Greater Ones*. See also Hom. vii and ix, etc.

[44] The organization of bishops, never quite consistently nor perfectly carried out, is (1) the Pope; (2) patriarchs; (3) exarchs (= primates); (4) metropolitans (= archbishops); (5) bishops; (6) chorepiscopi (something like our auxiliary bishops).

of Constantinople eventually swallowed them up into its patriarchate. But in Saint Basil's time no one dreamed of the future grandeur of Constantinople.[45] Cæsarea was an apostolic see[46] from which the great Church of Armenia had been founded.[47] The Primate (Katholikos) of Armenia always was ordained at Cæsarea, till Armenia became Monophysite in the fifth century. And the Exarch of Cæsarea ruled, over all northern and central Asia Minor, over Cappadocia, Pontus, Galatia and Pisidia. His boundaries touched the patriarchate of Antioch to the south (Cilicia belonged to Antioch) and the other exarchate of Ephesus to the west (the Roman province of Asia and Phrygia were under Ephesus). And he had jurisdiction over the great Church of Armenia to the east.

During the nine years (370–379) till his death, in which Saint Basil ruled this great province, he upheld the dignity of his see and was recognized throughout the Christian Church as one of her mightiest bishops. And when he died he left in his own name the chief glory of the see of Cæsarea. It is a dusty little Turkish town now; but of the few people who brave the hideously uncomfortable journey of five days' hard riding from Angora to *Kaisari*, most do so because it was the city of Basil. He was consecrated by the old bishop of Nazianzos, the father of his friend Gregory,[48] to the joy of all Catholics, to the great annoyance of Valens and the Arians. From distant Alexandria came a warm letter of congratulation from the old hero of the faith, Athanasius, who before he died (in 373) had the joy of seeing the work of his life taken up by that valiant band of younger men, of whom Basil was, perhaps, the chief.

---

[45] The first step in its advance was at the second general Council, in 381.
[46] Acts 2:9; 1 Peter 1:1.
[47] By St Gregory the Illuminator in the third century.
[48] The father was also named Gregory.

Very soon after the beginning of Basil's reign began one of the last efforts of Arianism, a violent persecution that was really the dying gasp of the great heresy. Domitius Modestus, the Pretorian Prefect, came to Cæsarea to force everyone to turn Arian. He summoned Basil and, in a long interview,[49] threatened him with confiscation, exile, torture and death unless he would accept the Cæsar's (Valens) religion. Basil withstood him so firmly that he said in astonishment, "No one has ever yet spoken to me so freely." "Perhaps", said Basil, "you have not yet had much conversation with a Catholic bishop." Then Valens came himself. The fame of Basil was so great throughout the empire that Valens wanted to see this man. So he went to the holy Liturgy in the Catholic church on the Epiphany of the year 372. There he saw the saint sitting on his throne facing the people, as eastern bishops do. The Cæsar was so impressed by his dignity that when the offertory came he brought up his gift with the other people. And to everyone's astonishment Basil took it, which shows that he could be conciliatory as well as firm. Two stories are told of this visit of Valens to Cæsarea. One is that his only son, Galatos, was dying and that his wife, Dominica, implored him to send for Basil to heal him. Valens, wishing to try every chance, did so. Basil came, cured him at once, but warned the Cæsar that God allowed this miracle only on condition that the boy be baptized by a Catholic. However, as soon as the boy was well, Valens went back to his usual friends and had him baptized by an Arian, with the result that Galatos at once died. The other story is that he prepared a sentence of banishment against Basil, and three times as he took up the pen to sign it his hand was paralysed and the reed

---

[49] Reported by Gregory of Nazianzos, *Oratio* xliii.

broke. So then in great fear he tore up the parchment.[50] Another time Valens engaged in a great theological discussion with the saint, and his cook kept chiming in and supporting the Cæsar's arguments. Basil made them all very angry by laughing at the cook's bad grammar.[51] Valens eventually learnt to respect the saint, after these interviews at Cæsarea, and so during Basil's campaign against the Arians as bishop he was not again troubled by the government.

7. The Affairs of the Province; Basil's Friends

During his reign, Saint Basil was constantly occupied not only with fighting Arianism[52] but also with various questions of secular and ecclesiastical politics. He was the natural protector of his fellow citizens, and they turned to him in their difficulties. One or two of these cases shall be described here. The government at that time was everlastingly cutting up provinces and making new ones, to the great hurt of stable administration. So Valens in 371 proposed to divide Cappadocia and form a new province in it, with a wretched little town called *Potanda*—a place no one had heard of before—as capital.[53] The people of Cæsarea were in despair at a proposal that would nearly ruin their city. They implored Basil to prevent this arrangement, so he wrote to the government and pointed out the arguments against it very reasonably. "If you cut a horse in two,"

---

[50] Gregory of Nazianzos, *Oratio* xliii, 54; Theodoret, *Hist. Eccl.* iv, 16. Both stories are told in the second nocturn of St Basil's office in the Roman breviary (June 14). It seems rather hard on Galatos to be killed for his father's sin.

[51] Gregory of Nyssa, *Contra Eunomium*, I; Theodoret, *Hist. Eccl.* iv, 16.

[52] His writings against the Arians are given below, p. 77 below.

[53] The same thing was going on all over the empire. It was really a roundabout way of getting more taxes out of the people.

he says, "you will not make two horses." [54] He could not
prevent the division, however, and the only effect of his
letter was that they made *Tyana* (about sixty miles south-
west of Cæsarea) the new capital instead of Potanda. This
led to further complications. Anthimos, the Bishop of Tyana,
hitherto a humble suffragan of Cæsarea, now thought that
as his city had become a capital equal to Cæsarea he ought
to be a metropolitan equal to Basil. [55] So he filched a great
part of Cappadocia to make himself a province, and when
Basil with his friend Gregory (of Nazianzos) went to levy
their dues from a monastery near his city he fell upon their
caravan, and there was a regular fight, in which Basil, Gregory and Anthimos all joined. The end of it was that Basil
and Gregory got through, but Anthimos captured a string
of mules laden with provisions. [56] In order to withstand this
truculent person, Basil then persuaded Gregory to accept
the Diocese of Sasima in the debatable land. He ordained
him himself. He also ordained his younger brother Gregory to be Bishop of Nyssa, hoping that both would help
him to put down Anthimos. But out of this double ordination arose a serious quarrel that for a time interrupted
the lifelong friendship of the three great Cappadocians. [57]
Eventually Basil and Anthimos became friends again; it seems
that Basil in the interest of peace gave up many of his
rights and allowed Anthimos to keep some of his ill-gotten
province. The saint then sternly put down a preposterous

[54] Ep. 74.

[55] It is one more case of the fatal tendency of eastern bishops to alter
ecclesiastical administration according to the changes of secular politics. The
rise of Constantinople and nearly all the troubles of eastern Christendom to
this day come from this misguided principle.

[56] Gregory of Nazianzos, *Oratio* xliii, 58; Ep. 48.

[57] See pp. 70 and 93–94 below.

deacon named Glykeros, who went about dressed like a patriarch, singing hymns with a choir of young ladies.[58] But he
was not a stern father. One of his chorepiscopi[59] named
Timothy had mixed himself up in politics, and Basil's letter
to him contains only the most delicate reproach mixed with
the kindest advice and the most affectionate interest in his
affairs.[60] He refused to use torture—the common punishment in those days—and continually, when a robber was
brought to him, sent him away with a sermon instead of
punishing him.[61] He writes constantly to defend an innocent person who had been accused unjustly to the magistrate, to plead for a remission of taxes in favour of poor
people, to intercede for a slave with his master, to persuade
the governor to build a bridge that the people want, to
soften the heart of a pagan father whose son has become a
Christian.[62] The great collection of the saint's letters shows
him always in the same light: stern and unflinching before
people in high places, gentle and merciful to the poor. It is
from these letters that we know him best, and in them that
we see the qualities that make Saint Basil one of the most
attractive and charming of all the Fathers.

He had naturally many friends. We have seen how closely
he was allied to Gregory of Nazianzos. Eusebeios, Bishop
of Samosata on the Euphrates (in Kommagene), was also
a dear friend to whom he wrote a number of letters;
Amphilochios, Bishop of Ikonion, was a disciple to whom

[58] Ep. 169, 170, 171.

[59] A chorepiscopus was a person who shared some of the bishop's work without having any jurisdiction—something like our [England's] rural deans. They
appear sometimes to have had bishop's and sometimes only priest's orders.

[60] Ep. 291.

[61] Ep. 286.

[62] Ep. 96, 107, 108, 109, 180, 273, 276, 305, etc.

he dedicated his treatise on the Holy Spirit (p. 77 below). Once Saint Ephrem (d. ca. 379) came from far Syria to visit the great metropolitan at Cæsarea. He could speak no Greek and Basil no Syriac; when Ephrem came to the church at Cæsarea Basil saw him during the office and came up to him afterward with an interpreter to say, "Are you Ephrem who have taken the yoke of salvation so excellently well upon yourself?" "I am Ephrem," he answered, "who walk so unworthily in the way of salvation." And they kissed each other, and Ephrem said, "Father, defend me against laziness and sloth, lead me in the right way, pierce my evil heart." They talked for a long time. Ephrem, when he went home, never forgot Basil, and long afterward wrote a panegyric about him. And Basil, too, remembered the Syrian deacon who had come all that way to see him.[63] "From my youth to old age," Saint Basil writes, "I have had many friends." [64] And again: "I have never sinned against friendship." [65] But one of these friends gave him great trouble. Eustathios of Sebaste in Armenia had been intimate with him for years. Basil loved Eustathios, and at first all went well. Then Eustathios, always shifty and uncertain, gradually went over to the Arians and repaid Basil's friendship with calumnies and accusations for three years. Basil spoke no evil of him, but always tried to make it up and to bring his old friend back to the faith. Only in the case of one flagrant calumny did he justify himself in a letter to the monks of his diocese.[66] Eustathios died an open heretic in 380; and Basil's brother Peter succeeded him as Bishop of Sebaste. The saint had continual relations with western

[63] Sozomenos, *Hist. Eccl.* iii, 16.
[64] Ep. 272.
[65] Ibid.
[66] Ep. 226.

bishops, too. When Valens was persecuting the Catholics, Basil sent to Pope Damasus (366–384), asking him to use his authority to make peace in the east. "The only remedy for these evils", he says, "is a visitation from your mercy." [67] He knew quite well that the Roman Bishop has jurisdiction over the whole Church of Christ. He writes at the same time to Saint Athanasius, "We thought it expedient to write to the Bishop of Rome that he should examine our affairs and to advise him, since it would be difficult to send anyone thence by the common decree of a synod, to use his lawful authority in the matter, choosing men fit to bear the fatigue of a journey and also fit to correct all perverse people in our parts gently and firmly." [68] During all this time he was treating with Damasus, continually imploring him to send help to the eastern Church, and showing in every letter how well he understood that Catholic bishops turn to Rome in time of great trouble. He was angry when he found that all the western bishops took the side of Paulinos in the schism at Antioch, whereas he, as all the easterns, was for Meletios. In one letter, he quotes Homer to express his annoyance at western pride.[69] But his annoyance passed away, and later he showed again how great a regard he has for his distant Latin brothers.[70] He was delighted at the election of Saint Ambrose at Milan (374), the western Father whose character is most like his own. When Ambrose wrote to ask him to send back the relics of Dionysius of Milan (who had died in exile for the faith in Cappadocia), he did so at once and wrote him a charming letter full of praise of the Milanese priests who had come

[67] Ep. 70.
[68] Ep. 69.
[69] Ep. 239.
[70] Ep. 265.

to fetch Dionysius' relics, and full of admiration for the bishop who had sent them. "Man of God," he says, "it is not from men that you have learned the Gospel of Christ; it is God himself who took you from the seat of the Roman magistrates to place you on the throne of the apostles. Fight the good fight. Heal the sickness of Arianism among your people. Renew the old paths of the fathers, and do not forget to write often to me, so that our friendship many never become weak. So shall we always be neighbours in spirit although a great distance divides us on earth." [71] One remembers these courteous and friendly relations between the two great Fathers at Cæsarea and Milan as one of the pleasantest examples of the old good feeling between eastern and western Christendom. How little either Basil or Ambrose foresaw that for more than eleven centuries a bitter schism could divide their successors.

During these years of Basil's reign as metropolitan, then, we see in him from every point of view the perfect model of a great Catholic bishop. Standing out valiantly for the faith against the Arians, ruling his province firmly and wisely, leader of his people, proudly conscious of the liberty of the Church against the state, gentle and kind to the poor, courteous, friendly and charming to his friends, best and most entertaining of letter-writers, submitting his difficulties to his rightful chief at Rome, from far Cappadocia he has left an example that any bishop in any land may pray to be worthy to follow.

8. Saint Gregory of Nyssa (ca. 331–ca. 395)

Since we left Basil's younger brother Gregory at home as a young man not very fond of prayers, we have almost lost sight of him. His life is too much overshadowed by that of

[71] Ep. 197.

his great brother for him to have a chapter to himself. One paragraph will be enough to give a short outline of his career. He, as well as the other brother Peter, had been educated chiefly by Basil, of whom he speaks as his "father and master".[72] His friends wanted him to be a priest, but at first he preferred the career of an orator, so that Gregory of Nazianzos says rather unkindly and unfairly that he "liked the name of orator better than that of Christian."[73] There is really no reason why an orator should not be as good a Christian as anyone else. At the same time, Gregory married a lady named Theosebeia.[74] She did not die till 381. He had, however, already served in church as a Lector.[75] Eventually he made up his mind to forsake the world and leave his wife.[76] He went to be a monk, apparently at Basil's settlement at Annesos. In 371, Basil ordained him Bishop of Nyssa, very much against his will, he says.[77] Nyssa was a little town in Cappadocia on the river Halys, about forty miles west of Cæsarea. He was, therefore, a suffragan of his brother. Basil thought he would find in him a valuable help in the affairs of the province. But, on the whole, it was rather a disappointment. No one questioned Gregory's virtues or good intentions; but his brother did not think him a success as a bishop. Basil has to complain of his "unwise and uncandid interference";[78] he says that by his "simplicity" he gave a great deal of trouble[79] and that he was "altogether without

[72] *De hominis opif.* 1 (*PG* 44, 125).

[73] Ep. 11.

[74] Gregory of Nazianzos, Ep. 197.

[75] Gregory of Nazianzos, Ep. 11.

[76] She seems to have joined him again later and to have lived with him like a sister (Gregory of Nazianzos, Ep. 197).

[77] Basil, Ep. 225 and 345.

[78] Ep. 58 and 60.

[79] Ep. 100.

experience in ecclesiastical affairs".[80] It would seem, then, that Gregory was a pious and irreproachable person, who was not, however, specially fitted to rule a diocese. It is his writings that give him a right to be remembered. However he had the honour of suffering for the faith. In 375, the Governor, Demosthenes—an Arian, of course, under Valens—deposed him as a Homooüsian and set up an Arian antibishop at Nyssa. Gregory of Nazianzos wrote to comfort him.[81] For years he then wandered about, "like a log floating on the water", says the other Gregory.[82] When Valens died (378), he came back to Nyssa. The next year he was at a synod at Antioch that tried to settle the great schism there (of Meletios). He outlived Basil, and was present at the second general Council (Constantinople I in 381). He was well-known as a staunch Catholic, so much so that Emperor Theodosius (379–395) ordered that the test of being a Catholic bishop in Pontus was to be in communion with three persons, Helladios of Cæsarea (Basil's successor), Otreios of Melitene in Armenia and Gregory of Nyssa. We hear of him last at a Synod of Constantinople in 394 under Patriarch Nektarios (381–397). Then he disappears; he probably died soon after. His last years were troubled by a quarrel with his metropolitan, Helladios.[83] For the writings that give him an important place among the Greek Fathers see below, pp. 79–82.

9. Saint Basil's Death (Jan. 1, 379)

There is little more to tell of Basil but his death and burial. During his last years, he had the pain of seeing the Roman

---

[80] Ep. 215.
[81] Gregory of Nazianzos, Ep. 72.
[82] Gregory of Nazianzos, Ep. 81.
[83] Gregory of Nyssa, Ep. 1.

arms defeated in a series of bloody battles with the Goths.[84] On the other hand, the cause he had fought for all his life, that of the Nicene faith against the Arians, triumphed completely under Theodosius. He just lived to see this triumph. In 378, only forty-nine years old, but worn out with austerities and the ill-health from which he had suffered all his life, he lay on his death-bed. The whole city was moved by the news of his sickness, and thousands besieged his house to speak to him once more. At the very end, they told him that certain persons, who should have been ordained deacon and priest, had waited over-long because of his sickness, so he roused himself once more and held a great ordination. Then he went back to die. On January 1, 379, he spoke the words with which we all hope to end our lives: "Into thy hands, O Lord, I commend my spirit", and went to his reward.[85]

Gregory of Nyssa buried his brother with such pomp as had never been seen before at Cæsarea. The whole city accompanied their great bishop to the grave, and everyone tried to touch the hem of his vestments as his body was borne on an open bier through the streets. Strangers, Jews and pagans lamented him as much as his own Catholics.[86] His lifelong friend, Gregory of Nazianzos, was too sick himself to be able to come; but two years later (in 381) he preached a great panegyric that is one of the chief authorities for Basil's life and a classical example of this kind of

---

[84] Valens allowed the Goths to settle in the empire in 376. But they soon began to fight. In 377, they defeated the Romans, and again in 378 at Adrianople. Valens himself was killed at this battle, but Gratian and Theodosius restored the honour of the Roman arms and drove back the barbarians for a time.

[85] Gregory of Nazianzos, *Oratio* xliii.

[86] Ibid.

sermon. He remembers the days long ago when they had sat on the same bench as young students: "O home of our friendship, beautiful Athens, where we loved each other in the comradeship of that really divine life!" [87] He wrote a beautiful letter to his namesake of Nyssa: "So I have lived to see the death of Basil and the departure of that blessed soul to the presence of God, to whom he had prayed all through his life." [88] "How great now", he says, "is the solitude of the Church that has lost his glory on earth, that is no longer adorned with his crown." [89] And Gregory of Nyssa, however inexperienced he may have been as bishop, during all the rest of his life never ceased honouring the memory of his great brother. He, too, preached a great panegyric about him; and soon afterward he went out to Annesos, where Makrine still lived as a nun. He found her very sick; they talked about Basil. He could not help weeping when he spoke of him, but she, more firm, gloried in his memory, spoke with pride of his life and would not mourn the brother she was soon to see again before the throne of God. She died very soon after.

One would like to have a picture of so great a Father as was Saint Basil. Gregory of Nazianzos describes him as tall, pale and thin, with a long beard; he was always absorbed in his thoughts and very shy. [90]

The great Church he defended during his life has not forgotten him after death. Every year in east and west the memory is kept of the saint whom we agree to call Basil the Great. His own Byzantine Church keeps his feast on the day of his death, January 1. On that day the monks

[87] Epitaph 119.
[88] Ep. 76.
[89] Ibid.
[90] *Oratio* xliii.

who look to him as their founder, the bishops who count him as a chief glory of their order, sing: "The Lord of all receives Circumcision, the Master of Life mercifully receives the wound and gives salvation to the world. And the high Priest of the Creator rejoices in heaven, the light-bearer and divine Bishop of Christ, Basil."[91] They have another feast of Saint Basil, with all his holy relations, the two Makrines, Emmelia, Gregory of Nyssa and Peter of Sebaste, on May 30,[92] and they honour him again together with Saint Gregory of Nazianzos and Saint John Chrysostom on January 30. Nor have his Latin cousins forgotten him. On June 14, the day of his consecration, the Roman Martyrology remembers: "At Cæsarea in Cappadocia the ordination of St Basil, Bishop, who, at the time of the emperor Valens, shone with wonderful wisdom and knowledge, was adorned with all virtues, and defended the Church with unchanging constancy against the Arians and Macedonians." And before our altars, white-robed for a Confessor Pontiff, we say on that day* the Mass of a Doctor of the Church: *In medio Ecclesiæ aperuit os eius; et implevit eum Dominus spiritu sapientiæ et intellectus: stolam gloria induit eum.*

10. Table of Dates

330 *Saint Basil born.*
ca. 331 Saint Gregory of Nyssa born.
ca. 345–355 Basil student at Cæsarea, Constantinople, Athens.

---

*In the post-Vatican II Church, the Latin rite celebrates the Feast of Ss. Basil the Great and Gregory Nazianzos on January 2.

[91] *Horologion*, Jan. 1, *Echos* [Οικος: A specific prayer—ED.] of the feast, 3.

[92] This is a Uniate feast. The Roman Martyrology commemorates his relations on the same day (Nicolaus Nilles, *Kalendarium Manuale* 2nd ed. [Innsbruck, 1896], I, pp. 167, 168).

355 Back home at Neocæsarea in Pontus.

355–357 Professor of rhetoric at Cappadocia.

357 *Baptized* by Dianeios of Cæsarea.

357–358 Journey to monasteries in Egypt, Palestine, Syria.

358–364 Head of monastic community at Annesos.

361–363 Julian emperor.

362 Dianeios of Cæsarea dies. Eusebeios succeeds him. Julian punishes the city.

364 *Basil ordained deacon and priest* by Eusebeios. He goes back to Annesos.

364–378 Valens Cæsar in the east.

365–370 Priest at Cæsarea.

367–368 Famine in Cappadocia.

370 *Basil Metropolitan of Cæsarea.* Domitius Modestus threatens to banish him.

371 Cappadocia divided into two civil provinces. Gregory ordained Bishop of Nyssa.

372 (Epiphany) Valens at Cæsarea.

374 Saint Ambrose Archbishop of Milan.

375 Gregory of Nyssa banished.

378 Valens dies.

379–395 Theodosius I Cæsar in the east (394–395 emperor).

379 (Jan. 1) *Death of Saint Basil.*

ca. 395 Death of Saint Gregory of Nyssa.

11. Works of Saint Basil

If Basil is famous as a saint, as the organizer of eastern monasticism, and a great Catholic bishop, he has a further title to fame as one of the chief classical writers of the fourth century. His language and style are immeasurably better than those of Saint Athanasius. Athanasius was hardly a stylist at all; but Basil had studied in the best school in the world and had been a famous teacher of rhetoric before he went to be a monk. His writing is less ornate than that of Saint John Chrysostom; perhaps for that reason it is more attractive to modern people. Through all his many works, especially in his sermons and letters, there is a restrained eloquence, a fire controlled by a very dignified and reticent self-command that makes them the most sympathetic and pleasant to read of all the works of Greek Fathers. He uses, of course, the language of his time. The dual and optative mood had disappeared long ago. It would have been an absurd affectation to revive them in the fourth century. Nevertheless, his writing is the best answer to the old idea that Greek letters were dead in the first Christian centuries.

His works were first published in Greek at Basel in 1532, in three folio volumes, reprinted at Venice in 1535 and at Basel in 1551. A learned Jesuit, Fronton le Duc,[93] edited them, and this edition was published by the Dominican F. Combefis at Paris in 1679, in two volumes. The best edition is still that of the Benedictines of Saint Maur, three folios at Paris, 1721–1730. L. de Sinners reprinted it at Paris in 1839. In Migne's collection (*Patrologia Græca*) his works fill four volumes, 29–32 (Paris, 1857). H. Hurter, S.J., has published a Latin version of the *De Spiritu sancto* in his *SS. Patrum opuscula selecta*, vol. xxxi (Innsbruck, 1875). Various works have been translated into many languages. Rufinus of Aquileia (d. 410) did ten sermons and both monastic rules into Latin. There is an Old English version of the *Hexaemeron* (H. W. Norman, *The Anglo-Saxon Version of the Hexaemeron of St Basil* [London, 1848]). Another work is G. Lewis, *The Treatise of St Basil on the Holy Spirit* (London, 1888).

---

[93] *Fronto Ducæus* in Latin.

DOGMATIC WORKS. The *Answer to the Apology of Impious Eunomios* (ἀνατρεπτικὸς τοῦ ἀπολογητικοῦ τοῦ δυσσεβοῦς Εὐνομίου, Libri v, *Quibus impii Eunomii apologeticus evertitur*, PG 29:497–773) was written about the year 363 or 364. It is his chief work against extreme Arianism. *Of the Holy Spirit* (περὶ τοῦ ἁγίου πνεύματ, *De Spiritu sancto*, PG 32:67–218), written in 375 and dedicated to his pupil Amphilochios of Ikonion, contains thirty chapters. It is a defence of the equality and consubstantial nature of God the Holy Spirit against the later Arians, who had begun to apply their theories about God the Son to the third Person of the Blessed Trinity (the Pneumatomachians). It has always been the standard work on the subject.

EXEGESIS. His most famous exegetical books are the nine homilies on the *Hexaemeron* (ἑξαήμερον, PG 29:3–208), that is, on the six days of creation. Saint Ambrose's Hexaemeron (*PL* 14:123–274) is practically a compilation from this and from a work of Origen with the same title. Basil explains the creation with the strangest theories of physics and many edifying applications. He also wrote fifty homilies on the *Psalms* (PG 29–30) some of which, however, are doubtfully authentic. A commentary on *Isaiah*, 1–16 (*PG* 30), is very doubtful.

ASCETIC WORKS. His two *Monastic Rules* have the first place here. There is a longer rule of 55 chapters (ὅροι κατὰ πλάτος) and a shorter one of 313 chapters (ὅροι κατ᾽ ἐπιτομήν, both in PG 31, *Regulæ fusius tractatæ, Regulæ brevius tractatæ*). The longer rule was written at Annesos, the shorter one—an epitome—later, at Cæsarea. He wrote a number of other treatises about the *Life of Monks* (βίος τῶν μοναχῶν), *De vita monachorum*, PG 31), the *Judgement of God* (περὶ κρίματος θεοῦ, *De iudicio Dei*, *PG* 31), *Rules of Morals* (τὰ ἠθικά, *Ethica*), eighty *Principles of Virtuous Life* (ὅροι, *Principia*), etc., all of which are collected under the general name, *Ascetica* (ἀσκητικά) in *PG* 31:619–1428.

HOMILIES. A number of Saint Basil's sermons, preached on various occasions, have been preserved. The best known are the ones *Against Usurers* (κατὰ τοκιζόντωυ, *Contra usuriarios*, *PG* 29:263–80) and at the time of the *Famine in Cappadocia* (367–68, see pp. 60–61 above). Twenty-four others (*PG* 31:163–618) treat of various questions of dogma, morals and exegesis or celebrate various saints and martyrs.

LETTERS. No one really knows Saint Basil who has not read his letters. There are 365 altogether (*PG* 32:219–1110), in which he writes of every kind of subject, details of his own life and events in the history of his time, dogma, polemics, practical advice and controversy. Sometimes he consoles someone for a loss, sometimes he asks a favour or thanks his correspondent for a favour already received. We find in them politics, discussions of points of scholarship, anecdotes of every kind. He corresponded with all sorts of persons from the Pope to heretics; he writes to governors, officers, monks, nuns, bishops; to the great Athanasius, his own relations, his clergy; most of all to Gregory of Nazianzos; even to Apollinaris of Laodicea, of unhappy memory. Sometimes he is angry and complains, sometimes he describes the country where he is; he constantly makes quiet fun. In his own time, these letters were famous; Gregory of Nazianzos began collecting them at once after his death.[94] There

---

[94] Gregory of Nazianzos, Ep. 53.

is certainly no collection of Greek letters so entertaining as these.[95]

LITURGY. The *Liturgy of St Basil* (*PG* 31:1629–78) is used throughout the eastern world, from Kiev to Alexandria and from Dalmatia to Japan. It is printed first in all the Orthodox and Melkite *Euchologia*. It is not the oftenest used, but the foundation of the Byzantine rite (see p. 60, n. 41 above). Liturgically, it occurs in thirteen translations besides the original Greek. How far it is really the saint's own composition is a question that will probably never be settled.

12. Works of Saint Gregory of Nyssa

Saint Basil's brother was a prolific writer, though none of his works reach the level of those of Basil. He is a philosopher and an ardent admirer and faithful disciple of Origen (d. 254), whom he follows exactly in his interpretation of Scripture. His most characteristic work is philosophical speculation about the Holy Trinity, the immortality of the soul and so on. Needless to say, as a disciple of Origen he is Neo-platonic.

The Jesuit Fronton le Duc first edited his works in two folio volumes at Paris in 1615; J. Gretser, S.J., published an additional volume of works omitted by le Duc in 1618. The next edition (complete with Gretser's additions) was at Paris in 1638, three volumes. Other works have been discovered by various people since, notably seven more letters by J. Caracciolo (Florence, 1731). Gregory of Nyssa fills

---

[95] They make a perfect parallel to the Latin letters of St Jerome (d. 420) both in their interest, humour and pleasantness, and in their beautiful style. For St Jerome, in spite of the shocks he sometimes gives us in the Vulgate, could write most beautiful Latin when he chose.

three volumes of Migne (*Patrologia Græca* 44–46 [Paris, 1858]). The *Oxford Select Library of Nicene and Post-Nicene Fathers* contains a selection of his works in English (ser. II, vol. v).

EXEGESIS. He wrote a *Defence of the Hexaemeron* (ἀπολογητικὸς περὶ τῆς ἑξαήμερου, *Explicatio apologetica in hexaemeron, PG* 44:61–124), a vindication and completion of his brother's work, and thirty chapters *Of the Creation of Man* (περὶ κατασκευῆς ἀνθρώπου, *De hominis opificio, PG* 44:125–256), We have also from him a *Life of Moses* (περὶ τοῦ βίου Μωυσέως τοῦ νομοθέτου, *De vita Moysis, seu de virtutis perfectione, PG* 44:297–430), in which he fills up the Biblical account with allegorical interpretations. The point of the life is that Moses should be a model to a friend of Gregory named Kaisarios. Further, an allegorical treatise *On the Inscriptions of the Psalms* (εἰς τὴν ἐπιγραφὴν τῶν ψαλμῶν, *In psalmorum inscriptionem*, libri II, *PG* 44:432–608), a commentary on *Ecclesiastes* (*PG* 44:616–753), in the form of eight homilies, twenty-five homilies on the *Song of Songs* (*PG* 44:756–1120), five on the *Lord's Prayer* (*PG* 44:1120–93) and eight on the *Beatitudes* (*PG* 44:1193–1301).

DOGMATIC WORKS. The most important is his *Great Catechism* (λόγος κατηχητικὸς ὁ μέγας, *Oratio catechetica magna*, forty chapters, *PG* 45:9–105), a defence of the Catholic faith against pagans, Jews and Arians. Then the *Twelve Books against Eunomios* (πρὸς Εὐνόμιον ἀντιῤῥητικοὶ λόγοι, *Libri XII, contra Eunomium, PG* 45:237–1121). Eunomios had answered Saint Basil's work against him (p. 77) after that saint's death; this is a refutation of the answer. His *Refutation of Apollinaris* (ἀντιῤῥητικός πρὸς τὰ ᾿Απολλιναρίου, *Antirrheticus adv. Apollinarem*, fifty-nine chapters, *PG* 45:1124–1269) and the sequel, *Against Apollinaris*, dedicated to Theophilos of Alexandria (κατ' 'Απολλιναρίου, *Adv. Apollinarem ad Theophilum*, *PG* 45:1269–77), are important authorities for the life and teaching of that heretic.[96] Then there are many shorter treatises on various dogmas, such as the Blessed Trinity, the immorality of the soul and Fate.

ASCETIC WORKS. He wrote a treatise on *Virginity* (περὶ παρθενίας, *De virginitate*, *PG* 44:317–416), letters to monks and short treatises on the *End of Man*, the *Life of a Christian* and so on, also a treatise *Against Those Who Put Off Their Baptism* (*PG* 46).

HOMILIES. Many of the works we have already noted are written in the form of sermons. There are others preached at Nyssa and Constantinople, panegyrics of saints, among which we note those on Saint Gregory Thaumaturgos, Saint Basil his brother, Saint Makrine his sister and the Funeral Orations of the princess Pulcheria and the empress Flaccilla. His sermons are very ornate and full of flowers of rhetoric. They cannot be compared to those of Saint Basil. All are contained in *PG* 46.

LETTERS. Migne (*PG* 46) contains twenty-six letters. The second letter about *Pilgrimages to Jerusalem* gives a vivid picture

---

[96] Apollinaris (Apollinarios), Bishop of Laodicea in Syria (d. ca. 392), was a famous heretic who, accepting the Neo-platonic theory that man consists of three elements, *body*, *soul* and *spirit*, taught that in our Lord the Divinity (the *Logos*, Word of God), took the place of this third element, the spirit. So he was not perfect man; he lacked one element of our nature, the human spirit. Apollinaris then was a kind of forerunner of the Monophysites. Nearly all the Fathers of this time wrote at least one treatise against him. Harnack thinks he was the only reasonable theologian of the fourth century, and he has become a quite appalling obsession to J. Dräseke. See my article s.v. "Apollinarism", in Hastings' *Encyclopedia of Religion and Ethics* (Edinburgh: T. and T. Clark, vol. 1.).

of the abuses and scandals that even then accompanied visits to the holy land. Gregory thinks that if people behave so badly when they get to Jerusalem they had better stay at home. This letter was often used by Protestants in the sixteenth century as an argument against all pilgrimages; a purpose that would have annoyed its author, since he made a very pious pilgrimage to the holy places himself. He is not the only Catholic who has been distressed at the quarrels that go on round our Lord's tomb.

CHAPTER THREE

SAINT GREGORY OF NAZIANZOS (330–390)

Gregory of Nazianzos, the intimate friend and companion of Saint Basil, fills a more important place in the consciousness of the eastern Churches than he does with us in the west. We should hardly name him among the very greatest Fathers, but in the east his writings are considered so important and so valuable that he is to the descendants of his own people the "Theologian" in a special and proper sense. That is his surname among them; they hardly ever speak of him as Nazianzene; when a Greek says "Gregory the Theologian" (Γρηγόριος ὁ θεολόγος) he means this saint. The Theologian was one of the three friends who redeemed the once not well-sounding name of Cappadocia.[1] He was not only a theologian but a philosopher, poet and a man of public political life as well. He had a chequered career and several unpleasant adventures before he at last settled down in peace to end his days in his own town. Less great than Basil, more so than Gregory of Nyssa, he has left the memory of an irreproachable, but not always very prudent saint, and of a voluminous, orthodox and edifying writer.[2]

---

[1] As mentioned earlier, the three great Cappadocians are St Basil, St Gregory of Nazianzos and St Gregory of Nyssa (Basil's younger brother).

[2] Most saints who were bishops are named after their dioceses; thus we speak of St Hilary of Poitiers, St Augustine of Canterbury, St Hugh of

1. Early Years (330–ca. 345)

Gregory was born in 330 at *Arianzos*, a property belonging to his father near Nazianzos. *Nazianzos* (Ναζιανζός), or *Dio-cæsarea*, in Cappadocia, was a small town about sixty-five miles south-west of the capital, Cæsarea.[3] And of this city his father, also called Gregory, was bishop. His mother, Nonna, was a saint, who brought her son up as carefully and as piously as Saint Emmelia was bringing up her son Basil at the same time.

The fact that Gregory's father was a bishop, and a very holy and orthodox bishop, which confronts us at the beginning of this life, will surprise most people, whether Catholic or Orthodox. How, one asks, could a bishop have a wife and family? And how could a bishop's wife be a saint?

The principle that is at the root of the law of celibacy certainly goes back to the time of the Apostles. Saint Paul tells us plainly that he considers virginity to be the higher state (1 Cor 7:28, 32–34, 40), and our Lord himself had taught the same thing (Mt 19:12). Inevitably, then, the Christian Church looked upon celibacy as a more holy thing. If anyone is to follow this higher and more austere path, surely it should be, in the first place, the clergy who are called to minister more closely to God. So clerics, as a general rule, preferred to remain unmarried; then nearly all did so. It began to be looked upon as unedifying if one did marry; then as almost, eventually, quite scandalous. It is a typical case of a law obtaining force by prescription.[4] But the law

---

Lincoln. This saint is an exception. He was Bishop of Sasima, but is always called after his native town, Nazianzos.

[3] Now a village, *Nenizi*.

[4] Even in the old law a temporary celibacy was required of priests before they sacrificed (Ex 19:15).

crystallized into different forms in east and west. In the west, at any rate since the fourth century,[5] the law is celibacy for all clerics in major orders. In the east, deacons and priests may keep their wives if they are already married, but bishops must be celibate.[6] There is no reason to suppose that the Bishop of Nazianzos ceased being a married man when he was ordained; on the contrary, our Saint Gregory had a younger brother, Kaisarios, who must have been born afterward. We must conclude then from this case that, at any rate in Cappadocia, celibacy was not yet considered a binding law for bishops, although in the fourth century the general feeling on the subject had already very nearly produced a law. The bishops, who took a foremost place at that time, the saints and Fathers such as Gregory the son, Basil, Chrysostom, and so on, were celibate as a matter of course.*

---

* More recent scholarly research has made it doubtful that the elder Gregory had any children after his ordination. Cf. *The Apostolic Origins of Priestly Celibacy*, by Christian Cochini (San Francisco: Ignatius Press, 1990), pp. 242ff. Cochini has shown that from apostolic times continence was required of married men as a condition of ordination.—ED.

[5] The first case of a definite law in the west seems to be the letter of Pope Siricius (384–399) to Himerius of Tarracona (Ep. 1, chap. 7, in the C.I.C. dist. lxxxii), Innocent I (401–417) repeats it (dist. xxxi), and from that time a number of councils (e.g., second Council of Carthage in 390, fifth Council of Carthage in 401) down to the first Lateran Council in 1123 (can. 21) and the second Lateran Council in 1139 (can. 40) form our present law.

[6] Obviously monks and nuns everywhere have always been bound by the same law. A solemn vow of chastity was always the essence of monastic life. The first Council of Nicæa (325) already maintained the "ancient custom" that forbade marriage after ordination. The Council of Constantinople in 692 (the *Quinisextum*, Trullanum II) insists on this law and forbids Bishops to be married. There has always been a strong feeling against bigamy for any clerics. *Bigamy* in Canon Law means not only having two wives at once (*bigamia simultanea*), but having two, one after another (*bigamia successiva*). This is always an impediment against Holy Orders. To marry a widow is a form of bigamy (*bigamia interpretativa*).

The elder Gregory was a well-known man, too, in a way. He had been a pagan and a statesman. His wife, Saint Nonna, converted him; he was baptized in 328 or 329. Soon after he became Bishop of Nazianzos, succeeding his baptizer, and he was a valiant defender of the Catholic faith against the Arians. His son in later years constantly referred to him with great veneration.[7] Our saint was apparently the eldest child, then came a sister, Gorgonia, and the brother, Kaisarios. The family lived chiefly at Arianzos, on their estate, a few miles south of Nazianzos on the road to Tyana. But they had a house in the city, too, and young Gregory began his education at school there. His mother, Nonna, easily formed his mind to love the Christian faith and the example of Christian saints. The boy was naturally docile and pious from the beginning. When he was quite little, he had a dream that two beautiful ladies came to him; their names were Temperance and Virginity.[8] And to these two ladies he promised to be true all his life, a promise he very faithfully kept.

2. Education at Cæsarea and Athens (ca. 345–357)

As soon as they were old enough, Gregory and Kaisarios went to Cæsarea, the capital of Cappadocia, to have a better education than could be obtained in so small a country town as Nazianzos.[9] At Cæsarea they met Saint Basil for the first time: Gregory formed a friendship with him that only one quarrel was to interrupt (see pp. 93–94 below) during all their lives. The friends parted for a time, and

[7] In the *Oratio* 18 especially.

[8] Gregory of Nazianzos, *Carmen* i, 45.

[9] Sokrates (*Hist. Eccl.* iv, 26, 13) says that Nazianzos was quite a small place of no importance.

Gregory went on to Palestine and Alexandria. Then he sailed to Athens. On the way, there was a frightful storm in which he was nearly drowned. He says afterward in what terror he was then at the thought that he was still unbaptized; the memory of that danger made Gregory, too, one of the most strenuous opponents of the dangerous custom of putting off baptism till a man is grown.[10] At Athens he met Basil again. Gregory remembered their years of friendship and study at "golden Athens" with as much pleasure as did Basil.[11] Years afterward, when his friend was dead and he preached his funeral sermon, Gregory recalled the distant days when they had shared the same lodging, the same studies, the same ideas.[12] He was the older of the two and had arrived at Athens first, so he was able to help his friend with advice about life at a university and to defend him from the practical jokes of the other students.[13] There was an amusing quarrel with the Armenians. Cappadocians and Armenians, being neighbours of different races, naturally did not like each other. The Armenians set various traps for these new Cappadocians, out of which Gregory assures us that they came victoriously. And he adds (on the word of a Cappadocian) that "the Armenian nation is not noble or frank; they are all sly and vicious."[14] After four or five years, in 357, Basil went back home to Cappadocia; Gregory stayed

[10] *Carmen de se ipso,* i, 324–26; xi, 162–74, etc.

[11] See p. 73 above.

[12] *Oratio 43, In laudem Basilii (PG* 36:493–605).

[13] Rough practical jokes on a freshman seem to be an inevitable element of universities everywhere. At Athens the most brilliant pleasantry was to seize your man and to throw him into the water (Gregory of Nazianzos, *Oratio* 43:16). It is also characteristic that the men should form themselves into companies according to their nationalities. There were the Cappadocians, Armenians, Syrians, etc.

[14] *Oratio* 43.

and continued his studies at Athens. But soon after he, too, left the university and started back for home.

This time, remembering the perils of the seas, he preferred a long journey by land round by Constantinople. Here he found his brother Kaisarios, who had studied medicine and was now making a fortune as a doctor in the capital. Gregory seems to have been all too eager to make everyone flee the world, as he himself was about to do. So he persuaded his brother to leave his practice and to come back to Cappadocia with him to be a monk. Kaisarios let himself be persuaded at first, but he never really wanted to change his life. We should say that he obviously had no vocation. So after a short time he went back to Constantinople and looked up his patients again. Gregory was disappointed; his disappointment turned into indignation when he heard that his brother still went on with his career under the pagan emperor Julian (361–363). Did not this inevitably mean at least a tacit apostasy? His suspicion was quite unjust. Kaisarios was a perfectly loyal Christian always, and when he found that by staying at the capital his faith was in real danger he again left his practice and went to Cappadocia. The end of Kaisarios was that he came back to Constantinople after Julian's death, became a government official under Valens (364–378), was baptized and died an edifying death soon after 368. He is an example of an entirely satisfactory Christian in the world. Gregory's everlasting girding that he should be a monk and his attitude of shocked surprise that his brother should choose rather to be a doctor are unreasonable and intolerant. Not everyone has a vocation to the "angelic life".[15]

---

[15] For the story of Kaisarios, see Gregory of Nazianzos, *Oratio* 7, Ep. 7 and *Carmen* ii.

3. Gregory's Baptism, Ordination and Flight
(357–ca. 372)

Meanwhile Gregory, who knew his own mind better than that of his brother, as soon as he came home to Cappadocia (357), began to see about being a monk himself. His father, the bishop, was now an old man, so for a time he stayed with him and looked after the estate at Arianzos. But each day he spent certain fixed hours in prayer and meditation. He was now twenty-seven years old, and it was quite time for him to be baptized, especially as he had not forgotten his narrow escape of death by shipwreck. So he was baptized, apparently by his father,[16] soon after he came home.

Meanwhile Basil was travelling about and learning from monks how to copy their life.[17] Soon after the community at Annesos in Pontus had been formed (358)[18] Gregory went to join it. He describes this first visit as a short one in which he only just tasted the sweetness of the ascetic life.[19] As his father still wanted him at home, he soon went back to Nazianzos. Then happened one of those curious cases of an ordination by force of which we often hear at this time. The people of Nazianzos wanted the bishop's son to be a priest. The father agreed, but Gregory himself was entirely against the plan. He wanted to be a monk with Basil, and monks were not priests. To be a priest meant to go on living in the world at Nazianzos. He felt unworthy

---

[16] According to our Canon Law, a man ought not to baptize his own son, except in case of necessity. But there is no such principle in the east. Besides, our Canon Law does not provide for bishops having sons.

[17] See p. 54 above.

[18] See pp. 54–55 above.

[19] *Oratio* 2, 6.

and unfit for so high and difficult a life. To flee the world, to meditate in silence and sing hymns at Annesos was easier and safer. So he resisted the proposal with all his might. In spite of his resistance, his father took him and ordained him priest by force, apparently on Christmas day in 361.[20]

The question of these ordinations in which the subject resists and is made a priest by force is a curious one. We should say that a mature person cannot receive a sacrament (except, perhaps, the holy Eucharist) validly, unless he has the intention of doing so. These Fathers never seem to think of that. We must suppose that, in spite of his resistance, Gregory had, at any rate, that very vague and implicit intention that is needed for the sacrament to be valid.[21] And in any case it is a question of moral force only.

As soon as the ordination was over Gregory, still very indignant and determined not to work as a priest even if he

---

[20] But was Christmas (December 25) kept in Cappadocia in the middle of the fourth century? In 385, it was still unknown at Jerusalem; St Ephrem (d. 379) does not know it, nor was it yet introduced into Armenia or Mesopotamia. Kellner (*Heortologie* [Freiburg im Breisgau, 1901]) thinks that Christmas was kept in Cappadocia first in 382 (pp. 84–85). St John Chrysostom announces it as a new feast at Antioch in 388 (Hom., *In nat. Christi*, PG 49:351). Before that the memory of our Lord's birth was kept on the Epiphany (Jan. 6). Bardenhewer (*Patrologie* [Freiburg im Breisgau, 1894]), who gives Christmas 361 as the date of this ordination, must mean the Epiphany. See Usener, *Religionsgesch. Untersuchungen* i (1889).

[21] People who are not theologians never seem to understand how little *intention* is wanted for a sacrament (the point applies equally to minister and subject). The "implicit intention of doing what Christ instituted" means so vague and small a thing that one can hardly help having it—unless one deliberately excludes it. At the time when everyone was talking about Anglican orders, numbers of Catholics confused *intention* with *faith*. Faith is not wanted. It is heresy to say that it is (this was the error of St Cyprian and Firmilian against which Pope Stephen I [254–257] protested). A man may have utterly wrong, heretical and blasphemous views about a sacrament and yet confer or receive it quite validly.

had been made one, ran away to Pontus to join Basil again.[22] But by Easter 362, Basil persuaded him that since he had been ordained he should go back to the world and help his father in the diocese.[23] He came back then to Nazianzos and was soon able to put an end to a serious disturbance there. His father, the bishop, was always really Catholic and Homooüsian. Only, he had given way once in a moment of weakness, like so many other good and well-meaning bishops in that time of persecution and hopeless confusion, when synods and anti-synods were everlastingly drawing up new formulas of various shades of Arianism, when the government was everlastingly demanding the acceptance of some new profession. The formula that Constantius (337–361) had forced on the great Synod of Ariminium (359) was semi-Arian. The emperor insisted that every bishop should sign it. There were very few confessors who had the courage to hold out still, after years of this sort of thing—it was the time of which Saint Jerome said that "the whole world groaned and shuddered to find itself Arian." [24] And old Gregory at Nazianzos gave way like the others and signed. At once there was great commotion in the diocese. The Catholics, and especially the monks, broke off all relations with a semi-Arian bishop (363). Gregory, the son, persuaded his father to retract his false step by a public confession of the Catholic faith (Homooüsianism); he then brought all the diocese back to its normal state of obedience. The dates of

[22] His *Apology of His Flight* (p. 102 below) was written in excuse and explanation of this flight to Pontus after his ordination.

[23] The conviction of all these Fathers that a man simply cannot be both a monk and a priest, that one state necessarily excludes the other, is very curious as showing what monasticism meant in the first stage of its development. See p. 53 above.

[24] *Contra Luciferianos*, 19.

these events are not certain. Some think that this schism and pacification took place before his ordination and flight.[25] During this first time, perhaps while they were both at Annesos, Gregory and Basil composed a selection from the works of Origen (d. 254) that they called the *Philokalia* (φιλοκαλία = Love of Beauty).[26] Then for about nine or ten years (362–372?) Gregory stayed at Nazianzos as a priest under his father. In 370, the father ordained Basil as Metropolitan of Cæsarea,[27] and the son assisted him, though he does not seem to have been too well pleased at his friend's promotion.[28] He had an invincible dread of the responsibility and dangers of such positions. But a very serious breach between the friends came when Basil made Gregory a bishop too.

4. Bishop of Sasima; His Hermitage at Seleucia (372–379)

Basil had great difficulties with his rebellious suffragan, Anthimos of Tyana.[29] In order to resist this person, he thought it a good plan to make his two staunchest supporters bishops of dioceses on the frontier of Tyana. So he ordained his own brother Bishop of Nyssa[30] and then wanted Gregory of Nazianzos to be Bishop of Sasima, a few miles south-east of Nazianzos. If Gregory had disliked the idea of being a priest, he was still more opposed to that of being bishop. So he refused absolutely. In spite of

[25] So Bardenhewer (*Patrologie*, p. 264) and Loofs in the Protestant *Realencyklopädie* ([1899], vii, 142). P. Clemencet (editor of the Benedictine edition of Gregory of Nazianzos. See p. 101 below) adopts the order I have given.
[26] Ep. 115, Clemencet, *Vita Greg.*, 65.
[27] See above, p. 62 above.
[28] *Carmen de se ipso*, 398ff.
[29] See p. 65 above.
[30] See pp. 65, 70 above.

that Basil took him and ordained him (it is another of these astonishing cases of forced ordinations), apparently in 372. Gregory's indignation knew no bounds this time. He absolutely refused to go near Sasima. He describes it as the most odious place in the world—barren, solitary, ugly and generally detestable.[31] He had never been there. Indeed, it is more than doubtful if he ever went to his diocese at all. So he ran away again to be a monk somewhere in the mountains, away from Basil and his father and Sasima.[32] He seems to have specially disliked the idea of being set up in a forepost to fight Anthimos, although he was so far loyal to Basil that he would not listen to Anthimos' arguments against the metropolitan.[33] For seven years, he bore a grudge against his old friend for this ordination and the plan of sending him to Sasima. It seems that Basil certainly made a mistake in ordaining Gregory against his will and that he had expected too much from his friend. On the other hand, it cannot be said that Gregory behaved well in this affair. The old father was very much annoyed at the whole business. He did not at all want his son to be Bishop of Sasima, but he did not want him to be a monk with useless bishop's orders either. He had been very glad to have him at Nazianzos, and now he wanted him back there to help in the affairs of that diocese. So he wrote and implored his son to come, not to Sasima, but to Nazianzos. He was a very old man now. If Basil had not taken this hasty step, he had hoped that his son might gradually undertake all the work at Nazianzos and eventually succeed him as bishop there. Gregory then

[31] *Carmen*, 386–485; Ep. 48 and 50.
[32] *Carmen*, 490ff.; 529ff.
[33] Ep. 48 and 50.

gave way to his father and came out of his hiding-place. Although he was still very angry with Basil and still refused to go to Sasima, he came back to Nazianzos and administered the diocese for his father. Old Gregory died in 374; Saint Nonna soon followed him to the grave. Our Gregory then went on taking care of the diocese. But he was still considered Bishop of Sasima; this connexion with a place he had never even seen was a trouble to him all his life. Soon afterward, in 375, the neighbouring bishops began to see about finding a successor to the dead bishop. His son, who had so long administered the diocese, was obviously the right man. But he was Bishop of Sasima. They were persuading the metropolitan, Basil, who now recognized his mistake, to accept his resignation of Sasima and to acknowledge him as Bishop of Nazianzos, when Gregory fled again, this time to Seleucia in Isauria. He must have had an invincible repugnance to be the Ordinary of any place, and he had not yet forgiven Basil. He stayed at Seleucia as a hermit for four years. While he was there, he heard the news of his old friend's death (Saint Basil, d. Jan. 1, 379). Death ends all quarrels. Gregory now forgot his grievance; all the rest of his life he was the most ardent defender of Basil's memory. He made the first collection of the great metropolitan's letters,[34] and later, in 381, he preached a splendid panegyric, in which he passes over the trouble about Sasima and remembers only the happy years they had spent together at "golden Athens".[35] This generous forgetting of his grievance is the pleasantest incident in Gregory's life. If saints do quarrel sometimes, they make it up again afterward.

[34] See p. 78 above.
[35] See p. 73 above.

5. Gregory at Constantinople (379–381)

If Gregory had made anything clear so far it was that he did not want to be a bishop. He seems to have been quite happy at Seleucia and only anxious to be let alone. But events now again brought him out of his hermitage and called him to use his orders at the capital. Under Cæsar Valens (364–378), the Arians had had it all their own way, especially at Constantinople. The Catholics were reduced to a little handful, who rejected the communion of the Arian bishop Demophilos (369–379). But when Theodosius I (379–395) succeeded as emperor, the situation changed. Theodosius was a determined Catholic always. So the faithful Homooüsians in 379 sent to Gregory, asking him to come and take charge of their community, at any rate till a regular bishop could be appointed. He was obviously just the person they wanted. He was a bishop who could use any episcopal function, and he was not engaged at any diocese. He could not resist this appeal, himself one of the first champions of the Nicene faith in eastern Christendom. So again he gave up his ideal of leading a monk's life and came to take charge of the Catholics at Constantinople (379). Here he arranged everything, restored order, ordained and fulfilled all a bishop's duties till a bishop should be elected in the usual way. For so far, at any rate, he did not consider himself, nor was he considered by anyone, to be Bishop of Constantinople, but rather still titular of Sasima. He also preached; his sermons were so famous that Saint Jerome (d. 410), already an old man, came to the capital to hear them. Theodosius came to Constantinople in 380 and at once restored to the Catholics the chief church of the city (either the Hagia Sophia or the church of the Apostles) that the Arians had seized. Meanwhile the

Egyptians—always disturbers of the peace in the Church of Constantinople—irregularly ordained one of themselves, a certain Maximos, as Ordinary. The greater number of the Catholics refused to acknowledge this person and wanted Gregory formally to resign the see he had never even visited and to accept an election as Ordinary in the capital. He seems to have been disposed to do so; for a time now he apparently claimed to be Bishop of Constantinople.

6. The Second General Council (381)

At this time came the meeting of bishops at Constantinople that was eventually recognized as the second general Council. Out of the great Arian movement, then dying out fast, two new heresies had grown. Some Arians applied their theories about God the Son to the Holy Spirit too, saying that he, too, is a creature, less than God the Father. These people are the *Pneumatomachians* (πνευματόμαχοι = fighters against the Spirit). The semi-Arian Bishop of Constantinople, Makedonios (344–348, 350–360), who had been driven out and had come back, was their chief leader; with him a monk named Marathonios defended this heresy.[36] The Pneumatomachians had been condemned by an Alexandrine synod in 362; soon afterward they themselves held one at Zele in Pontus,[37] in which they separated themselves from both Catholics and Arians to form a sect of their own. They were now disposed to admit the Divinity of our Lord and his equality with God the Father; but they transferred all the Arians' ideas about him to the Holy Spirit. Several

---

[36] From these two people the heretics are also called *Macedonians* or *Marathonians*.

[37] Its date is uncertain.

Fathers, Didymos the Blind,[38] our Gregory[39] and others had already written against this heresy. As a result of the opposition to Arianism, the famous *Apollinaris*, Bishop of Laodicea in Syria, had evolved his system, according to which our Lord had a human body and soul, but no human spirit, since the Word took its place.[40] In 381, Theodosius summoned all the bishops of the empire to a council at Constantinople, to declare the faith on these points and once more to wipe out whatever was left of Arianism. Only 150 eastern bishops came. There were no Latins and no legates from Rome. This is the council, œcumenic neither in its summons nor its sessions, to which the ratification of the Roman See and of the Church long afterward gave the right of being numbered among the œcumenical synods.[41] At first, Meletios of Antioch[42] presided; he died during the council, and our Gregory of Nazianzos then took his place. If the addition to the Nicene creed was made by this council,[43] it shows its condemnation of the Pneumatomachians in the clause about the Holy Spirit, "the Lord and giver of

[38] *Didymos* (310–395), a layman, was the leader of the Catechetic school at Alexandria. He had become blind when four years old, but was nevertheless one of the most famous scholars of his time, and an ardent Origenist. St Jerome, Rufinus and other Fathers learned from him. His works are in *PG* 39:131–1818. Against the Pneumatomachians, he wrote *On the Holy Spirit*. Of this work, only St Jerome's Latin translation has been preserved (*PL* 23:101–54).

[39] In his fifth theological Oration (thirty-first Oration).

[40] See above, p. 81, n. 96.

[41] That is as far as its dogmatic definitions are concerned. Its four canons were never received in the west. Its third canon is the first step in the advance of Constantinople to patriarchal rank (see my *Orthodox Eastern Church* [London: Catholic Truth Society, 1907], pp. 32–33).

[42] The famous bishop about whom the Meletian schism arose (ibid., pp. 90–92).

[43] Mgr Duchesne (*Églises séparées* [Paris, 1905], pp. 77–80) and others doubt this. If they are right, the second general Council did nothing at all.

life, who proceeds from the Father, who, together with the Father and Son, is adored and glorified, who spoke by the prophets". The synod refused to acknowledge Maximos at Constantinople and took the side of Meletios at Antioch. Both decisions gave offence to Rome and the west.[44] The fathers of Constantinople then recognized Gregory as bishop of that city. So he must for a short time be considered Ordinary of Constantinople. But his enemies, especially the Egyptians, still used their old argument against him. He was Bishop of Sasima, and no one can hold two sees at once. By this time, Gregory must have loathed the very name of that barren and detestable town that he had never even seen. Still no doubt there was something in their argument. He does not seem to have ever formally resigned his old see, or perhaps the Metropolitan of Cæsarea (where Helladios had succeeded Saint Basil) had not accepted his resignation.[45] No other Bishop of Sasima had been appointed; if that see had an Ordinary at all it was Gregory.

The saint was further annoyed by the action of the council with regard to the Antiochene affair. He had hoped to

[44] Rome acknowledged Paulinos, Meletios' rival at Antioch. As for Maximos, Rome was disposed to acknowledge him too. It is another case of that alliance between Rome and Egypt that influences all eastern Church history for centuries (*Orth. Eastern Church*, p. 92). If ever a philosophical account of ecclesiastical politics in the east is written, the alliance between Rome and Alexandria as against Antioch and Constantinople will be seen to be an important factor throughout.

[45] As a matter of fact, translations from one see to another were the rarest things at that time. There was for many centuries an idea that the symbolic marriage of a bishop to his see should be as indissoluble as a real marriage— till the see was widowed by his death. The analogy recurs in all kinds of forms. To usurp another man's diocese was adultery. So even in the case of the highest sees—the patriarchates, Rome itself—a vacancy was filled, not by translating a bishop from somewhere else, but by ordaining a priest or deacon of the diocese.

arrange matters peaceably now that Meletios was dead; but the extravagant partisanship of most of the fathers led to the appointment of Flavian as a successor in the Meletian line, whereby the trouble was continued and the friction with the west increased. So Gregory was now only anxious to leave Constantinople and the council. He felt, no doubt, himself the force of the argument against his position there; perhaps he had never really meant to become permanently bishop of the capital. Nektarios was chosen bishop peacefully and canonically (381–397), and Gregory retired. Before he left the council, he preached a sermon to the fathers in which he bade them farewell and gave them good advice as to their duties. Then, tired of all these disputes and wishing only to end his days in peace, he went home to Nazianzos.

7. Last Years and Death (381–390)

He ended his days quietly by the city where he had spent his first years. Since his father's death no successor had been appointed at Nazianzos. Our saint did not consider himself to be that successor—he still bore the burden of that title of Sasima—but he declared that he would administer the diocese till an Ordinary should be elected. He did so for two years. Then by his advice a certain Eulalios was chosen canonically and consecrated in 383. Gregory then lived in retirement on the estate he had inherited at Arianzos. Here again he was able to realize his old ideal of living like a monk, being as much a monk as a bishop could be. He spent the last seven years of his life in prayer and great mortification and found a relaxation in writing poetry. Besides various hymns and poems written for edification, he composed a long *Song of His Life* (see p. 102 below). He died in peace in 390 (others think it was in 389).

We have seen that he fills a larger place in the memory of eastern Churches than he does with us. To them he is by a special title the *Theologian*. We remember him chiefly as Saint Basil's friend and as a man of strangely uncertain character whose want of consistent purpose was caused mainly by the fact that all his life he could never do as he wanted. It was Basil's ill-considered impulse about Sasima that ruined his life. He is the patron saint of people who do not want to be bishops. The Byzantine Church keeps his feast on January 25, again on January 30 with Saints Basil and John Chrysostom,[46] the Syrian Uniates and Jacobites on January 25 and the Latins on May 9.* He is a Doctor of the Church.

8. Table of Dates

330 *Gregory born at Arianzos* by Nazianzos in Cappadocia.

ca. 345(?). Student at Cæsarea, then at Athens with Saint Basil.

357 Baptized at Nazianzos. Monk at Annesos.

361 *Ordained priest* at Nazianzos. He escapes to Annesos.

362 Priest at Nazianzos.

363 Schism at Nazianzos.

372 *Ordained Bishop of Sasima*. He again escapes. Back at Nazianzos.

374 Gregory the father dies.

375–379 At Seleucia in Isauria.

---

* Since Vatican II, in the Roman Church, the feast of St Gregory Nazianzos is celebrated with that of St Basil the Great on January 2.—ED.

[46] These three are the "three holy Hierarchs and Œcumenical Doctors". This feast dates from 1081 or 1084, when it was instituted by the emperor Alexios Komnenos (1081–1118). Cf. Nilles, *Kalendarium Manuale* 2nd ed. (Innsbruck, 1896), I, p. 87.

379–381 *Administers the See of Constantinople.*

381 SECOND GENERAL COUNCIL (First Council of Constantinople). Gregory goes back to Nazianzos.

383 Eulalios Bishop of Nazianzos. Gregory at Arianzos.

390 (or 389) *Gregory* dies.

9. Works

J. Billius and F. Morellus edited the works of Saint Gregory of Nazianzos in two folio volumes at Paris in 1609–1611. The Benedictine edition was begun before the French Revolution (vol. 1 by P. Clemencet [Paris, 1778]) and finished after it (ed. A. B. Caillau [Paris, 1840]). In Migne's *Patrologia Græca* his works fill four volumes (35–38 [Paris: 1886 and 1862]). All these editions are in Greek and Latin. J. Goldhorn published selections of Saint Gregory of Nazianzos with Saint Basil in the *Bibl. Patrum Græca dogmatica*, vol. 11 (*S. Basilii et S. Greg. Naz. opera dogm. selecta* [Leipzig, 1854]). E. Dronke edited some of his poems (*Carmina Selecta S. Greg. Naz.*) at Göttingen in 1840; another selection in W. Christ and M. Paranikas, *Anthologia græca carminum christianorum* (Leipzig, 1871), pp. 23–32. The *Oratio apologetica de fuga sua* was published separately by J. Alzog in 1868 (Freiburg); the *Oratio in fratrem Cæsarium* (Paris, 1885), and *Oratio in laudem Machabæorum*, by E. Sommer (Paris, 1891). H. Hurter, S.J., in his *SS. Patrum opuscula selecta* (Innsbruck) includes Latin versions of the five *Orationes theologicæ* (XXIX) and the *Oratio apologetica de fuga sua* (XL). Rufinus of Aquileia had already translated some of his sermons into Latin (publ. at Strassburg in 1508). Other works are the two Orations *Against Julian* in an English version by C. W. King (*Julian the Emperor* [London, 1888]).

ORATIONS. There are forty-five Orations or sermons spoken by Saint Gregory of Nazianzos on various occasions (*PG* 35–36). Of these, the numbers 27–31 form a group apart, that he himself describes as *Theological Orations* (οἱ τῆς θεολογίας λόγοι, in *Oratio* xxviii, 1). These are often numbered apart, 1–5 (as by Hurter, above). They were preached at Constantinople in 379 and 381 to defend the Catholic faith about the holy Trinity against Arians and Pneumatomachians. Among the others, the most important are numbers 4 and 5, two *Accusations against Julian* (λόγοι στηλιτευτικοὶ κατὰ Ἰουλιανόν), prudently held after the emperor's death; also number 20, *On the Appointment of Bishops*, and number 32, *On Moderation in Dispute*. Number 2, the famous *Apology of His Flight* (ἀπολογητικὸς τῆς εἰς τὸν Πόντον φυγῆς ἕνεκεν, *Oratio apologetica de fuga sua*), is not properly an Oration but a treatise. It is his most valuable work. Written about the year 362 as a justification of his flight after he was ordained priest (see pp. 90–91 above), it contains a very ideal and splendid description of the priesthood; it was probably the model on which Saint John Chrysostom formed his treatise.

POEMS. The longest poem is the *Song of his Own Life* (ᾆσμα περὶ τοῦ βίου ἑαυτοῦ, *Carmen de vita sua*, *PG* 37:1029–1166). In this, he tells the story of his life in a succession of lines in every kind of metre—hexametres, pentametres, trimetres, iambic and anacreontic, with many lines that do not scan at all. It is the chief source for his biography. Some of his shorter poems approach nearer to poetry. The *Evening Hymn* and *Exhortation to Virgins* (*PG* 37:511–14, 632–40) are in rhythmical prose. In the poem, *About His Verses* (*PG* 37:1329–36), he gives his reasons for writing in this form. The tragedy, *Christ Suffering* (Χριστὸς πασχών,

Christus patiens, PG 38:133–38), once attributed to him is a late medieval composition.[47]

LETTERS. Of these, 243 are preserved, most of them written at the end of his life at Arianzos (383–390). He began making a collection of them himself for a friend named Nikobolos (Ep. 52, 53, XXXVII). They are contained in Migne, *PG* 37. Nearly all are very carefully written, and many are evidently meant to be read by others besides the person to whom they are addressed. They treat of events in his life, and in that of his friends, or they discuss points of theology.

---

[47] Of the eleventh or twelfth century (Krumbacher, *Gesch. der Byzantinischen litteratur* [Munich, 1891], p. 746ff.). Naturally Dräseke attributes it to Apollinaris, as he does every doubtful work in Greek.

CHAPTER FOUR

SAINT JOHN CHRYSOSTOM
(344–407)

John of Constantinople, to whom by universal consent has been given the surname of Chrysostom,[1] "Golden-mouthed", is, perhaps, of all Greek Fathers the best known in the west. He is (together with Photius) the most famous Patriarch of Constantinople, one of the only three saints[2] who sat on that soul-endangering throne. He suffered persecution and exile, not for the faith, but for the equally sacred cause of morality; he is remembered by his own people as the author of the liturgy they commonly use, and by everyone as the most eloquent and perfect orator of the

---

[1] Χρυσόστομος (χρυσοῦν στόμα), *Chrysóstomus* (pro-paroxytone in both Greek and Latin). So much has this name been joined to his original one, that his is almost the only case in which a surname occurs in our liturgy. As a rule, saints are called only by their Christian name in prayers. Thus we speak of St John Damascene, St Thomas Aquinas, St Francis de Sales; but in their collects they are only "Johannes", "Thomas", "Franciscus". On the other hand, on January 27, we pray God to increase by grace his Church "quam beati Johannis Chrysostomi, confessoris tui atque pontificis illustrare voluisti gloriosis mentis et doctrinis" [now his feast is September 13—ED.]. So again in the secret and post-communion. The only other case of a surname in the text of the Roman Missal is that of St Peter Chrysologus (Golden-speeched) Archbishop of Ravenna (d. 450), the western counterpart of our saint (Dec. 4) [now celebrated on July 30—ED.].

[2] The others are St Gregory of Nazianzos (390) and St Ignatius of Constantinople (d. 877), the lawful patriarch when Photius was intruded.

Christian Church. To Catholics as to the Orthodox he remains for all time the great model and patron of preachers.

1. Early Years (344–369)

Saint John was born about the year 344 in the city which was the centre of the first half of his life, Antioch on the Orontes, the capital of Syria. Antioch in the fourth century was still one of the greatest cities of the empire. Before Constantinople arose, it had been one of the three chief towns, with Rome and Alexandria. Founded in 301 B.C. by Seleukos I (Nikator), the first of the line of Seleucid Kings of Syria,[3] and named by him after his father Antiochos,[4] under the Romans it still kept its natural place as the head of Syria. It was an enormous city; the great colonnade from the eastern to the western gate was over five miles long. About fifteen miles to the west was the harbour Seleucia; four miles further down the Orontes was the sacred grove of Daphne, to which pilgrims came from every part of the empire to the oracle of the far-darting Apollo. But Antioch became a great centre of Christianity too. Saint Paul and Saint Barnabas here "stayed the whole year in the Church and taught a great crowd; so that at Antioch the disciples were first called Christians" (Acts 11:26). At the time of Saint John Chrysostom, of its two hundred thousand inhabitants half were Christians. The Antiochene school of

[3] The empire of Alexander the Great (B.C. 336–323) broke up after his death and was divided among his generals (the διάδοχοι = successors). Of these successors, the chief were Ptolemaios in Egypt, who founded the kingdom of the Ptolemies with Alexandria as capital, and this Seleukos in Syria. Both lines were of course Greek, and their capitals were outposts of Hellenism among barbarians. The Romans conquered Syria in 64 B.C. and Egypt in 30 B.C.

[4] Ἀντιόχεια, *Antiochía*.

theology was very famous, although suspect as unsafe in doctrine, and the Bishop of Antioch was one of the three older patriarchs.

The splendour of the great Seleucid capital has gone now. You may ride from the port of Iskanderun to *Antakiye* in a day, and you will find a little town, half Turkish, half Arab, that does not fill up a tenth part of the space enclosed in the old walls. Among the thick olive-woods around it, you will see broken columns, by the mosque in the chief street ruins of the old colonnade. Going out through the Moham-medan tombs you come to the grove of Daphne. Her laurels still tremble in the cool winds as if she feared the god; but Apollo has gone long ago. Even the Christian memories hardly linger here; of the five persons who bear the splen-did title of Patriarch of Antioch not one now lives here.[5] From the tombs across the river you see the town with its minarets and the great wheels that churn up the brown water under the mountains on which you may trace the ruins of the old walls against the sky. You may try to call up the old glory of the "great and God-protected city" in which John Chrysostom preached. While the distant wail of the Mu'ezzin tells you that there is no god but Allah and Mohammed is the prophet of Allah, you will think that here we first got our name of Christians.

Our saint's family was very wealthy and powerful. His father, Secundus, died young, soon after John's birth, so the child was educated by his mother, Anthusa. Saint Anthusa is one of the great Christian mothers who brought up their sons to be famous saints. As we who honour Saint Augustine

---

[5] The Orthodox and Melkite patriarchs live at Damascus, the Maronite at Bkerki in the Lebanon, the Jacobite at Diarbekr on the Tigris, the titular Latin patriarch at Rome. [The author wrote this in 1908.—ED.]

remember Saint Monica, as the glory of Saint Gregory of
Nazianzos is bound up with that of Saint Nonna, so does
Anthusa share the honour of John Chrysostom. He remembered always what he owed to her, and later he quoted the
words said to him by one of his pagan teachers: "What wonderful women these Christians have!" Then John went to
hear the professors who made Antioch famous as a centre
of education. Of his masters the most famous was Libanios,
one of the last of the old pagan philosophers and orators,
and one of the greatest. Libanios, a worthy and excellent
person, who was one of Julian's special friends, still clung
to the worship of the dying gods. He shared the feeling of
those last Hellenes that this new religion, which glorified
asceticism and dreaded the world, would mean the death of
everything that is beautiful and pleasant. They could not
understand the worship of a crucified God; all the fasting
and flagellations, the black gowns and downcast faces of
monks, poverty, chastity and obedience seemed dismal and
horrible to them. They loved Hellas and sunlight, the pleasant old feasts that scattered roses over the steps of temples
while the glorious statues gleamed in the clear light. And
they wanted the old gods, Apollo and Aphrodite and Artemis, the ideals of perfect beauty, and the dear homely gods
of wood and fountain and roadside that were so easily pleased
and so content to see their children happy. One is not surprised that the mystic glory of the Lord who reigns from
the cross, the strange joy of pain for Christ's sake, the silent
love of the good Shepherd, were as much beyond them
as the awful majesty of the Lord of Hosts reigning alone
above the distant heavens. And yet they were not all intolerant, these last pagans, who still pitifully burnt their incense
before the dead gods. Some of them, at any rate, seem to
have lived fairly peacefully among the growing crowd of

Galileans. Even poor Julian, who would have persecuted had he dared, seems sometimes to be reaching out blindly toward the Stranger who draws all things to himself.

And Julian's friend, Libanios, was so little prejudiced that it is said that when he saw the genius of his pupil he wanted to resign his chair in favour of John. The story shows, at any rate, that our saint already then was looked upon as the most distinguished student at Antioch. During this time, he made friends with a certain Basil, who was, perhaps, the future Bishop of Raphaneia.[6] Afterward he began his famous treatise *On the Priesthood* by saying: "I have had many friends both true and dear, who kept the laws of friendship very exactly. But there was one of these who was as much dearer to me than the others as they were dearer than mere acquaintances." This one was Basil. "We followed the same studies", he goes on, "and heard the same masters. We shared the same enthusiasm for our studies, the same cares, the same life in everything."[7] During these first years, then, he acquired that skill in oratory that made him so famous; he learned to use the most perfect language in the world as a skilful workman uses a pliant tool, to persuade, frighten, amuse or rouse enthusiasm. He learned, too, to read the Greek classics, as his later allusions, especially to Plato, show. But John, who is the master of late Greek eloquence, was by no means an unstinted admirer of rhetoric. Later he has very severe things to say against the art of speaking for its own sake,[8] and on one occasion at least he even ventures to attack Homer.[9]

---

[6] In any case not to be confused with St Basil the Great of Cæsarea.
[7] *De Sacerd.* i, 1.
[8] *In Joannem* i, *In Genesin* 22, etc.
[9] *In Ep. ad Ephes.* 21.

During these years in the world, his religious education was not neglected either. At first this was the care of his mother, Anthusa. Later he came very much under the influence of two famous bishops. The first of these was the man whose name is connected with a great and lamentable schism—Meletios of Antioch. It would take too long to tell the whole story of the Meletian schism here.[10] The Arians had banished Eustathios, the lawful Bishop of Antioch, in 330 and had set up a certain Eudoxios as Arian bishop. Eustathios died in 337, so the Catholics were left without a lawful pastor. When Eudoxios also died, in 360, the Arians chose Meletios, Bishop of Sebaste in Armenia, to succeed him. But he turned out to be a Catholic, so they deposed him and set up a real Arian, Euzoios, instead. Meletios came back claiming to be the true bishop, and no doubt all the Catholics would have acknowledged him, had not Lucifer of Calaris (in Sicily) ordained Paulinos as successor to Eustathios. There were then two Catholic bishops, Paulinos and Meletios; after their deaths the rival lines were continued for some eighty-five years. Rome and Alexandria were on the side of the line of Paulinos; most of the Greek Fathers stood by Meletios and his successors. But this did not produce any really bad feeling; eventually it was Saint John Chrysostom who arranged a reconciliation between the Meletian line and the Pope, after the Eustathian succession had died out.[11] Meletios was undoubtedly a very good and holy person: the Roman Church has admitted

[10] The best account of it is F. Cavallera, *Le Schisme de Mélèce* (Paris: Picard, 1906). The author takes Meletios' side throughout.

[11] St John and Theophilos of Alexandria arranged that Flavian, the Meletian bishop, should send an embassy to Pope Siricius (384–399) under Akakios of Berrhoea in 398 and that the Pope should acknowledge him (Sozomenos, *Hist. Eccl.* viii, 3; Sokrates, *Hist. Eccl.* v, 15; Theodoret, *Hist. Eccl.* v, 23).

him to her canon of saints. And he was the first teacher and always the devoted friend of Chrysostom. The other master was Diodore, afterward Bishop of Tarsus (378–394), one of the founders of the famous theological school of Antioch. John's writings, and especially his commentaries on the Bible, show how much he was influenced by Diodore.

Our saint had no period of worldliness to regret in after years. On the contrary, from the beginning, he was very pious and exact in his duties, and already in these first years he felt strongly drawn to join one of the communities of monks that were set up all over Syria. It was his mother, Anthusa, who persuaded him not to leave her "doubly a widow"[12] as long as she lived. John may then have contemplated the career of an orator at first, though it is more likely that he was only waiting till Anthusa died to leave the world and be a monk. And all this time he was, according to the strange and dangerous practice of that time, not yet baptized. In later years he, too, like all the Greek Fathers, protested against the custom of putting off baptism till a man was an adult.[13]

2. Baptism; Life as a Monk (369–380)

In 369, when he was about twenty-five years old, he was baptized by Meletios, who ordained him Lector (ἀναγνώστης) soon after. A certain Karterios at that time had a kind of monastery at Antioch itself.[14] Diodore was one of the leaders of

[12] *De Sacerd.* i, 5.

[13] *In Act. Ap.* i; *In Ep. ad Hebr.* 13.

[14] Sozomenos, *Hist. Eccl.* viii, 2. It would hardly be considered a real monastery since one of the first principles of monasticism then was literally to go away from the world to some place in the desert. And Karterios' establishment was in the middle of the city. At any rate, it was a school of perfection in which people lived like monks.

this congregation. John was influenced by these holy men, too, and confirmed in his wish to flee the world. Then Anthusa died, apparently about the year 373. At the same time, there was a proposal to make both friends, John and Basil, bishops. This scheme led to a quarrel between them. John thought that Basil would make a very good bishop, but was diffident about his own worth. So he let Basil think that he fell in with the scheme and then, as soon as Basil was ordained, John ran away and hid in the mountains.[15] Basil was very much annoyed, thinking that his friend had played an unworthy trick on him.[16] They made up the quarrel eventually, and Saint John's treatise *On the Priesthood* was written as an excuse for what he had done, and dedicated to Basil as an apology.

He was then able to realize his old wish to be a monk. For four years, he lived in a community somewhere in the mountains not far from Antioch; then he retired still more and spent two years as a hermit quite alone in a cave. During all the rest of his life he suffered from ill-health as the result of his over-great mortifications during this time. But he was not destined to remain a monk always. On the contrary, he was to fill a very important place in the world. These six years must be considered as a time of preparation for the great career that was to follow. In about 380, he came back to Antioch, either because his health could not stand a hermit's life or because he understood that he had a work to do in the Church. He had now conquered his former fear of being ordained and took his place as the most important priest in his own city, till he left it to be Patriarch of Constantinople.

[15] *De Sacerd.* i, 6.
[16] Ibid., i, 7.

3. Ordination; Preacher at Antioch (381–397)

In 381 Meletios ordained John deacon. In 386 Flavian, successor of Meletios (d. 386) in that line, ordained him priest.
He was then about forty years old. Some of his earliest works,
notably his treatise *On Virginity* (see p. 140 below), were written before he was known, during the very first years of his
career as a deacon and priest. Then Flavian gave him a special mission as preacher, and for twelve years, till he went to
Constantinople in 398, he was the most famous Christian orator of Antioch, gradually becoming the most famous preacher
in the world. He preached weekly on Sundays, sometimes on
Saturdays too. His sermons were held in all the churches of
the city, but especially in the great Golden Church built by
Constantine.[17] During this time then, especially, he earned
his name of "Golden-mouthed". And the Antiochenes, eager
lovers of eloquence like all Greeks, were in raptures about
their preacher. We have a long series of homilies on different
books of the Bible from these years at Antioch, catechisms
addressed during Lent to the *competentes*, who were to be baptized on Easter eve, and sermons preached on special occasions, of which the most famous is that about the statues.
Gradually he felt his power, and he did not hesitate to allude
to it. Everyone knew that his sermons were the great events
of the week. "You wait for my words like little swallows looking for food from their mother", he said,[18] and another time,
when he had been away for a short time, he said that it

---

[17] This Golden Church was the chief pride of Christian Antioch; it was a
round, or rather eight-sided, building, looked upon as the most splendid
church in the empire. The Patriarchs of Antioch still bear a representation of
it as their arms. Eastern bishops have no cathedrals in our sense; or rather
every church is their cathedral. Each has a permanent bishop's throne against
the south side of the Ikonostasis, facing the people.

[18] *Hoc autem scitote.*

seemed long to him and he was quite sure it seemed long to them too.[19] It would take much space to tell in detail all the qualities of his eloquence. In splendid and sonorous Greek he produces his effect each time irresistibly. His flow of words is amazing; he adorns his speech with every ornament of rhetoric. Sometimes he is majestic and splendid, and then he suddenly comes down to pleasant familiarity. He is indignant, and the sentences roll like thunder; he is pathetic, and it is all tears and woe. Or he argues subtly, persuasively, he pleads tenderly, he threatens awfully. He weaves chains of argument or paints pictures, teaches, exhorts and carries everyone with him up to some crashing climax. One is not surprised that every Greek preacher down to our own time tries to model himself on Chrysostom and that still, on the rare occasions when you may hear a sermon in an Orthodox church, you are surprised to notice that the homely language of the preacher suddenly stops, and that under the low cupolas rolls a splendid sentence, pompous and magnificent, that he has learned by heart from Chrysostom. We are told that our saint, in order to have more opportunity for his effects, in order to be seen by everyone, instead of standing in the usual place in the presbytery before the Ikonostasis, went up into the ambo. This ambo, degraded from its original use as the place from which the readings are made, has become our modern pulpit.

His most famous sermons of all are about the statues.

4. The Affair of the Statues (387)

In 387 happened one of the riots against the government that continually disturbed the Syrian towns, especially Anti-

---

[19] *In facie ei restiti.*

och. These Syrians, like the Egyptians, were never very loyal to the empire into which they had been forced. Later, Syria and Egypt fell away at once when the Moslems came (637 and 641). This time it was some grievance about the taxes—probably a very real one—that made the people commit a mad offence. They rushed to the agora, burnt down a part of the town and knocked over the statues of the emperor Theodosius (379–395), his wife, and sons. Now as for burning down houses, that mattered less, but to upset the emperor's statue! Theodosius was not a man to pass over *lèse-majesté* lightly. It was sheer high treason. As soon as the people had done so, they seem to have realized their danger. A few years later, Theodosius killed every man, woman and child in Thessalonica for a sedition of this kind,[20] and the Antiochenes seem to have known their master's character. So they went to their bishop's house and implored him to set out at once for Constantinople to intercede for them. Flavian, the patriarch, was a very old man, but he did not hesitate to do as they wished. Meanwhile the governor, the "Count of the East", began to apply the punishment. All the members of the Senate who had not fled were at once put in gaol, and awful threats were heard of what Cæsar would do to people who upset his statue. To lose their rights as citizens forever, to have Antioch reduced to a village, and long prison for all the leaders was the very least they could expect. They would be lucky if a troop of soldiers was not sent to hang and burn them.

During the Lent of 387, while Flavian was away and everyone trembled at their danger, John preached his twenty-one homilies on the affair of the statues. He begins by reminding them that he had already complained of their

---

[20] It was for this crime that St Ambrose made him do public penance.

unruly habits. He says that many citizens are decent, law-abiding folk, but that a crowd of lazy, riotous strangers has long disturbed the city, and now they see the result. "If today we are all in such fear, it is the fault of these people. If we had driven them out or made them behave decently, we should not now be in this danger. I know quite well that good manners are practised here, but these strangers,[21] a crew lost to all shame, who have long given up trying to save their souls—these are the people who have brought about all this trouble. You suffer for their crimes, and now God has allowed this insult to the emperor in order to punish us for our carelessness."[22] But all through that Lent he comforts the people, tells them to bear whatever may happen as a punishment for their sins, but to hope for the best, and, above all, to trust in God. And then at Easter came the most glorious news. Flavian had seen the emperor and had persuaded him to forgive the rebellion. The commissioners, who had already started to inflict a most awful punishment on the city, were recalled; the affair would be passed over this time. The messengers from Flavian arrived as the first dawn of the Easter sun lightened the sky; he himself was on his way back and would arrive very soon. So on that Easter morning, Saint John went up into his ambo and preached the *Homily on the Return of Flavian*. One would like to quote nearly all of what is the most perfect example of his eloquence and from every point of view his most famous sermon. "With the word with which I began to

[21] The strangers are the barbarous Syrians from the country round; the decent citizens are the Greeks of the city like himself. No Greek, not even a Greek saint, could ever stand the native population of the place where he was. This passage is amusingly like the way Macedonian Greeks talk of Bulgarians and Serbs and Vlachs.

[22] Hom. i, *De statuis.*

speak to you during the time of danger I begin again today, and I say with you: Blessed be God. Blessed be God who allows us to keep this holy feast with so great joy and delight, who gives the shepherd [Flavian] back to his sheep, the master to his disciples, the bishop to his priests. Blessed be God who has done more than we either asked or even hoped." [23] "Who would have thought", he says, "that our father in so short a time would be able to see the emperor, take away all danger and come back to keep the holy Pasch with us?" "God has used this danger to give greater honour to the city, to the bishop, and to the prince." He develops these three points. The city has acquired honour by the patience and courage of the citizens in so great a danger and because they sought comfort from God. "When those who are in prison heard on all sides that the emperor's fury was growing, that he would destroy the city from top to bottom, they still kept up their courage. They said: 'We trust not in man, but in Almighty God. We are sure that all will end well, for it cannot be that this hope be in vain.'" Then comes glowing praise of the bishop who in his great age put aside every fear to try to save his people, as Moses offered himself for the Jews. And the emperor, too, has acquired undying honour. "What has happened gives him more glory than his diadem, for he has shown that he will listen to a bishop where he would not hear any one else, and he has at once forgiven so great an injury and has silenced his own just anger." [24] Then comes an account of Flavian's interview with Theodosius, how he pleaded and how the emperor forgave. And Theodosius, by his noble generosity, built himself a monument in the hearts of the people of Antioch

---

[23] *In reditum Flav.* i.
[24] Ibid., 3.

that no riot could ever overturn; his mercy was mightier than his armies, more precious than his treasures. Never again would the citizens of this great city forget what they owed to so noble a prince. The emperor had told Flavian to hurry back with the good news. "Go", he said, "at once and reassure them. I know that they are frightened. When they see you again, they will forget the storm. And pray for me that all these wars and troubles may come to an end, and some day I will come to visit Antioch myself." "Let the heathen", says the preacher,

> be confounded, or, rather, let them be instructed, now that prince and bishop have shown them what our philosophy is.[25] ... Now let Antioch adorn her squares with garlands, let torches blaze and green boughs wave throughout the city, rejoice as if it had been founded again! ... Teach this story to your children, and let them tell it to future generations, that all may know for all time how great is the mercy of God to this city.... And let us always give thanks to God the Lover of men[26] both for our safety now and for the danger he allowed, since we know that he ordains all things for our good. And may we always taste of his mercy in this world and come at last to the kingdom of Heaven through Jesus Christ our Lord, to whom be glory and power for ever. Amen.[27]

5. Chrysostom's Theology

During the next ten years, Saint John went on with his office as preacher and, in a long series of sermons, developed his ideas on every part of the life of a Christian. He

---

[25] Ibid., 16.

[26] ὁ θεὸς ὁ φιλάνθρωπος is a favourite expression with Chrysostom; it continually occurs in his liturgy.

[27] *In reditum Flav.*, the end.

preached continually on the duty of *helping the poor*; he was indignant at the luxury of the rich. He told his people to be ashamed of property that they had amassed by pettifogging traffic, by buying cheap and selling dear, or, worse still, by lending out money at usury.[28] He had no tolerance for social distinctions; God gave us all the same father, Adam.[29] Rich people were worse than wild beasts. "Weep," he says to those down in the world, "weep as I do, not for yourselves, but for those who despoil you. Their lot is worse than yours."[30] He wanted people who were well off to keep a permanent guest-house for poor travellers. "Have at least such a place by your stables. Christ comes to you in the form of the poor. Let Christ, at least, use your stable. You shudder at such an idea. It is still worse not to receive him at all."[31] He did not like *slavery*, though no one then thought it absolutely incompatible with Christianity. At least persons should treat their slaves justly and kindly. As for the crowd of useless servants who hung round a rich man's house, "teach them a trade by which they can earn their living honestly and buy their freedom."[32]

He had much to say about the *sanctity of marriage* and about the duties of parents toward their children. Marriage should not be put off till too late, because of the danger of such a course to young people. He insisted on the equality of husband and wife. Infidelity was just as bad, just as disgraceful in a man as in a woman.[33] He thought that each had his proper duties: "God has not given the same life to

[28] E.g., *In Ep. i, ad Thess.* 10; *In Ep. i ad Cor.* 39; *In Matth.* 56.
[29] *In Ep. i ad Cor.* 34.
[30] *In Ep. i ad Tim.* 12.
[31] *In Act. Ap.* 45.
[32] *In Ep. i ad Cor.* 40.
[33] *Ad Stagirum.* ii.

men as to women. The house for the wife, the public square
for the husband. The man works in the field, the woman
weaves her children's clothes." [34] He thought that a man's
wife had to have great influence over him; the husband
would listen to her when he would not take advice from a
stranger. She had to use this influence in the right way.[35]
But he had great and splendid things to say of *celibacy* and
of the higher path of those who gave up all these things to
live only for God. He wrote, besides his treatise *On Virginity*, another, *Against Those Who Attack the Monastic Life* (see
p. 140 below). He was indignant against the old *pagan customs* that still survived at marriages and funerals, and for
funerals especially, he explained exactly what rites were really
Christian, and how people might show their grief without
mourning like those that had no hope.[36] He preached very
strongly against *theatres* and *circuses*. It should be added that
both at that time were still at the level of the late Roman
performances, in which the place of the old Greek poetry
and skill was taken by luxurious extravagance and gross
indecency. Saint John's homily *On Shows*,[37] even if one allows
a margin for rhetoric, contains descriptions of a quite shameless state of things. He saw in the theatre the source of
idleness, of dissatisfaction with real life and especially of
immorality. One can then understand how indignant he
was when on one occasion he found his church almost
empty because everyone had gone to the circus.[38] Saint
John was one of the most enthusiastic admirers of the *Bible*.
By far the greater number of his sermons are explanations

[34] *In Ep. i ad Cor.* 34.
[35] *In Joann.* 61.
[36] *De dormientibus*, passim, etc.
[37] *Contra circenses ludos et theatra* (PG 56:263–70).
[38] Hom. vi, *In Gen.*

of parts of it; taken together, they form a complete commentary on the chief books, from the sixty-seven homilies on Genesis to the thirty-four on Hebrews. In the middle ages, his exposition of the Psalms, and especially the thirty-two sermons on Romans, were the most admired. Isidore of Pelusium (d. ca. 440) says of these: "Had St Paul himself explained his ideas in Attic Greek, he would not have used other language than this." [39] Chrysostom had a special devotion to Saint Paul; it was he who made the saying that became a proverb, "The heart of Paul was the heart of Christ." [40]

Most of the Doctors of the Church have some one point of the faith of which they are the classic exponents; thus, Saint Athanasius is the Doctor of the Divinity of Christ, Saint Augustine is the "Mouth of the Church about Grace". By universal consent, Saint John Chrysostom is looked upon as the great defender of the *holy Eucharist*. He is the *Doctor Eucharisticus*. The Blessed Sacrament and the Real Presence are the subjects to which he turns most often; his writings on this question form a complete defence and exposition of the teaching of the Catholic Church about her most sacred inheritance. In his homilies *On the Sixth Chapter of St John*, he develops the ideas that our Lord has given us "Bread from Heaven, that he who eats it may not perish", that he himself is the "Living Bread that came down from heaven", that we are to "eat his Body and drink his Blood". "We must listen", says Chrysostom, "to this teaching with fear, because what we have to say today is very awful." [41] He points to the altar and says, "Christ lies there sacrificed", [42]

[39] Ep. v, 32 (*PL* 78:1348).

[40] *Cor Pauli cor Christi erat* is constantly quoted in the middle ages.

[41] Hom. xlvii, 1.

[42] Hom. i, *De prod. Judce.* (*PG* 49:381).

"His Body lies before us",[43] "That which is there in the chalice is what flowed from the side of Christ. What is the Bread? The Body of Christ."[44] "Think, man, what sacrifice you receive in your hand [people took the Blessed Sacrament in their right hands], what altar you approach. Consider that you, dust and ashes, receive the Body and Blood of Christ."[45] We not only see the Lord, "we take him in our hand, eat, our teeth pierce his flesh, that we may be closely joined to him."[46] "What he did not allow on the cross, that he allows now at the Liturgy; for your sake he is broken, that all may receive."[47] "It is not a man who causes the Offering to become the Body and Blood of Christ, but he himself who died for us. The priest stands there as his minister when he speaks the words, but the power and grace come from the Lord. This is my Body, he says. This word changes the Offering."[48] "With confidence we receive your gift," he says in a prayer, "and because of your word we firmly believe that we receive a pledge of eternal life, because you say so, Lord, Son of God, who live with the Father in eternal life."[49]

In other points of the faith, Chrysostom stands where we should expect an orthodox and Catholic Father of the

---

[43] Hom. l, *In Matth.* n. 2. (*PG* 58:507).

[44] Hom. xxiv, *In 1 Cor.* 1, 2 (*PG* 61:200).

[45] Hom. *In nat. D.N.I.*, chap. 7 (*PG* 49:361).

[46] Hom. xlvi, *In Joh.* 3 (*PG* 59:260).

[47] Hom. xxiv, *In 1 Cor.* 2 (*PG* 61:200).

[48] Hom. i and ii, *De prod. Judce.* 6 (*PG* 49:380 and 389). This text shows plainly that St John believed that the words of Institution and not the Epiklesis consecrate.

[49] Hom. xlvii *In Joh.* See also Hom. xxiv *In 1 Cor.* 1; *De Sacerd.* iii, 4 ("You see the Lord lying sacrificed and the priest offering and praying, and the tongue reddened with the Precious Blood"—a favourite expression with Chrysostom); Hom. lxxxii, *In Matth.* Catech. ii, 2, etc.

fourth century to stand. One need hardly say that he is uncompromisingly *Homooüsian* and that he anathematizes the Arian heresy, which indeed was dying out fast in his time. He was a friend of Theodore of Mopsuestia (d. 428), who afterward was looked upon as the father of the Nestorian heresy, but there is no trace of Nestorianism in Chrysostom. He believed that our Lord had two natures as firmly as that he was one person. "When I say one Christ, I mean a union, not a mixture, so that one nature was not absorbed in the other, but was united to it." [50] One could not wish for a more accurate statement. The two chief heresies in his time were *Mardonism* and *Manicheism*, and against both he preached continually. He spoke very strongly against pagan superstitions, amulets, auguries, omens and so on. He honoured *saints* [51] and *relics* and gave *absolution* from sins. When he was accused at the Oak-Tree Synod (see pp. 130–31 below), one charge was that he was even too lax in teaching the ease with which sins can be forgiven. "If you sin again," he is reported to have said, "do penance again; as often as you sin come to me and I will heal you." Only on one point does he sometimes use doubtful expressions. He knew nothing of the Pelagian heresy, which did not begin (411) until after his death. He always spoke strongly against the Manichees, who said that all matter is bad, and in his zeal to defend the holiness of nature he sometimes uses

---

[50] Hom. vii *In Phil.* 2, 3 (*PG* 62:231, 232).

[51] For instance in his sermon on SS Berenice and Prosdoce: "Not only on this their feast, but on other days too, let us cling to them, pray to them, beg them to be our patrons. For not only living but also dead they have great favour with God, indeed even greater favour now that they are dead. For now they bear wounds suffered for Christ, and by showing these there is nothing that they cannot obtain of the King" (Hom. *De SS Berenice et Prosdoce*, 7).

expressions that seem to exalt it at the cost of grace.[52] The Pelagian Julian of Eclanum afterward quoted such passages so as to claim Chrysostom for his side. To him, Saint Augustine opposes texts from the same saint that prove the contrary, and says very truly: "What is the good of scrutinizing the works of persons who had no need of caution in this difficult question, since they wrote before the heresy had begun. Certainly they would have been more careful if they had been obliged to answer objections in this matter." [53]

That Saint John believed in the *Primacy* and universal jurisdiction of the Pope of Rome, he showed vary plainly when his own trouble came and he appealed to the Holy See to judge between him and his enemies (below, pp. 133–35). On one point especially, his ideas will please a modern reader. He was on the whole tolerant, much more so than anyone else at that time. "Least of all", he writes, "should Christians try to convert sinners by force. Judges punish criminals and make them change their ways, even if unwillingly. But we must call such people to better things, not by force but by persuasion. The law gives us no right to punish, and even if it did we might not use such a right, because God will not reward people who are compelled to change their lives, but only those who freely do so from conviction." [54]

So John spent eleven years preaching as a priest at Antioch. Then came the great change in his life when he was

[52] Hom. *In Rom.* v; Hom. xii, *In Hebr.*; Hom. xlii, *In Gen.* i. I have quoted some such passages in my *Orthodox Eastern Church* (London: Catholic Truth Society, 1907), p. 109.

[53] *De prædest. SS.* xiv, 27. He quotes as anti-Pelagian passages in Chrysostom, Ep. iii, *Ad Olymp. De Resurr. Lazari*; Hom. ix, *In Gen.*; Hom. *De Baptizatis*; Hom. x, *In Rom.* It is curious to note that Chrysostom, the Eucharistic Doctor, has some doubtful passages about Grace, and that Augustine, the Doctor of Grace, has some inaccurate places about the Eucharist.

[54] *De Sacerd.* ii, 3. He did not always quite act according to these principles.

called away to fill what was already practically the chief place in eastern Christendom.

6. Patriarch of Constantinople (398)

In 397, Nektarios of Constantinople died. There were several candidates for the succession. Theophilos of Alexandria, representing the former chief eastern see that had been reduced in rank by the advance of New Rome (who, like all the Egyptians, was jealous of the new patriarchate of Constantinople) had a candidate of his own, through whom he hoped to rule over that see as well as over his own. But John of Antioch was already a very famous man throughout the east. The news of his wonderful power as orator, of his holiness and unquestioned orthodoxy, had long reached the capital; so he was elected by the clergy to fill the place Nektarios had left. Theophilos concealed his annoyance and himself ordained the new bishop on February 26, 398. So popular was John at Antioch that they had to smuggle him away in secret, lest the people should make a rebellion rather than lose him. It is curious that the two people concerned in his appointment at Constantinople, Theophilos, who ordained him, and the eunuch Eutropios, the favourite of the emperor Arcadius, were the very two men who became his chief enemies afterward.

As Patriarch of Constantinople,[55] John continued his work as preacher. He preached here, too, constantly; but from

[55] The title *patriarch* was used loosely for a long time (*Orth. Eastern Church*, p. 8). Constantinople did not, perhaps, become strictly what we should call a patriarchal see till the Council of Chalcedon (451, can. 28; which even then was not recognized by Rome). But it was already (since can. 3 of the second general Council, 381) practically the chief see in the east, "having the primacy of honour after Rome". It does not appear that St John ever spoke of himself as patriarch.

this moment the main interest of his life was no longer in his sermons, but in the grave political troubles that led to his two banishments. Theodosius the Great (379–395) was dead. The empire was divided between his two sons: Arcadius (395–408) ruled in the east, Honorius (395–423) in the west. Theodosius was the last emperor who ruled the whole empire; this division of east and west, first made by Diocletian (284–305), joined together again by Constantine (323–337), now becomes a permanent state of things. The two halves were never united again.[56] There is not much good to be said of Arcadius. He was at the mercy of a succession of court favourites; and his wife Eudoxia, who was thoroughly bad, gradually got hold of the administration. This Eudoxia became the great enemy of the patriarch.

7. Eutropios' Disgrace (399)

The first trouble was the affair of the eunuch Eutropios. He was the all-powerful favourite. In 399 he made the emperor name him consul, and for a time he practically ruled the empire. Like all such court favourites, he ruled abominably badly. He sold offices and justice, robbed the public funds and was an example of every kind of shameless immorality. The patriarch was not likely to bear with such a person, even if he were a consul; so soon after John's ordination we find him alluding plainly to these scandals in his sermons.[57] He remonstrated with Eutropios personally,

[56] The western half of the empire came to an end with Romulus Augustulus in 476. The right over the whole then fell back on the eastern line at Constantinople. But, in spite of the heroic efforts of Justinian I (527–565), the emperors never got back any real authority in the west, except intermittently in southern Italy and Sicily. And in 800 with Charles the Great began a rival line of emperors in the west.

[57] In Hom. vii, *In Ep. ad Coloss.* and Hom. ii, *In Ep. ad Philipp.*

but that only led to a greater quarrel. The consul especially found the right of sanctuary inconvenient. At that time, as still in many eastern lands, certain places of refuge were allowed, so that criminals who could reach them were safe. These sanctuaries had been the temples; then naturally churches took their place. The right was recognized by the government; how far such a chance of escape for criminals would be an advantage to society in a well-ordered state is another question. At any rate, in a troubled and violent time it gave a man a chance of escaping the first burst of rage against him. He could take sanctuary, prepare his defence at leisure and then, if he were judged innocent, come out. The right of taking sanctuary existed in the west, too, all through the middle ages. To violate sanctuary and drag a man away from his refuge in the church was a specially heinous form of sacrilege.[58] Saint John then stood up for the right of sanctuary; on several occasions, people attacked by Eutropios managed to escape him by taking sanctuary. So Eutropios found the law inconvenient and persuaded Arcadius to abolish it. The patriarch refused to recognize its abolition, and the question further embittered the consul against him. Now comes the dramatic moment of this story. Suddenly Eutropios fell, as such favourites do fall. He had offended the empress, the court gave him up, and all the long list of his crimes were on his head—treason, bribery, evil administration, robbery, corruption, injustice, violence and murder. He had no chance for his life, except one. He fled from the guards who sought him and took sanctuary in John's church. And the patriarch, true to his principles, in this case, too, defended the right in favour of

---

[58] Among the forms of *sacrilegium locale* in the old books of law will be found *violatio asyli*.

the man who had abolished it. The soldiers surrounded the church and clamoured for Eutropios; they did not dare break in. John refused to give him up and protected him until he could get away to Cyprus. The picture of the fallen eunuch, who had abolished sanctuary, cowering at the altar, and Chrysostom, his enemy, standing over him and protecting him, is one of the vivid scenes that has taken hold of the imagination of people in those parts.[59] Nor did the saint fail to improve the occasion in two Homilies *On the Fall of Eutropios*.

8. The Oak-Tree Synod and First Exile (403)

A more serious trouble was the quarrel between the patriarch and the empress. Eudoxia offended the saint in many ways. She was vain and frivolous; she set the fashion of wearing false hair, painting cheeks and aping the manners of a young girl among matrons. These were the very vanities that had long moved the saint's indignation at Antioch. He did not abate a jot of his denunciation of them at Constantinople, in spite of the danger of offending the empress. Worse still, she misgoverned the empire. She had robbed a widow of her field; there were other cases of tyranny and injustice committed by her. Against all these things the patriarch spoke openly. So very soon he knew that he had to count this lady as his enemy. She hated him and began to consider how she could get rid of him. Then came a great quarrel with Theophilos of Alexandria. We have seen that Theophilos had had other plans for the succession at Constantinople. Although he had pretended to give in

---

[59] I have seen boys at a Greek school playing at this scene; it is constantly reproduced in pictures.

and had himself ordained John, he was always secretly his enemy. Now his enmity broke out openly.

Origen (d. 254), the greatest scholar of the eastern Church, perhaps the most wonderful genius of all Christian writers, was destined to be the source of endless disputes for centuries after his death. He is the father of the Fathers of the Church. Every school had learned from him; but, on the other hand, he was more than suspect of various heretical opinions. He had been a Subordinationist[60] and a Chiliast[61] and had taught the pre-existence of souls. So for centuries the Fathers were divided between his ardent admirers, who forgave or ignored these errors, and his enemies, who looked upon him as the father of all heresies.[62] This question, then, was the immediate

[60] That is, he taught that the Son of God was less great than the Father; Subordinationism was the forerunner of Arianism.

[61] *Chiliasm* (= Millennialism) was the belief in the end of all evil, a reign of Christ for one thousand years on earth, the conversion of the devil and all evil spirits, the end of hell and a final restoration of all things in God.

[62] The question of Origen comes up again and again and continually severs the best friends. Gregory Thaumaturgos (d. 270), Pamphilos of Berytos (d. 309) and Dionysios the Great (of Alexandria, d. 264) were his most devoted disciples and admirers. In a less degree, Basil (d. 379), Gregory of Nazianzos (d. 390), Gregory of Nyssa (d. ca. 395), our John Chrysostom (d. 407) were counted Origenists, so was the whole school of Antioch, and countless monks everywhere. Among his uncompromising enemies were Methodios of Olympios (d. ca. 312), Theophilos, this Patriarch of Alexandria (d. 412), most of the Alexandrine school, and many Latins. St Jerome (d. 420) had been an Origenist, but became a violent partisan of the other side and had a tremendous quarrel with Rufinus (d. 410) about this question. Origen comes up again all through the troubles of the sixth century, and once more the burning question was whether he should be considered a heretic or a Father of the Church. Eventually the fifth general Council (Constantinople II in 553) declared against him (can. 11). For all that, Origen's influence, on eastern theology especially, has been enormous; all their metaphysics and still more their exegesis can be traced back to him. Even the men who most attacked him (including St Jerome) owed far more to him than they would ever confess.

ostensible cause of the quarrel between Theophilos of Alexandria and John of Constantinople. Theophilos had in his patriarchate many monks, and monks were nearly always Origenists. Chief among these Origenist monks were four who were called by the strange name of the "Tall Brothers".[63] The patriarch held a synod in 399, condemned Origen and forbade his writings. The Tall Brothers then refused to accept his decision. They were joined by a priest named Isidore, who had quarrelled with Theophilos. The brothers and Isidore escaped from Egypt, where their patriarch meant to punish them, came to Constantinople and begged John to protect them. Saint John behaved very prudently. When he had heard their tale, he allowed them to lodge in a monastery, but would not admit them to communion till he had heard from their own bishop. So he wrote to Theophilos asking him what it was all about. Meanwhile there was already a strong party in his own city against him. The leader was the empress. She was furious because she had heard the patriarch in a sermon speak of Jezebel, and she thought he meant her. Very likely he did. That she was a Jezebel is abundantly evident. Then there were three bishops, some monks and a good many ladies who did not like the patriarch's sermons. The bishops and monks thought him too severe, and the ladies could not bear his ideas about wigs and painted faces. Two deacons whom he had suspended for bad conduct joined the party. So the empress persuaded Theophilos to come to Constantinople, on the strength of this affair of the Tall Brothers, and to hold a synod against John. Theophilos came in 403. He had, of course, no shadow of right to

[63] Οἱ μακροὶ ἀδελφοί. Their real names were Dioskoros, Ammonios, Eusebios and Euthymios.

judge the patriarch of Constantinople; it was an additional insult to do so in that patriarch's own city. He brought a number of his Egyptians with him; joined with the rebellious Byzantines they held a synod of thirty-six bishops. They sat at Chalcedon,[64] across the water, in a property that possessed that rare adornment in those parts—a splendid oak tree. This is the famous *Oak-Tree Synod* (σύνοδος ἐπὶ τὴν δρῦν, *Synodus ad quercum*) in 403. From the saint's sermon after his return from exile and Photius' collection,[65] we know what the case against Saint John was. The points are so absurdly frivolous that it is quite evident that he was condemned really only because the empress wanted to get rid of him. He was charged with having suspended a deacon who had beaten his slave, with being friendly toward pagans, with squandering Church property in almsgiving, with treating his clergy harshly and saying they were not worth three oboles, with being too easy in forgiving sins, eating honey-cakes, making classical allusions in his sermons, exciting the lower classes and interfering in Theophilos' jurisdiction by receiving the Tall Brothers. This last accusation is a most brazen piece of impudence. He had done nothing of the kind, as we have seen. And if Theophilos was so jealous of patriarchal independence, what was he doing at Chalcedon? Lastly comes the real matter, a vague allusion to treason against the empress. John naturally refused to attend this entirely uncanonical synod. So he was declared contumacious, deposed and sentenced to banishment. When he heard his

---

[64] *Chalcedon*, where the fourth general Council was held in 451, lies opposite Constantinople across the Bosphorus—now *Qadi Köi* and *Haidar Pasha*. The Baghdad railway starts here. [These details as of the early twentieth century.—ED.]

[65] *Bibliotheca Photii*, 59.

sentence, he preached a famous sermon. "Tell me, what am I to fear? Death? Christ is my life and death my gain (Phil 1:21). Banishment? The earth is the Lord's and the fullness thereof (Ps 24[23]:1). The loss of goods? Naked I came into the world and naked I shall leave it (Job 1:21)." But still, he says, even in exile nothing can separate him from the Church of which he is lawful bishop, for "whom God has joined together, no man can put asunder" (Mt 19:6).[66] He gave himself up to the officer who came to take him away, and a great crowd of his faithful people accompanied him to the ship on the Bosphorus that was to carry him to Bithynia.

But this first exile did not last long. Soon after he was gone, there was a great earthquake at Constantinople, and Eudoxia was frightened at what she took to be a judgement of God. Also the people, faithful to their patriarch, began to show signs of revolt. So she sent for him very soon after, inviting him back. At first John declared that he would not return till another and greater synod had pronounced his innocence.[67] But the insistence of the empress, who was now as anxious to have him back as she had been to get rid of him, and the rumour of trouble among the people overcame his scruple. He came back in triumph (403), Eudoxia herself came down to the quay to receive him, and this first trouble was over. As usual, he preached his next sermon on the subject, the *Homily at his Return*.[68] He tells the whole story of his trial and

---

[66] Hom. *Ante exilium* (PG 52:427–30).

[67] This was in accordance with the decree of the *Synod of Antioch* in 341, namely, that if a bishop were deposed by a council, he should not be restored till a larger council had declared for him (can. 4 and 12). The law did not apply in this case really, because it supposes that the first synod was a canonical one.

[68] Hom. *Post reditum* (PG 52:443–48).

banishment and then praises Eudoxia, for bringing him back, in a way that seems almost too flattering.

9. The Second Exile (404–407)

But the reconciliation did not last long. A few months afterward the quarrel broke out again, and this time, like the old disturbance at Antioch (see pp. 113–17 above), it was about a statue. Eudoxia had a silver statue of herself set up just outside the Hagia Sophia, the great church of the Holy Wisdom.[69] The erection of the statue was celebrated with a great feast, dancing, racing, drinking and play-acting. The patriarch had always hated this sort of thing, especially the acting (p. 119 above), and now he saw in it, as an additional profanation, a desecration of the church. People trying to say their prayers inside were disturbed by ribald choruses and a shouting racecourse mob. So he protested to the prefect of the city and demanded that the statue should be set up somewhere else, further from the church door. Eudoxia saw in this demand a personal offence against herself and her statue and was mightily offended. Already she began to think about sending the patriarch back into exile. He heard of her plan, and then things came to a climax when he preached a sermon on Saint John the Baptist. For he began his homily by saying: "Once again Herodias rages, once again she screams and dances, again she asks for the head of *John*."[70] The allusion was obvious, for not only the Baptist was named John. Eudoxia was furious. She had been called a Jezebel before, and now she was a Herodias.

---

[69] That is, of course, the older church built by Constantine. The present Holy Wisdom at Constantinople was built on its site by Justinian (527–565) after the old church had been burned down in 532; it was finished in 537.

[70] Sokrates, *Hist. Eccl.* vi, 18; Sozomenos, *Hist. Eccl.* viii, 20.

So she wrote to Theophilos at Alexandria, to ask him to come back and hold another synod against his brother of Constantinople. Theophilos did not want the trouble of making another long journey, so he answered that John could be got rid of in a much simpler way. Let the government invoke that very Synod of Antioch about which he had had a scruple[71] and, since he had come back without having been restored by a synod, his restoration could be described as unlawful, and he could be sent back into exile at once. Eudoxia took this advice. Just before Easter in 404, John was arrested in his own house; all the catechumens who had assembled for their last preparation for baptism were driven away by soldiers. The patriarch was kept a prisoner till after Whitsunday. On June 20, he was again put on a ship and sent away. He was taken across the Black Sea and Asia Minor to Cucusus at the extreme end of Cappadocia, near the Cilician frontier, in little Armenia. A certain Arsakios was set up as anti-patriarch of Constantinople. Saint John still had a large following of faithful subjects in the city. These people, the "Joannites", were then fiercely persecuted; but their lawful bishop kept up relations with them by letter. Eudoxia died soon after she had succeeded in finally banishing her enemy (404). Arsakios died too in the next year; but the government at once set up another intruder, Attikos (406–425). Saint John did not come back alive from this second exile.

10. Appeal to the Pope (404)

Like Athanasius in his trouble, and so many other saints of the eastern Church, John Chrysostom then, finding

[71] See above p. 131, n. 67.

himself banished and persecuted by the empire, solemnly and formally appealed to the great Patriarch at Old Rome, whose rule stretches over the whole Church of Christ.[72] Saint Innocent I (401–417), a very great and splendid Pope, then held the keys. The saint's enemies had appealed to him, too, asking him to agree in John's deposition and to acknowledge Arsakios. Innocent, having heard both sides, on this occasion, too, stood out firmly for the lawful patriarch; and this time, too, as in the later affair of Ignatius and Photius (857), when the appeal to Rome went against them, the government and the usurper at Constantinople dragged the eastern Church into formal schism.

Innocent wrote to John comforting him in his trouble and promising to do all he could for him.[73] Then he wrote to Theophilos of Alexandria reproaching him for his uncanonical proceedings at the Oak Tree and saying that a general Council had better be summoned to settle the affair.[74] But the general Council never came about; there were too many difficulties. So the Pope then wrote again to Honorius, the emperor in the west, asking him to remonstrate with his brother Arcadius. Honorius did so, but received only an offensive reply, in which he was told to mind his own business.[75] There was no possibility of restoring the patriarch by force; so the Pope refused to admit the usurper to his diptychs. Arsakios and then Attikos retorted by breaking communion with the west, and a schism began that lasted eleven years (404–415). Rome then was not able to

---

[72] Palladios, *Dialogus* 9, *Hist. Laus.* 121 (*PG* 34:1233). John's letter to the Pope in Palladios, *Dialogus* 10–22.

[73] Palladios, *Dialogus* 4.

[74] Ibid., 1.

[75] Honorius' letter in Baronius, *Annales* ann. 404 §80ff. (Mansi, iii, 1122ff.).

help Saint John materially; the incident would be unimportant were it not one more example of the acknowledgment of the Primacy by the eastern Fathers and one more case in which the Holy See unhesitatingly defended the right side, even at the cost of a schism.[76]

11. Death and Final Triumph (407–438)

We now come to the end. From Cucusus, the saint was moved to Arabissos, and then the government sent him on again to the north of Asia Minor. But on the way, worn out with the privations of his exile in a wild and desert country, he stopped at Komanes in Pontus, too sick to go any further. A martyr of the Diocletian persecution, Saint Basiliskos, was buried here, and when John arrived and spent the night sleeping by the martyr's tomb, in a dream he saw Basiliskos, who seemed to say to him, "Brother, take comfort, tomorrow we shall be together." The next day Chrysostom rose, vested himself and said the holy Liturgy. After his communion, he lay down and died (Sept. 14, 407).[77] His last words have always been remembered by those who honour his memory, *Glory to God for everything*, δόξα τῷ θεῷ πάντων ἕνεκεν.

And then, as in the case of Saint Thomas of Canterbury, God allowed the final triumph of his saint after death. Arcadius the persecutor died in 408. His son, Theodosius II (408–450), succeeded him, and Theodosius repented of the harm done by his parents. In 438, he sent for the saint's

---

[76] There were four great schisms, making up altogether 203 years, between east and west before the greatest of all under Photius. In each of them Rome was right, without any question; see Mgr Duchesne, *Églises séparées* (Paris, 1905), p. 163, and *Orth. Eastern Church*, pp. 96–97.

[77] Palladios, *Dialogus* c. 11.

relics, that they might be brought back to Constantinople. He himself went down to the shore to meet them, with all his court. In the evening of January 27, the procession of boats came up the Golden Horn, lit by blazing torches that gleamed from the Bosphorus to the Propontis. The emperor kneeling before the barge on which the body rested "asked forgiveness for his parents and for what they had done in ignorance".[78] The waves of the Golden Horn, lit up by the light of the torches, flowing out into the Hellespont and into the great sea beyond, are a symbol of the glory of the golden-mouthed preacher that spread out from his patriarchal city to the ends of the Christian world. For not only in his own country is he honoured. Throughout the great Latin Church, too, across the ocean to lands of which he had never heard, wherever a Catholic priest stands before his people to preach, we remember our patron and example, the one who spoke in season, out of season, reproved, rebuked, exhorted with all patience and learning.[79] The day on which his relics were brought back (January 27) is his feast among his own Byzantines and to us Latins.* They sing: "The holy Church rejoices mystically at the return of thy sacred relics, and receives them as a golden treasure. She never ceases teaching her children to sing of thee, and of the grace obtained by thy prayers, John of the Golden Mouth."[80]

She never does cease. She teaches her Latin children, too, on that day to sing of the "High Priest who in his day

---

* Since Vatican II his feast has been celebrated on September 13.—ED.

[78] Theodoret, *Hist. Eccl.* v, 36 (*PG* 82:1266).

[79] 2 Tim 4:1, 2.

[80] *Kontakion* (*Echos* I) in the Byzantine *Horologion*, Jan. 27. The Byzantine Church honours St John Chrysostom on Jan. 30, with SS Basil and Gregory of Nazianzos (these three are the "three holy Hierarchs"), and by himself on Nov. 13 as well.

pleased God. For there is none other like him who kept the law of the Most High. Blessed is the man who suffered hardship, because when he has been tried he shall receive a crown of victory." [81] And when we sing of Chrysostom in our language while they praise him in theirs, [82] we may look out across the sea and think of his people, his own Byzantines, cut off by this lamentable schism from the throne that defended him, and groaning under the heel of the unbaptized tyrant whose presence still defiles the city of eighty Roman Cæsars. If anything can trouble the peace of the saints, he must be troubled to see his successors rebel against those of Innocent, and to hear the Mu'ezzin cry from the place he would not have defiled by Eudoxia's statue. And if any saint has a special reason to pray to God for the end of these evils, it is John who appealed to Old Rome as lawful Bishop of New Rome, who, where Islam is now preached, spoke for the gospel of Christ with his golden mouth.

12. Table of Dates

ca. 344 Saint John Chrysostom *born at Antioch*. Educated at Antioch.

369 Baptism.

374–380 Monk near Antioch.

381 Ordained deacon by Meletios.

386 Ordained priest by Flavian.

386–397 *Preacher at Antioch*.

387 Affair of the statues at Antioch.

398 *Patriarch of Constantinople*.

---

[81] Gradual in the Roman Missal, Jan. 27. [This is the pre-Vatican II Missal.—ED.]

[82] It is the same day really, but for the dislocation of the calendar that makes their Jan. 27 come thirteen days after ours.

399 Eutropios' disgrace.

403 *Oak-Tree Synod*. First exile.

404–407 Second exile.

407 (Sept. 14) *Death at Komanes in Pontus*.

438 (Jan. 27) His relics brought to Constantinople.

13. Works

Saint John Chrysostom has left more works than any other Greek Father. Most of these are Homilies preached at Antioch and Constantinople. The Jesuit Fronton le Duc (*Fronto Ducæus*) edited the first complete collection in Greek and Latin in twelve folio volumes (Paris, 1609–1633). An Anglican, H. Savile, published an edition in eight volumes (Greek only) at Eton in 1612, and the Benedictine B. de Montfaucon did so at Paris in thirteen volumes (Greek and Latin [1718–1738]). The editions of Le Duc and Montfaucon have often been reprinted since. The works fill eighteen volumes of Migne (*Patrologia Græca* 47–64). Separate treatises have been published on many occasions. Especially the most read work, *On the Priesthood*, has gone through countless editions. J. A. Bengel edited it in Greek and Latin in 1725 (Stuttgart); there is an edition of the Greek text only published by Tauchnitz (1825, often reprinted, last in 1887) and an excellent one in the *Cambridge Patristic Texts* by J. A. Nairn (Cambridge, 1906).[83] H. Hurter, S.J., gives a Latin translation of it in the series, *SS. Patrum opuscula selecta*, vol. XL (Innsbruck, 1879); W. R. W. Stephens did it into English for the *Select Library of Nicene and Post-Nicene Fathers* (ser. 1, vol. IX [1892]), and T. A. Moxom has done so for the *Early Church Classics* (S.P.C.K., 1907). The *Homily on the Return*

---

[83] This is the best modern text. There is a little mild Protestantism in the introduction and notes.

of Flavian was edited in Greek by L. de Sinner (Paris, 1842), the one *On Eutropios* by J. G. Beane (Paris, 1893). Hurter's *SS. Patrum opuscula selecta* also include his treatise *On the Divinity of Christ* (*Quod Christus sit Deus*, vol. xv) and his five *Homilies against the Anomeans* (*De Incomprehensibili*, vol. xxix). Most of the homilies on the New Testament were collected and published at Oxford in five volumes (1849–1855) by F. Field. Lastly, useful selections are *Johannis Chrys. opera præstantissima*, by F. W. Lomler ([Rudolstadt, 1840], Greek and Latin); *S. Joh. Chrys. opera selecta* by F. Dübner ([Paris, 1861], Greek and Latin, only one vol. published); and Mary Allies, *Leaves from S. John Chrysostom* (Burns and Oates, 1889).

HOMILIES ON THE BIBLE. Saint John preached long courses of sermons on various books of the Bible, so that, taken together, they form a continuous commentary on most of the books. At Antioch in 388, he preached sixty-seven homilies *On Genesis* (*PG* 53–54) and nine others *On Genesis*, too (*PG* 54:581–630). Various passages in *Kings* are explained by eight homilies (*PG* 54:631–708, at Antioch in 387), and sixty *Psalms* (*PG* 55). The homilies on Job and Proverbs (*PG* 64:503–740) are doubtfully authentic. In 386, he preached *On the Difficulties in the Prophecies* (*PG* 56:163–92), in 386 and 397 on parts of Isaiah (*PG* 56:11–142). Fragments on Jeremiah (*PG* 64:739–1038) and Daniel (*PG* 56:193–246) are collected from Catenas. In the year 390, he explained St Matthew in ninety sermons (*PG* 57–58). Of his commentaries on St Mark and St Luke, only seven homilies *On the Parable of Lazarus* (Lk 16:19–31, *PG* 48:963–1054) are preserved. Eighty-eight sermons on *St John* (*PG* 59) were preached in 389. At Constantinople, in 400 or 401, he preached fifty-five homilies on the *Acts of the Apos-*

tles (*PG* 60), and he explained all *St Paul's Epistles* in long series of sermons (*PG* 60–64).

OTHER SERMONS. The most famous are those *On the Statues* (see pp. 113–15 above, *PG* 49:15–222) and *On Eutropios* (see pp. 125–27 above, *PG* 52:391–414). He preached *Against the Jews* (eight homilies, *PG* 48:843–942), *Against the Anomoeans* (extreme Arians, twelve homilies, *PG* 48:701–812), *On the Resurrection* (*PG* 50:417–32), *On Penance* (nine homilies, *PG* 49:277–350), *Against Circuses and Theatres* (*PG* 56:263–70) and on most of the great feasts of the calendar (*PG* 49, 50, 52, 64). We have seven sermons *On St Paul* (*PG* 50:473–514) and others *On Martyrs* and various saints (*PG* 50). The sermons *Before* and *After His First Exile* are famous (*PG* 52:427–30, 443–48).

OTHER WORKS. Although preaching was Saint John's special vocation, he wrote books too. In 382, he composed a treatise *Against Julian and the Heathen* (κατὰ Ἰουλιανοῦ καί πρὸς ἕλληνας, *Adv. Julianum et gentiles*, *PG* 50:533–72), and in 387 a *Defence of the Divinity of Christ against Jews and Pagans* (πρὸς ἰουδάιους καὶ ἕλληνας ἀπόδειξις ὅτι ἐστὶ θεὸς ὁ Χριστός, *Demonstratio qd. Christus sit Deus adv. iudæos et gentiles*, *PG* 48:813–38). He defended monasticism in his work *Against Those Who Attack the Monastic Life* (πρὸς τοὺς πολεμοῦντας τοῖς ἐπὶ τὸ μονάζειν ἐνάγουσιν, *Adv. oppugnatores vitæ monastiæ*, *PG* 53, 47:319–86), written in 376, and wrote ascetic treatises *On Virginity* (περὶ παρθενίας, *De virginitate*, *PG* 48:533–96) and *On the State of Widows* (περὶ μονανδρίας, *De viduis*, *PG* 48:533–96). He was rightly indignant against the dangerous and scandalous custom that clerics should live in the same houses as nuns (πρὸς τοὺς ἔχοντας παρθένους συνεισάκτους, *De virginibus subintroductis*,

PG 47:495–514 and 514–32). But the most important of all his ascetic works are the six books *On the Priesthood* (περὶ ἱερωσύνης, *De Sacerdotio libri vi*, *PG* 47:623–92).[84] We have seen on what occasion this little treatise was written (p. 111 above). It is, with Saint Gregory I's *Regula Pastoralis*, the classical work on the dignity of the priesthood and the responsibility and duties of priests.

LETTERS. Volume 52 of Migne's Greek series contains 238 letters written by Chrysostom to various people, which give a number of valuable details about his own life, as well as a lively and interesting picture of society in his time.

LITURGY. The Service of the holy Eucharist used throughout the Orthodox Church and among the Catholic Melkites for nearly every day in the year[85] bears the title: *The Divine Liturgy of Our Father among the Saints John Chrysostom*. It is a shortened form of the older Liturgy ascribed to Saint Basil. How far it is really the work of Chrysostom is a question that has not yet been settled. We know that at Antioch our saint was much concerned about the right celebration of the holy Liturgy and anxious to make any modifications that would cause a more reverent attendance.[86] It is also certain that the Liturgy was very long, and that this form is an abridgement of the older one. As Patriarch

---

[84] Ἱερωσύνης (*sacerdotium*) means *bishophood* rather than *priesthood*. *Sacerdos* in Latin and ἱερεύς in Greek practically always mean a bishop in the age of the Fathers. But most of what the saint says about bishops applies equally to priests.

[85] On some days, the older use of St Basil is followed (see p. 60, n. 41 above), and for Lent (except Saturdays and Sundays), they use the Liturgy of the Presanctified, which they ascribe to St Gregory Dialogos (our Pope Gregory the Great, 590–604).

[86] *In Ep. 2, ad Thess.; In Act. Ap.* 29; *In Ep. 1 ad Cor.* 36; *In Gen.* 4; *In Matth.* 73.

of Constantinople, John would naturally apply the same principles; from the chief church in the east, his reform would
spread very quickly over all those parts. In the Liturgy,
there are forms and expressions that are evidently his. But
whether he really drew up and imposed a complete Liturgy
is another question. The first part, the preparation of the
gifts (προσκομιδή), is certainly much later than his time. And
for the rest, also, Liturgies are modified too gradually, there
are too many influences at work for their final and definite
form ever to be really the work of one man.[87]

[87] I have given an outline of this Liturgy in the *Orth. Eastern Church*,
pp. 412–18.

CHAPTER FIVE

SAINT CYRIL OF JERUSALEM
(ca. 315–386)

Cyril of Jerusalem was one of the many Catholic bishops who suffered persecution and exile for the faith at the time of the Arian troubles. Of the thirty-five years during which he was bishop, he spent altogether sixteen in banishment. He was the witness of Julian's attempt to rebuild the temple and was known to the other Greek Fathers of that time as a valiant and steadfast defender of the faith of Nicæa, as well as a zealous and irreproachable bishop; but his chief title to fame is the series of catechisms he held as a priest at the Holy Sepulchre in Jerusalem.

1. First Years (ca. 315–345)

Cyril[1] was born in or near Jerusalem about the year 315. We know nothing of his parents, and for these early years of his life we have only one or two passing references and what can be deduced from allusions in his writings. He was evidently brought up as a Christian, but there is no reference to his baptism anywhere. One may conjecture that he was baptized, probably by Makarios, Bishop

---

[1] Κύριλλος (Cyrillus) is a common Greek name. It means *little Lord* (diminutive of Κύριος).

143

of Jerusalem,[2] as a young man. He seems to have lived alone somewhere as a monk for a time; at least his repeated references to the monastic life[3] seem to imply that he had some experience of it. And he had certainly studied holy Scripture, the older fathers, Origen (d. 254), the teaching of various heretics (notably of the Manicheans)[4] and to some extent profane letters. It was probably his reputation as an austere and virtuous person and a theologian that induced Makarios to take him away from his solitude and ordain him deacon in 334 or 335. For ten years, he then served as deacon in the Church of Jerusalem. Meanwhile Makarios died and was succeeded by Maximos.

2. Priest and Catechist (345–350)

Maximos ordained Cyril priest in 345 and gave him the important duty of teaching the faith to the catechumens before their baptism, and then of preparing them for their first communion. It was during these five years that Cyril held the series of catechetical instruction that have made him famous. He wrote down what he said, and this series of twenty-three homilies form practically all we have of his works. They were held during Lent and Easter week to the people who would be baptized on Easter eve. In those days, the preparation for baptism was a very long and serious business. Practically everyone was baptized as an adult. Many were converts from Judaism or paganism, and even people born of Christian parents generally waited till they were

---

[2] This Makarios was present at the first general Council (Nicæa I, 325) and received a long letter from Constantine about building the Church of the Holy Sepulchre (Eusebeios, *Vita Constant.* iii, 29–32). He died between 335 and 345.

[3] E.g. Catech. iv, 24; xii, 33, 34, etc.

[4] Catech. vi, 34.

grown up before they applied for baptism. We have seen how the Fathers of just this time were baptized at a late age themselves, and how they afterward protested against that custom.[5] A person then who wished to be a Christian passed through a long time of preparation, divided into stages by solemn rites, before he was immersed in the font on Easter eve. Of this period of preparation with its rites, most curious and interesting traces remain in our present rite of baptism[6] and in our services for Lent and Holy Week. Naturally, the arrangements were not everywhere the same. In this matter as in others, different churches followed different rites. At Jerusalem, where the use of Antioch prevailed,[7] no doubt many things were different from the Roman practice; but the main outline of the long process of Initiation seems to have been much the same everywhere. The convert was first solemnly admitted to the class of catechumens.[8] This was done by an exorcism, breathing on his face and the sign of the cross.[9] He then remained a member of that class for a long time, often for years. Meanwhile he learned the rudiments of the faith, although everything that belonged to the *discipline of the*

[5] See above, pp. 52, 87, 110.

[6] There are two rites of baptism in the Roman ritual. The more primitive one, in which most of the old ceremonies are preserved, is rarely seen now—the *Order of the baptism of adults*. This service, itself a compendium of the old ceremonies for catechumens, is further abbreviated in the *Order of the baptism of infants* that we usually see. [Written in 1908, before the Church revived some of the ancient baptismal customs.—ED.]

[7] The use of Antioch was itself taken from Jerusalem. The parent rite of this family of liturgies is that of *St James* in Greek, certainly composed for the city of Jerusalem (see my *Orth. Eastern Church* [London: Catholic Truth Society, 1907], p. 115).

[8] Κατηχούμενος is the present participle passive of κατηχῶ (to resound, then bewitch, then teach) and means *he who is being taught.*

[9] This is the first rite of our baptismal service.

secret[10] was still carefully kept from him. When at last the catechumen was considered firmly established in the faith, had shown that he would live like a Christian and himself wished to be baptized,[11] he was admitted into the next class and became an elect, or competent (*competens*, φωτιζόμενος, "being enlightened").[12] This was always at the beginning

[10] The *disciplina arcani* was an important element in the teaching of the Church. In order to shield the most sacred mysteries from profanation, they were not revealed till just before or just after baptism. The Jews treated their proselytes in the same way, and the mysteries of the heathen sects from the east that flourished during the first centuries (of Mithraism especially) were only revealed gradually to the initiated. The Christian discipline reserved the baptismal creed and the Our Father till just before baptism; and especially the mystery of the holy Eucharist and the Real Presence was not taught till after baptism. The discipline of the secret seems to have begun toward the end of the second century. St Justin's (d. 166) clear allusions to the holy Eucharist (*Apol*. i, 65, 66) argue that he did not know it. But St Irenæus (d. 202, *Adv. hær*. iii, 4, 1, 2) and still more plainly Tertullian (d. 240, *Apol*. vii, 1) allude to it. About the sixth century, when there were practically no more heathen in the empire, and the whole process of Initiation had become modified, the practice died out. Mgr Batiffol is disposed to minimize its observance (*La discipline de l'Arcane*, in his *Études d'Histoire et de Theologie positive* [Paris, 1902], pp. 3–41). We constantly find that the Fathers of the fourth and fifth centuries, when preaching to mixed congregations of faithful and catechumens, find that they can make only a mysterious allusion to the holy Eucharist and add "the initiated understand what I mean"—*norunt initiati*. We have a classical example in the [pre-Vatican II] Roman breviary (in the eighth lesson for the *Finding of the Holy Rood*, May 3) where St Augustine in his sermon (*Tract. II in Joannem*) says that if you ask a catechumen whether he eats the Body of the Son of Man and drinks his Blood the catechumen will not understand what you mean.

[11] To be a catechumen involved fewer responsibilities than to be baptized and fewer duties; so many people, as notably Constantine and Constantius the emperors, preferred to put off baptism to the end of their lives. See Mgr Duchesne, *Orig. du Culte chrétien* (Paris, 1898), chap. ix, "L'Initiation chrétienne".

[12] Mgr Duchesne (ibid.) and Dr Funk (*Theol. Quartalschr.* [Tübingen, 1883], p. 41ff.) show that these were the only two classes before baptism—those of the catechumens and competents. They were allowed to come to church for

of Lent,[13] since baptism was administered on Easter eve. Halfway through Lent came another service of exorcisms and the first teaching of part of the discipline of the secret. They learned and had to repeat the creed and Our Father.[14] At Rome, at any rate, the giving of the salt (*sal sapientiæ*, as they learned the new wisdom) was part of the rite.[15] Later came a signing (*consignatio*) with oil or saliva, a last profession of faith (Dost thou renounce Satan? etc.) and an anointing with the oil of catechumens.[16] At last, during the long Easter vigil, after the Prophecies had been read[17], the bishop blessed the font, and the long line of competents one by one took off their clothes and went down into the font. They were baptized by a triple immersion,[18] and then confirmed with chrism at once.[19] When they came out of the

---

the first part of the Liturgy (the *Missa catechumenorum*), but were dismissed by the deacon before the offertory. This dismissal is still a ceremony in all eastern liturgies. In the oldest extant liturgy (of the *Const. Apost.*), the deacon cries out: "No one of the catechumens, no one of the hearers (= competents), no one of the unbelievers, no one of the heretics" (viii, 12). Then begins the *Missa fidelium*.

[13] There is a very close connexion between the observance of Lent and the preparation of the competents for baptism. See Duchesne, *Orig. du Culte chrétien*, and Fr Thurston, *Lent and Holy Week* (Longmans, 1904), pp. 169ff.

[14] This is the *traditio symboli* that forms the second part of our baptismal service, when the child is brought into the church.

[15] Thurston, *Lent and Holy Week*, p. 172.

[16] It will be seen, then, that we still carry the child through all these stages before baptism. We make it a catechumen, then an elect, and do all the rites that prepare for baptism; though it is now all done in a few minutes, instead of stretching over months.

[17] These Prophecies on Holy Saturday are considered by some people to be the last instruction of the catechumens before baptism. Fr Thurston thinks not (*Lent and Holy Week*, pp. 426ff.).

[18] In all eastern churches, baptism is still administered only by immersion.

[19] Certainly at one time in the west too, confirmation was given at once after baptism. Our ritual contains a curious survival of this in the anointing

font they did not put on their old clothes again, but new white garments. There was a last imposition of hands, and they each received a burning light. They were now the enlightened (*illuminati*, φωτισθέντες). For one week they kept their white robes, and meanwhile were taught the last part of the secret discipline—about the holy Eucharist. On Low Sunday, they made their first communions and put off their white robes.[20] After this they belonged to the class of the faithful (*fideles*, πιστοί) for the rest of their lives, unless through a grave crime, such as especially murder, idolatry or adultery, they fell from it into that of penitents. It was then to these competents during Lent and then to them again in Easter week when they had become the "enlightened" that Cyril held his catechetical instructions. The first eighteen are for the competents, the last five for the enlightened (p. 160 below).

3. Was Cyril Ever a Semi-Arian?

That our saint in later years as bishop was a most steadfast defender of the faith of Nicæa, for which he suffered continual persecution, is a fact that no one denies. It has, however, been suggested that as a priest he conceded so far to the times as to profess one of the many varieties of semi-Arianism, rather than the whole uncompromising Catholic

---

with chrism that follows baptism. All eastern churches still confirm immediately after baptism. The priest confirms as well as the bishop; and we acknowledge their confirmation as valid. [The author is writing in 1908.—ED.]

[20] Hence the name *Dominica in albis* (scil., *deponendis*) = *Sunday of the taking off of white robes*. Whatever reasons of sentiment there may be for choosing Corpus Christi or any other feast for the day of general first communion, undoubtedly from the point of view of tradition and antiquity the right day would be Low Sunday.

faith. His metropolitan, Akakios of Cæsarea, as we shall see, was a bitter and persistent Arian; and Arianism was the religion of the court under Constantius (337–361). Times were bad for Homooüsians. Did Cyril bend to the storm? Or was it even as a semi-Arian that he succeeded to the see of Jerusalem when Maximos died? The reason for this theory is that in his catechisms he never uses the word *Homooüsios*. The fact cannot be said to have no significance. That word was the standard of the Catholic faith. It is undoubtedly striking that he—evidently purposely—avoids it. That he did so seems to argue a kind of economy on his part. But, on the other hand, although he does not use the term, he teaches what it means so clearly that no one who heard him could have the slightest doubt that he was entirely on the side of the Nicene fathers. He says that Christ our Lord is "God born of God, Life of Life, Light of Light, like in all things to his Father." [21] The allusion to the Nicene symbol is obvious. Again, our Lord has the same glory as the Father,[22] he has the "Father's divinity" himself,[23] He is "God in nature and truth",[24] born "from eternity", "God of God, eternal of the eternal Father",[25] He is "God born of the virgin",[26] has the same divine nature as the Father.[27] "A perfect Father begot a perfect Son." [28] "From the one perfect Father is one perfect Son." [29] And Cyril explicitly rejects the Arian formula: "There was a time when the Son was

[21] Catech. iv, 7, xi, 4.
[22] Catech. vi, 1.
[23] Catech. vi, 6.
[24] Catech. vii, 5.
[25] Catech. xi, 4.
[26] Catech. xii, 1.
[27] Catech. xi, 18.
[28] Catech. vii, 5.
[29] Catech. xi, 13.

not." [30] Whatever reason, then, he may have had for avoiding the word *Homooüsios*, however much one may think that he would have done better to use it boldly, it is obviously impossible to doubt that he was as much a Catholic and a Homooüsian at this time as afterward as bishop. Moreover, we may notice that though Akakios of Cæsarea was an Arian, his own bishop, Maximos, under whom he taught his catechism, was altogether correct and Nicene. And if a priest has his bishop on his side, he need not much trouble to conciliate a distant metropolitan. Certainly Maximos would not have entrusted this important office of catechist to anyone whose faith was in the least suspect. That he afterward compromised in order to be ordained bishop is certainly false. The second general Council, which was unswervingly anti-Arian throughout, acknowledged his ordination as lawful and canonical, as we shall see (p. 158 below), whereas it deposed Arians and semi-Arians.

4. Cyril's Theology

With regard to other points of theology, we may note that Cyril very strongly insists on the *Real Presence* and on *Transubstantiation*, of which he gives a most accurate definition: "That which seems bread is not bread but the Body of Christ; that which seems wine is not wine but the Blood of Christ." [31] "It is not ordinary bread (ἄρτος λιτός), but the Body of Christ." [32] "As Christ changed water into wine, so does he change (μεταβάλλει) wine into his Blood." [33] Christians who receive holy communion become "of one

[30] Catech. xi, 17–18.
[31] Catech. xxii, 9.
[32] Catech. xxi, 3.
[33] Catech. xxii, 3.

Body and of one Blood with Christ" (σύσσωμοι καὶ σύναιμοι Χριστοῦ) and are "Christbearers (Χριστοφόροι)." [34] Transubstantiation takes place, he says, "by the invocation of the Holy Spirit." [35] The holy Eucharist is a "spiritual sacrifice" and a "sacrifice of atonement".[36]

Like all the Greeks, Saint Cyril insists very much on *free will* and the value of good works.[37] But the precious Blood shed on the cross is our Redemption.[38]

5. Bishop of Jerusalem, to Julian's Accession (350–361)

Maximos died in 350, and Cyril was at once elected as his successor. In a letter to Constantius, he says that soon after he was consecrated a great shining cross was seen in the sky above the holy city and that everyone watched it for several hours.[39] The cross was a fit symbol of his reign as bishop. For almost at once he got into trouble with his metropolitan. The first general Council (Nicæa, 325, can. 7) had given to the see of Jerusalem a not clearly defined "succession of honour", meaning, apparently, a place of honour next after the patriarchs, because it is the holy city; but the council had carefully added that the "domestic rights of the metropolis" must be preserved. The metropolitan see over Palestine was Cæsarea. It was not till the fourth Council (Chalcedon in 451) that Cyril's successor Juvenal (420–458) succeeded in getting this vague place of honour changed

[34] Ibid.

[35] Catech. xxi, 3; xxii, 6. This would argue his belief that the Epiklesis consecrates: contrast with this St John Chrysostom, p. 121, n. 48.

[36] Catech. xxiii, 8. See also all xxii and xxiii for the real Presence, or the quotations in Bardenhewer, *Patrologie* (Freiburg im Breisgau, 1894), pp. 250–51.

[37] Catech. ii, 1; iv, 2, 18–19, etc.

[38] Catech. ii, 5.

[39] Ep. *Ad Const.* (*PG* 33:1165–76).

into a real independent patriarchate.[40] Meanwhile the purely titular "succession of honour" inevitably led to friction with Cæsarea. The metropolitan, naturally, was not pleased to see one of his suffragans placed far above himself in dignity, and the bishops of Jerusalem were not always disposed to obey their metropolitan quite so meekly now that they themselves had so high a rank. This difficult position led to a quarrel between Saint Cyril and his superior, Akakios of Cæsarea. A much more important reason for the quarrel was the question of faith. Cyril was a Catholic, and Akakios was a most pronounced and determined leader of the Arians. Akakios had succeeded Eusebeios,[41] the father of Church history, in 340 and had at once distinguished himself by his opposition to Athanasius and the Homooüsios. He was present at the Arian Synod of Antioch in 341 (ἐν ἐγκαινίοις). Later, in 359, he was the acknowledged head of the forty extreme Arians at Seleucia.[42] But it was Akakios who here founded a third party, as a compromise between the Arians and semi-Arians, on the basis of the word *similar* only—the Son of God is to be called neither "of the same" nor "of a different" nor "of a like substance" with the Father, but only "similar (ὅμοιος)" in general, without any use of the word "substance" at all. This third party, the Homoians, are also called Acacians after their founder.

[40] *Orth. Eastern Church*, pp. 25–27.

[41] Eusebeios (d. 340) was also an Arian, but of a milder kind; had he lived he would have joined the semi-Arian party. Akakios had been his pupil.

[42] Constantius in 358 summoned a synod to Nicæa, and then to Nikomedia. Eventually two synods met, one for western bishops at Ariminium (Rimini in Italy) and the other for easterns at Seleucia in Isauria. Both synods condemned the Nicene faith. This year, 359, marks the height of the Arian flood. "Ingemuit totus orbis et se esse arianum miratus est" (St Jerome, *Contra Luciferianos*, 19). The tide turned almost at once after this. St Hilary of Poitiers (d. 366) was present at Seleucia, being then in exile for the faith.

It was then inevitable that there should be trouble between Akakios and Cyril. In 358, Akakios summoned a synod at Cæsarea, over which he himself presided. Saint Cyril refused to go to it, either because he thought that his "succession of honour" after the patriarchs gave him a right to be judged only by a patriarchal synod,[43] or because he knew that he had no chance with what was a purely Arian assembly. So Akakios and his synod deposed Cyril, in his absence, for these reasons: that he had in some way disobeyed or behaved with insubordination toward his metropolitan,[44] that he had sold vestments and vessels belonging to his church in order to feed the poor at a time of famine, that he was a Homooüsian. For these offences, he was banished to Cilicia. Cyril appealed to a greater council, according to the right given to deposed bishops by the Synod of Antioch in 341 (can. 4 and 12); meanwhile he was hospitably received by Silvanus, Bishop of Tarsus. The next year the situation was reversed. The Synod of Seleucia, like the twin assembly at Ariminium, was semi-Arian, disposed to be conciliatory and opposed to such extreme people as Akakios. It also made a point of restoring bishops who had been unjustly deposed.[45] Akakios and Cyril both attended. Cyril was

[43] The canon of Nicæa had left the whole question of the place of Jerusalem in a confusion. It certainly meant to leave the canonical rights of Cæsarea exactly where they had been before. But the Bishops of Jerusalem almost inevitably thought that the situation had changed now that they held so high a place. The further promotion given at Chalcedon was the inevitable result of can. 7 of Nicæa.

[44] This is the whole question—which was it? Sozomenos (Hist. Eccl. iv, 25) says it was because he had disobeyed and refused to acknowledge Cæsarea as his metropolis, in which case he would have been wrong; Theodoret (Hist. Eccl. ii, 22) says it was only because he had taken precedence, which he had a perfect right to do.

[45] It restored St Hilary to Poitiers. The [pre-Vatican II] Roman breviary on his feast (Jan. 14, Lectio v) is not quite fair about the motives of his

restored, and Akakios deposed; but Akakios went to Constantinople, where he had the ear of Constantius, held an entirely Arian synod there in 360 and, by the emperor's favour, again deposed Cyril.

6. The Attempt to Rebuild the Temple (ca. 362)

Constantius died just as he had set out to fight his cousin in 361. Julian (361–363) at once proclaimed the restoration of all banished bishops. Like Saint Athanasius,[46] Saint Cyril, too, profited by this edict and came back to Jerusalem (361).

The next event in his life was Julian's attempt to restore the temple. Julian, who had been outrageously treated by his Christian cousin,[47] and who loathed the endless Arian and semi-Arian quarrels and worshipped the glorious memory of old Greece, spent his short reign in a hopeless attempt to destroy Christianity and restore the old gods. Himself a philosophic pantheist, with a strong tendency toward monotheism in the form of Sun-worship and a taste for the mysteries of the eastern religions[48] as symbols of profound truths, he did us the unwilling honour of trying to revive his synthetic paganism with specifically Christian ideas,[49] while he as nearly persecuted Christians as his magnificent and

---

restoration. [St Hilary's optional memorial is now celebrated on January 13.—ED.]

[46] See p. 32 above.

[47] Constantius had murdered Julian's father, uncle and two brothers. Julian himself spent the early part of his life in a dreary castle in Cappadocia, as a prisoner in daily fear of being murdered himself.

[48] Mithraism especially. He was initiated by the *Taurobolion* in Gaul in 361, just after he had kept the Epiphany in the Christian church at Vienne. Mithra, identified with Apollo and the Sun, was to him the Logos of the Neo-platonists.

[49] See the fragment of his letter to a heathen priest in Hertlein's edition (2:552–55).

contemptuous principles of tolerance would allow.[50] But while he hated Christianity, which would allow no rival, he gladly protected all the old national religions that were to him simply local expressions of the same philosophic truth. The Roman peasant should go on worshipping his Roman nature-gods; the Greek found in Apollo, Artemis and Aphrodite externally beautiful symbols of the many-sided hidden reality; the Egyptian inherited from an immense age his dark mysteries; the Phrygian turned to Attis and Cybele, the Syrian to Adonis and Astarte, the Persian to Ahura-Mazda and the Babylonian to Marduk.[51] If that were so, why should not the Jew turn to the God of Israel. Jews had as much right to a national god as any one else; and although Julian never concealed his contempt for this "barbarous" sect, although he hated their intolerance and still more the proselytizing spirit of later Judaism, he undertook to protect them as well as all the other religions. Only Christians

---

[50] For the story of Julian, see P. Allard, *Julien l'apostat* (3 vols.—an exhaustive life [Paris: Lecoffre, 1900]); G. Negri, *L'Imperatore Giuliano l'apostata* (Milan: Hoepli, 1902); Harnack's admirable summary in Herzog and Hauck's *Realencyklopädie für prot. Theol. u. Kirche* (3rd ed. [Leipzig: Hinrichs, 1901], x, 609–19); Gibbon's *Decline and Fall*, chap. xxii–xxiv; and the excellent monograph by Alice Gardner in the *Heroes of the Nations* series (*Julian, Philosopher and Emperor* [Putnam, 1895]).

[51] For a brilliant summary of these eastern religions that toward the end of paganism had ousted the original Greek and Roman mythologies, see F. Cumont, *Les Religions Orientales dans le Paganisme Romain* (Paris: Leroux, 1905) and *Les Mystères de Mithra* (Paris: Fontemoing, 1902). It should be remembered that people like Julian who wanted to restore "Hellenism" were as far removed from the old simple polytheism as their Christian rivals. Philosophy had destroyed the old beliefs among educated people entirely. Their ideal was rather pantheism; and the forms of their religion were these mysteries (Attis, Adonis, Mithra) from Asia that had invaded Rome and Greece. For Julian's own ideas, the sources are his *Oratio* iv, *To King Sun* (πρὸς τὸν βασιλέα ἥλιον, ed. Hertlein, 1:168–205) and *Oratio* v, *To the Mother of the Gods* (εἰς τὴν μητέρα τῶν θεῶν, ed. Hertlein, 1:206–33).

were too utterly intolerant and arrogant in their claim of
being the only faith to have any mercy. He wrote a friendly
letter to a Jewish high priest,[52] whom he condescends to
call his "brother", and in another letter he asks for Jews'
prayers and promises to come to Jerusalem after the Persian
war and there to pray to their god too. A result of this
protection to the Jews was that he ordered the rebuilding
of their temple.[53] He gave large sums of money for this
purpose and appointed one Alypios of Antioch to superintend
the work. And naturally Jews from every part of the empire
contributed lavishly to the triumph of their religion. What
happened? It is certain that the whole scheme came to nothing, and that strange portents put an end to the work. Ammianus Marcellinus, the heathen historian, who is, therefore,
not suspect in this matter, says that globes of fire burst from
the ground and killed the workmen.[54] So the temple was
never rebuilt. The Christian writers[55] naturally saw in this

[52] The priest's name was *Hillel*, which Julian makes into Ἰουλός (ed. Hertlein,
2:512–14).

[53] Possibly another reason for this scheme was that it would prove our
Lord's words false: "not a stone shall be left upon a stone" (Mt 24:2; Mk
13:2; Lk 21:6). All the Fathers of this time (Gregory of Nazianzos, *Invectiv. c.
Jul.* ii, 4; Sokrates, *Hist. Eccl.* iii, 20; Sozomenos, *Hist. Eccl.* v, 22) describe
this as his only motive. But none of them are fair to Julian. The two *Invec-
tives* of Gregory of Nazianzos are simply unrestrained abuse. Julian is one of
the people whom no one seems able to treat fairly. Till quite lately every
Christian writer poured abuse on the Apostate. Now there is a reaction (since
Gibbon especially), and enemies of Christianity make him into a fabulously
perfect person. Paul Allard (*Julien l'apostat*) has set an example of a really
scientific, moderate and sympathetic treatment of a man who was almost a
genius, always extraordinarily interesting, very ideal in his character and
irreproachable in his morals, rather mad and in any case a hopeless failure. If
only poor Julian had taken up any less hopeless cause than that of the gods,
he would have been the greatest emperor since Constantine.

[54] Ammianus Marcellinus, xxiii, 1.

[55] Sozomenos, Gregory of Nazianzos, Sokrates (see n. 53 above).

the hand of God against the attempt to falsify his Son's words. Sokrates says that Saint Cyril, when he saw the preparations, foretold exactly what would happen.[56]

7. From Jovian's Accession to Cyril's Death (363–386)

Julian died fighting valiantly against the Persians in 363. Jovian (363–364), who succeeded him, was a Catholic. Then came Valentinian (364–375), who named his brother Valens (364–378) Cæsar in the east. Valens was an extreme Arian; so he at once ordered that all bishops who had been banished by Constantius and restored by Julian should again go into exile.[57] Saint Cyril was one of these bishops, so he had to leave Jerusalem in 367. He did not come back for eleven years, when Valens died (378). We do not know where he spent those years of exile. After Valens, Gratian (375–383), Valentinian's son, who was already emperor in the west, made Theodosius I (379–395) Cæsar for the east. Gratian and Theodosius were Catholics, and they ordered that all Catholic bishops—that is, those who were in communion with the Pope and the Bishop of Alexandria[58]—should be restored. Cyril profited by this and came back to his see, where he ended his days in peace. We hear of him once

---

[56] Sokrates iii, 20. There is an interesting article about this attempt to rebuild the Temple by M. Adler in the *Jewish Quarterly Review* (July 1893). He thinks that it was never more than a project, and that the whole story of the attempt was made up by Gregory of Nazianzos, from whom everyone else (including Ammianus!) copied it.

[57] See above p. 33.

[58] That was their test of a Catholic: "those who embrace the communion of Damasus and Peter of Alexandria" (Theodoret, *Hist. Eccl.* v, 2). Cf. *Cod. Theod.* xvi, Tit. I, l, 2.

again at the second general Council (Constantinople I, 381),[59] at which he was present. Akakios of Cæsarea, his old enemy, was dead; Cyril's own nephew, Gelasios, a firm Catholic, was now metropolitan. The difficult and delicate situation between the metropolitan and the suffragan who had a precedence of honour led to no friction between nephew and uncle. The council acknowledged Cyril's ordination as Bishop of Jerusalem as canonical and praised him for his steadfast opposition to Arianism.[60] That is the last event in his life of which we know. That he ruled his see as a zealous and holy Catholic bishop we see from a letter of Saint Basil, who says that in his time the Diocese of Jerusalem had greatly flourished.[61] Saint Cyril died on March 18, 386. March 18 is his feast in both rites, Byzantine and Latin.[62] On that day our Martyrology names: "At Jerusalem Saint Cyril, Bishop, who, having suffered many injuries from the Arians for the faith, and having been many times driven from his see, at last rested in peace, illustrious with the glory of holiness; of whose untarnished faith the second œcumenical synod, writing to Damasus, gave a splendid witness." And the collect for his Mass, with its allusion to the chief subject of his catechism, is specially beautiful: "Grant us, Almighty God, that by the prayers of blessed Cyril, the Bishop, we may so know thee, the only true God, and Jesus Christ whom

[59] For this council see pp. 96–99.

[60] Theodoret, *Hist. Eccl.* v, 9.

[61] Basil, Ep. 4, *Ad monach. lapsum.*

[62] Also to the Syrians, both Jacobite and Uniate, and the Maronites. The Armenians keep St Cyril of Jerusalem on the second Sunday of Lent, the Copts on March 22; the Nestorians on the fifth Friday after the Epiphany, in a very miscellaneous collection of "holy Greek Doctors", who include Nestorius and St Ambrose!

thou didst send, that we may always be counted among the sheep that hear his voice."

8. Table of Dates

ca. 315 *Cyril born at Jerusalem.*

334 or 335 Ordained deacon.

345–350 Priest and *catechist at Jerusalem.*

350 *Bishop of Jerusalem.*

358 Akakios of Cæsarea's synod. Cyril banished.

358–359 First exile at Tarsus in Cilicia.

359 Restored by the Synod of Seleucia.

360 Synod at Constantinople under Akakios. Cyril's second exile.

361 Restored by Julian.

ca. 362 Julian's attempt to rebuild the temple.

367 Valens banishes Catholic bishops.

367–378 Third exile.

378 Restored by Gratian.

381 Present at the second general Council.

386 (March 18) *Death at Jerusalem.*

9. Works

Saint Cyril's complete works were first published by J. Prévot (Paris, 1608, quarto, reprinted 1631 and 1640), then by T. Milles at Oxford in 1703 (folio). W. Morell had already edited the seven first and the five "mystagogic" catechisms (Paris, 1564). John Grodeck made a Latin translation at Köln (1564). The best edition is that of the Benedictine A. A. Touttée ([Paris, 1720], folio, with Grodeck's Latin version). This is reprinted by Migne, *Patrologia Græca* 33 (Paris, 1857). W. K. Reischl and J. Rupp published the works in two octavo volumes at Munich in 1848–1860, and Photios

Alexandrides at Jerusalem in 1867–1868 (two vols, with notes by Dionysios Kleophas). H. Hurter, S.J., includes a selection in Latin in *SS. Patrum opuscula selecta*, vol. VII (Innsbruck, 1885).

THE CATECHISMS. These are Cyril's only important work. The twenty-three instructions (*PG* 33) were held at Jerusalem to competents and then to the neophytes between 345 and 350 (see above, pp. 144–48). The introductory catechism (προκατήχησις) is about the great grace his hearers were about to receive (baptism) and the importance of this instruction. The first repeats the same ideas; the second is about sin and repentance, the third about the effects of baptism; the fourth is a short compendium of the chief points of the Christian faith (avoiding all that comes under the *disciplina arcani*), and the fifth describes the virtue of faith. Catechisms 6–18 give an exact commentary on the creed, as professed by the catechumens at their baptism. This is the end of the first part. On Easter eve, his hearers were baptized and confirmed. The last five instructions (19–23) are addressed to them as neophytes. There was no longer a *disciplina arcani* to be observed, and they had to be prepared for their first communion on Low Sunday. These five are called the *Mystagogic Catechisms* (κατηχήσεις μυσταγωγικαί), because they treat of the Mysteries (sacraments). Numbers 19 and 20 explain again the rite of baptism without any reticence; number 21 is about confirmation, numbers 22 and 23 about the holy Eucharist.

This series of catechisms is famous as the most complete ordered course of instructions on the faith we have from the first centuries and as containing incidentally very valuable references to the rites of Jerusalem in the fourth century.

OTHER WORKS. Besides the catechisms, we have only one complete sermon by Saint Cyril (*PG* 33:1131–54), on the healing of the man with palsy at the pool of Bethsaida (Jn 5:1–9); a *Letter to the emperor Constantius* (*PG* 33:1165–76), about the cross that appeared when Cyril was ordained bishop (p. 151); and three short fragments of sermons (1181–82).

CHAPTER SIX

SAINT CYRIL OF ALEXANDRIA
(d. 444)

Cyril, after Athanasius the most famous Patriarch of Alexandria, has incurred an undeserved unpopularity chiefly because during his reign a Christian mob murdered Hypatia. He is not the most attractive of the Fathers. He had something of the despotic nature of his uncle, Theophilos; he behaved badly to Saint John Chrysostom, and in his earlier years especially ruled at Alexandria in a way that gave offence to the civil government; but he was a very great theologian and the leader of the Catholics in his time. He is the Doctor of the Church against Nestorianism. In his time again, as in that of Saint Athanasius, orthodoxy reigned from Alexandria; what Athanasius was in Arian times, that was Cyril against the Nestorians. As the last of the chain of Fathers who follow each other since his great predecessor,[1] he is called by Greeks the *Seal of the Fathers* (σφραγὶς τῶν πατέρων). His name is bound up always with that of the Council of Ephesus. If not exactly lovable, he is a most imposing and princely figure, typical of the great line of "Christian Pharaohs"[2] who

[1] St John Damascene (d. ca. 754) comes long afterward and stands alone in a different age.

[2] This was a common name for the Patriarchs of Alexandria (see my *Orth. Eastern Church* [London: Catholic Truth Society, 1907], p. 13).

held the second place in Christendom and ruled the mighty Church of Egypt from their throne by the sea. And the chief work of his life was not murdering Hypatia, but fighting for the person of Christ and the honour of the Mother of God against the Nestorians.

1. Saint Cyril before He Was Patriarch (?–412)

We do not know in what year Cyril was born. He belonged to one of the greatest of the Greek families in Egypt, and he was the nephew of the Patriarch Theophilos, whom we know as Saint John Chrysostom's enemy.[3] He must have received the education both in sacred and profane letters, of which he made such great use afterward, at his own city, Alexandria. The Alexandrine schools were still the most famous in the world. During this first period, he made friends with Saint Isidore, abbot of a great monastery near Pelusium[4] (d. ca. 440). This Isidore had a very salutary influence over Cyril all his life. Cyril calls him his father even when he himself had become patriarch, and it was under Isidore that he spent some years as a monk.[5] The first certain date in our saint's life is 403, and here he appears in no saintly light, for he accompanied his uncle to the Oak-Tree Synod and took his part in the deposition of Saint John Chrysostom.[6] For many years after he still had a grudge against Saint John. It was not till 417 that Isidore persuaded him to add his former victim's name to the diptychs of

[3] See above, pp. 124, 127–31.

[4] Pelusium was a town on the most eastern branch of the Nile, just outside the Delta, near where the Suez Canal now is. Isidore of Pelusium was a disciple of St John Chrysostom and belonged to the Antiochene school. About two thousand of his letters are preserved in *PG* 98:1273–1312.

[5] Isidore of Pelusium, Ep. i, 310, 323, 324, 370.

[6] See pp. 130–31.

Alexandria.[7] This reconciliation after death with Chrysostom is one example of many cases in which Isidore used his influence over Cyril for a good purpose.

2. Patriarch (before Nestorianism, 412–428)

Theophilos died in October 412. The government wanted a certain Archdeacon Timothy to succeed,[8] but Cyril was elected canonically and became patriarch. The governor of Egypt was Orestes, who pretended to be a Christian to the Christians and talked philosophy to the pagans. And the last remnant of the Hellenism that Julian (361–363) had in vain tried to revive, clustered round the school by the Serapion, where Hypatia taught her Neo-platonism.

Hypatia[9] was the great heathen influence in the city and was believed to be all powerful with Orestes.[10] Very soon after Cyril's consecration, there was trouble between him and the governor. Orestes feared the patriarch's masterful disposition—for Cyril was like his uncle in many ways—and was annoyed to see that he, the bishop, and not himself, the governor, was the real master of the city. First Cyril shut up a Novatian church at Alexandria and confiscated

---

[7] Cyril of Alexandria, Ep. i, 370.

[8] Sokrates, *Hist. Eccl.* vii, 7.

[9] Hypatia was the daughter of a philosopher named Theon. "She had acquired so great a learning that she was far superior to all philosophers of her time. She had been led by Plotinos to the school of Plato, and she taught all the lessons of philosophy to her hearers. So students of philosophy crowded to her from all sides. Because of the confidence and authority she had acquired by learning she was able to appear even before governors with great effect. Nor was she ashamed to show herself among a crowd of men; for everyone reverenced her and honoured her for her great modesty" (Sokrates, *Hist. Eccl.* vii, 15).

[10] "For, since she very often conversed with Orestes, a calumny against her spread among the Christian people to the effect that she hindered a reconciliation between Cyril and Orestes" (ibid.).

the goods of the Novatian bishop Theopompos.[11] Then he expelled all Jews from the city, apparently because they had massacred Christians. Orestes protested against this to the emperor (Theodosius II, 408–450), but Cyril got his way. Lastly came the murder of Hypatia. In March 415, a mob of Christians, led by the Parabolani[12] and by a Lector named Peter, cruelly tore her to pieces on the steps of a church.[13] Various writers have suggested more or less plainly that the patriarch was involved in this crime. Sokrates does not say so plainly, but he implies it and adds a solemn moral reflection.[14] As a matter of fact, not only is there no sort of

[11] Ibid., i, 7. It must be remembered that Sokrates, the authority for all this account, is greatly prejudiced against Cyril. Novatian was an African priest who had made a schism in Rome at the time of Pope Cornelius (251–253). His followers took a line of extreme strictness. They said the Church consists only of the pure, forbade second marriages and rebaptized all their converts. Novatianism became practically a form of Montanism, of which Tertullian (d. 240) was the chief defender.

[12] The *Parabolani* (παραβολάνοι) were people who tended the sick, especially in time of plague, thereby endangering their own lives (παραβολὴ τῆς ψυχῆς). They were counted as forming a minor order, like the *Fossores*, who buried the dead, the *Notarii*, who wrote down acts of martyrs, and other classes that have since disappeared. They were chosen and commissioned by the bishop. Being rough and sturdy fellows of a low class, they seem to have often filled up the time between plagues by making political disturbances. At one time, they were expressly forbidden to attend political meetings. After Justinian's time (527–565), they disappear (see Kraus, *Realenz.* II, 582).

[13] "Certain men of fierce character whose leader was a Lector named Peter made a conspiracy and watched the lady. They caught her coming back from some house, tore her from her saddle and dragged her to a church called the *Kaisarion*. Here they stripped her and killed her with broken shells. When they had torn her to pieces they burned her limbs at the place called Kinaron" (Sokrates, *Hist. Eccl.* vii, 15). It will be seen that the Parabolani, as a class, were not nice people.

[14] "This affair brought no small disgrace to both Cyril and the Church of Alexandria, for murder and slaughter and all such things are altogether opposed to the Christian religion" (ibid.). Damaskios, a heathen who wrote a life of Isidore the Philosopher, long afterward insinuates the same thing (quoted in

evidence that he had anything to do with it, there are positive reasons for knowing that he had not. After the murder, a deputation of citizens went to Constantinople to petition the emperor to prevent such horrors for the future and to put down the disorderly Parabolani, and the first means they urge for that purpose is that the patriarch should stay in the city (Orestes wanted him banished).[15] Moreover, if ever a man had bitter enemies it was Cyril. Wilful murder was considered just as unsuitable conduct for bishops in the fifth century as it is now. Why, during all the fierce conflict with the Nestorians, when they brought every possible charge against him, did no one think of calling him Hypatia's murderer? Although to accuse our saint of this horrid story is a gross calumny, there is no doubt that in other ways he did give annoyance to the government. A number of monks from the Nitrian mountains (Sokrates says five hundred!) had insulted and wounded Orestes in the streets of Alexandria.[16] He had their leader[17] seized and tortured, under which torture the monk died. Cyril then brought this person's body to the church and solemnly buried

---

the notes of Henri de Valois—Henricus Valesius, on Sokrates vii, 15. ed. Gul. Reading [Cambridge, 1720], ii, 361). Charles Kingsley in *Hypatia* repeats the insinuation and is responsible for the dislike of St Cyril among many people who have never heard of him nor of Hypatia, except through that singularly silly novel (e.g., the monk's apology of Christianity to the heroine just before she dies, Raphael's argument against celibacy, Hypatia's philosophic discourse, etc.).

[15] *Cod. Theod. De episc.* xvi, 2 (quoted by J. Kopallik, *Cyrillus von Alexandrien* [Mainz, 1881], pp. 20ff.).

[16] They called him a "sacrificer and a pagan (θυτὴρ καὶ ἕλλην) and many other offensive names". He declared that he was a Christian and had been baptized at Constantinople by Attikos. But the monks would not believe him, and began throwing stones, one of which wounded him severely on the head (Sokrates, *Hist. Eccl.* vii, 14).

[17] Named Ammonios.

it, while he preached a panegyric on him, declaring him a martyr who had died for the faith and "praising his high soul with many words".[18] "But", says Sokrates, "even the Christians, or at least the more reasonable ones, did not approve of Cyril's enthusiasm for Ammonios, for they understood that this man had paid the penalty of his own folly, and had not suffered because he would not deny Christ. And at last Cyril himself gradually let the whole matter be buried in silence,"[19] which was, perhaps, just as well. We hear no more about Saint Thaumasios the martyr; but one can understand that Orestes, who heard of the service and the sermon while he was nursing his broken head at home, was annoyed, and that for these various reasons "between him and Cyril an unrelenting feud existed".[20]

But the patriarch was not destined to spend his life in a series of petty quarrels with a shuffling magistrate. Soon a cause arose that was worthy of his high spirit, and he was able to direct his restless energy against a danger that threatened the whole Church.

3. Nestorius and His Heresy

We have seen that when Saint John Chrysostom was banished (404) the government at Constantinople set up first Arsakios (404–405), and after his death Attikos (406–425) as anti-bishops.[21] After Saint John's death (407), Attikos seems to have been generally accepted as lawful occupier of the see till he, too, died in 425. Then came one Sisinios

---

[18] Sokrates, *Hist. Eccl.* vii, 14. He changed the martyr's name to Thaumasios.
[19] Ibid.
[20] Ibid., vii, 13.
[21] [Note missing from 1908 edition. It probably was a cross-reference to pp. 133–34 above.—ED.]

(425–427), and after him, not without dispute, Nestori-us[22] (Νεστόριος, 428–431),[23] the most important of the many bishops who have left to the Byzantine Church a fame with which their successors would gladly dispense.[24] Nestorius was an Antiochene who had been a monk in a laura out-side the walls of Antioch. He had then been ordained priest and had a great reputation as a preacher. When he became Patriarch of Constantinople, the people thought they were to have a second Chrysostom as bishop. In his first sermon preached before the emperor, he showed his zeal against heretics, "Give me", he said, "a world free of heretics, and I will give you heaven; help me to destroy heretics and I will help you to destroy Persians" (presumably by his prayers).[25] He further showed this pious zeal by shutting up an Arian conventicle, attacking Novatians, Apollinarists, Quartodecimans[26] and all manner of enemies of the true faith. Sokrates says he was a calumniator and a firebrand[27] and that his tongue was unreserved and petulant.[28]

---

[22] Nestorios is so well known under this Latin form, Nestorius, that one must leave it for the present.

[23] The story of the quarrels as to the succession after Attikos is told by Sokrates, Hist. Eccl. vii, 26–29.

[24] Among the heretics who occupied the see of Constantinople are Make-donios I (344–348, 350–360) the Pneumatomachian; this Nestorius; Akakios (471–489) who made the Acacian schism; the Monothelete Sergios I (610–638); Pyrrhos (638–641, 652); Paul II (641–652); a number of Iconoclasts in the eighth century; and Cyril I (Lukaris) in the seventeenth century. I count only those whom the Orthodox too admit to have been heretics.

[25] Sokrates, Hist. Eccl. vii, 29—where the early life of Nestorius is described.

[26] The Quartodecimans (Quattuordecim = fourteen) were people who, in spite of the decree of the Nicene Council, kept Easter on Nisan 14 instead of waiting till the following Sunday. They made a schism that lasted till the fifth or sixth century.

[27] Sokrates, Hist. Eccl. vii, 29. I conceive that Πυρκαϊά (or Πυρκαιεύς?) means this and not a man who set fire to houses.

[28] Ibid.

Very soon after his accession, Nestorius began to give his favour to the particular heresy that is called after him. At this time, Arianism was practically dead, and Apollinarism,[29] too, was universally condemned. Every Catholic believed that the Word of God is equal and consubstantial to the Father and that our Lord had a perfect human nature complete with body and soul. There remained the question *how* the Logos, the Word, was joined to this human nature. It was, apparently, as a result of Antiochene theology that Nestorius and his friends defended a *moral* union only.[30] The Logos came down from heaven and dwelt in the man Jesus Christ, very much as the Spirit of God had filled the prophets. Christ was really and wholly a man (this against the Apollinarists), the Logos was not part of his human nature, but was in some way joined to it. What other way is possible but some close moral connexion, some indwelling of the Divinity that did not affect his person, but made that person its temple? That is the Nestorian heresy. Gradually Nestorius and his party went further, evolved their theory more consistently and so wandered still further from the Catholic faith, as is the way of heretics. Is there any reason for supposing that the Logos dwelt in Christ always? When did the Logos descend into him? Is it not probable that this is what happened at our Lord's baptism when "the Holy Spirit came down on him in the figure of a dove",[31] and "stayed in him",[32] so that before his baptism there was no union at all? Nor did they fail to produce arguments for their new theory. Christ was born as a little child, grew in

---

[29] See p. 81, n. 96, above.

[30] Nestorius had been a disciple of Theodore of Mopsuestia, who was, perhaps, the original father of this heresy (p. 185, n. 68).

[31] Lk 3:21.

[32] Jn 1:33.

wisdom and age and grace,[33] was surprised,[34] wept,[35] suffered pain, died. None of these things can be true of God. In the language of our philosophy, Nestorianism can be put in one very short sentence: there are *two persons in Christ*, a Divine person, the Logos, dwelling in a human person, the man Jesus. The use of the word *person*, or rather of its Greek equivalents *hypostasis* (ὑπόστασις) and *prosopon* (πρόσωπον)[36] was not technically so clear in the fifth century as it became in scholastic times. The Catholic Fathers, Saint Cyril himself, sometimes use the word *hypostasis* for what we call nature, and sometimes for person. But the issue is quite clear. The Nestorians divided Christ into two separate beings only joined by a moral tie; the later Monophysites, going to the other extreme, said that Christ's humanity was absorbed and swallowed up by his Divinity, so he would not be really man at all. Against both, the Catholic faith is that our Lord is really and completely God, really and completely man, and yet he is really, physically, indissolubly *one*. As we say, he is *one person with two natures*, the nature of God and the nature of man.[37] The Nestorians liked the word *Theophóros*

[33] Lk 2:52.

[34] Mt 8:10.

[35] Lk 19:41.

[36] Since practically the whole controversy was carried on in Greek.

[37] We may as well understand what *nature* and *person* mean. Our *nature* is what makes us what we are essentially. If you are a man, that is because you have a human nature, a horse has an equine nature, etc. Since it is naturally impossible for anyone to be two essential things at once, we, and all things, have one nature each. An essential change means a change of nature, the old nature goes and a new one comes. A *person* is the individual being who has a rational nature. We do not use the word for beasts or plants or stones. But among men (and angels) we are each of us a person complete in himself. I *have* a human nature, I *am* a human person. The person is the real *me*. The person acts and is responsible. You may always substitute the word *person* for a proper name or a pronoun. "John does so and so", that is, "that person

(θεοφόρος); it expressed exactly what they meant: the man Christ was "God-bearing"—had God in him. But it was another word that became the standard of either side, according as it was used or rejected, and in this heresy, as on other occasions, the honour of our Lord's Mother was the defence of his honour: people who were really attacking him did so by attacking her. What the term *Homooüsios* had been in Arian times that was the word *Theotókos* (θεοτόκος) now. Theotókos means *Mother of God*, and all Catholics, everyone who believes in our Lord's Divinity and is not a Nestorian, calls the blessed Virgin so. It follows obviously from the hypostatic union: she is the mother of Christ, the mother of a person, and that person is God. The relation of mother and son concerns persons. The mother of a person who is God is just as much Mother of God as the mother of a

---

does so and so." "He is wicked", namely, "a wicked person". You cannot say that of nature. He is not a wicked nature, though you may say (loosely) that he has a wicked nature. Obviously then, since our Lord by the miracle of the hypostatic union is both God and man, he is the only case of two natures in one person. He has both natures, divine and human; but it is the same *he*, the same person. He died (as man) and he (the same person) is almighty and immortal (as God). So far all Catholics have always agreed, from St Irenæus (d. 201), who says: Jesus, who suffered for us, he himself is the Word of God (*Adv. Hær.* iii, 16, 1–3), or rather from St John, who says: "the Word *became* [not "took up his abode in"] flesh [= man]", and our Lord himself: "I and the Father are one" (Jn 10:30) and "I [the same I, the same person] spoke openly to the world" (Jn 18:20). Anyone who is not a philosopher says the whole truth quite accurately by the statement: "He is both God and man." It is the same subject ("He", therefore one person), and the two predicates express the two natures. It is only when we come to the philosophical terms that we find that they, like all philosophical words, have not always been used in the same sense. Now we say that substance, essence (and in Greek, φύσις, οὐσία) mean exactly the same thing as *nature*. On the other hand, *suppositum, hypostasis* and πρόσωπον mean person. In earlier times, the words *hypostasis* in Greek and *substantia* in Latin were often ambiguous, meaning sometimes nature and sometimes person.

person who is man is mother of man. The title that expresses the great and unique honour of our Lady was not new in the fifth century. It was used by all Catholics and had been used for centuries.[38] Here, as always, it was the heretics who were the innovators. They began, as we shall see, to preach against this title and to demand that it should be changed into *Christotókos* (χριστοτόκος), Mother of Christ, which is noncommittal either way. And against them the watchword of all the Catholics, led by Saint Cyril, was that Mary is the Mother of God.[39] We may then sum up the

---

[38] Origen (d. 252) uses it: *Comm in Ps.* i (Sokrates, *Hist. Eccl.* vii, 32), so also Eusebeios (d. ca. 340), *Vita Const.* iii, 43; Athanasius (d. 397), *Oratio* iii *Adv. Arian.* 14, 29, 33; Cyril of Jerusalem (d. 386), Catech. x, 19; Didymos (d. ca. 395), *De Trin.* i, 31, 94; ii, 41, etc.; Gregory of Nazianzos (d. ca. 390), *Oratio* xxix, 4; Ep. 101 *Ad Cledon.*, etc.

[39] It is curious that most Protestants resent this word, apparently from a general dislike to any honour given to Christ's Mother. If they knew anything about it, they would realize that by refusing it they are letting themselves in for Nestorianism as well as their other heresies. I have heard from High-Church Anglicans of that type that loves anything Eastern but hates everything Roman that the word *Theotókos* is right, but not *Mater Dei* or *Mother of God*. Miss I. Hapgood, who has translated a selection of Orthodox services into the funniest mixture of Prayer-book English and American slang (*Service Book of the Holy Orthodox-Catholic Apostolic Græco-Russian Church* [Boston: Houghton, Mifflin, 1906]) puts for *Theotókos* the portentous form: *Birth-giver of God*. Such scruples are superfluous. *Dei Genitrix* is an exact version of θεοτόκος and *genitrix* is simply a *mother*. It is an accident of language that Latin does not lend itself to a compound form so well as Greek in this case. *Deipara* is not pretty. German Catholics translate the word beautifully: *Gottesgebärerin*. On the other hand, in the case of Orthodox who speak a language that does not form compounds, the Liturgy puts simply *Mother of God*, as we do. So Arabic: *wālidat allāh*. The Orthodox themselves never conceive the possibility of there being a difference of meaning between these two forms. They constantly say: μήτηρ τοῦ θεοῦ in Greek too. This pretended distinction is like that imagined between μετουσίωσις and *transsubstantiastio*, a figment of the prejudiced mind. If Miss Hapgood were a theologian, she would not have troubled about this point, and she would not have put such appalling heresy as: "did lay aside his godhead" for ἐκένωσε σεαυτόν (p. 103).

Nestorian heresy in these six points: (1) The man Christ is not God, God is not the man; but the man is most intimately joined to God. (2) Therefore the mother of Christ is not Mother of God. (3) The Word in Christ alone can really be adored; the man receives the name "Only-begotten Son of God" only in an improper sense, by participation. (4) God did not himself become our high priest. (5) God did not suffer nor did he die. (6) God was in Christ in the same way as he was in the Prophets (but rather more intimately); God speaks through Christ. The man Christ is the temple, organ, instrument of God.

4. Before the Council of Ephesus (428–431)

Having explained the issue, we now come back to the history. Soon after Nestorius had become patriarch, one of his followers, a priest named Anastasios, began the fight by preaching a sermon at Constantinople in which he denied our Lady's title. "Let no one call Mary *Mother of God*," he said, "for she was merely a human being, and God cannot be born of a human being." He proposed the word *Christotókos* instead. Then a bishop, Dorotheos of Markianopolis in Asia Minor, who was in the city, preached a sermon of the same kind and excommunicated everyone who called Mary the Theotókos. Naturally, people were surprised, and it was not long before other priests and laymen spoke in defence of the traditional teaching. We notice that at the very beginning, or during the whole time of this dispute, the question turns around our Lady's title of *Theotókos*. Already people were divided according as they attacked or defended this word. It was when they gave their reasons for what would seem an unimportant detail that the fundamental difference of their views about Christ appeared. Nestorius himself then took the side of his friends Anastasios and

Dorotheos and preached a course of sermons against the
Theotókos, explaining that it is idolatrous and blasphemous, God cannot have a mother, Mary's son was not
the Logos, but a man in whom the Logos dwelled, and so
on—in short, explaining and developing the heresy of
which from this moment he becomes the champion.[40]
On Lady-day 429, a Catholic bishop, Proklos of Kyzikos,
preaching before the patriarch at Constantinople, defended
the title that everyone was already discussing and showed
that it is only a corollary from the Catholic faith about the
hypostatic union. As soon as the sermon was over, Nestorius stood up and denied all that Proklos had said. There
seems to have been something of the nature of a scene in
church. Nestorius further ratified the excommunication
against everyone who said Theotókos. The quarrel now
spread all over the east. In Egypt too, people began to
discuss it; Egyptian monks read Nestorius' sermons, and
some of them said they agreed with him. So Saint Cyril
in his Paschal letter of 429[41] explained the matter to
them and refuted the arguments of the sermons, but without naming Nestorius. Soon after he wrote a long encyclical letter in which he again defends and explains the word
Theotókos. Copies of this encyclical got to Constantinople,
and the Theotokians there comforted themselves by reading it.[42] Nestorius was very angry and complained of Cyril's

[40] The sermons in Mansi, v, 763: "Has God a mother? Only a pagan (ἕλλην)
speaks of the mother of the gods without being reproved. Mary did not give
birth to the Divinity [of course not; no one said she did], ... but she gave
birth to a man who was the organ of the Divinity."

[41] The *Paschal letters* of the Alexandrine patriarchs were published each
year to announce the day on which Easter would fall; and at the same time
they used the opportunity of discussing any question that concerned their
patriarchate at the time. See p. 41 above.

[42] Cyril of Alexandria, Ep. xi, 4 (*PG* 77:81).

interference.[43] Cyril had not interfered at all as yet; both the Paschal letter and the encyclical were addressed only to his own subjects, who were puzzled by the news from Constantinople. But now he wrote to Nestorius and remonstrated with him,[44] to which letter Nestorius sent an unconciliatory answer.[45] The champions of the two sides had now taken up their arms. The story of the Nestorian heresy became one of a conflict between Cyril and Nestorius, and so, incidentally, between the sees of Alexandria and Constantinople. There was that side to the quarrel too. Apart from the theological question, this story is one chapter in what was a long history, the mutual enmity of these two sees.

Alexandria had been—was still canonically—the second see in Christendom, the first in the east. Since the second general Council (381), Constantinople had been scheming and intriguing to get that place herself and to reduce Alexandria to the third rank—a plan in which she finally succeeded, chiefly after the Council of Chalcedon (451) and the fall of Dioskoros of Alexandria (the Monophysite).[46] We shall see that Nestorius got sympathy from other bishops in many cases, not because they cared about his views but because they were instinctively on the side of Constantinople against Alexandria. Next certain excommunicate

[43] Cyril of Alexandria, Ep. ii (PG 77:40).

[44] Ibid.

[45] Cyril of Alexandria, Ep. iii (PG 77:43).

[46] The quarrel between these two sees is an important element throughout eastern Church history from the fourth century till the final fall of Alexandria at the Moslem conquest of Egypt in 641. See my Orth. Eastern Church, pp. 11–15, and 28–46. Three great incidents in that fight were Theophilos' deposition of St John Chrysostom (see pp. 129–31 above), Cyril's deposition of Nestorius, and, later, the deposition of Dioskoros. In the first and third, our sympathies are with Constantinople, in the second with Alexandria. But they are all parts of one long rivalry.

clerics of Egypt, who had run away to the capital, stirred up feeling there against their patriarch. Cyril then wrote a second letter to Nestorius in 430. This is known as his *Dogmatic Letter*, in which he more fully explains the faith;[47] at the same time he wrote sternly to the rebellious clerics who were calumniating him.[48] Nestorius wrote to various people too. He tried to persuade Isidore of Pelusium and John, Patriarch of Antioch, to take his side. In John's case, he appealed of course to the alliance between Constantinople and Antioch against Alexandria.

Meanwhile the emperor, Theodosius II (408–450), had heard of the matter. Nestorius at the court counted on his support. Cyril wrote to explain the matter to him, to his wife, Eudokia, and his sister, Pulcheria.[49] The question had now become so important that both sides, following the traditional practice of eastern as well as western Christendom, appeal to the Pope of Rome. It was Saint Celestine (422–432) who was called upon to settle this matter: he fills the same place as judge in Nestorian times as does his successor, Saint Leo I (440–461) in the later Monophysite disturbance—in which, however, the positions were reversed, and Alexandria was wrong. Saint Cyril then, "compelled", as he says, "by the command of God who demands vigilance, and by the ancient custom of the Church", sent a long account of the matter to Celestine by one of his deacons, Posidonios.[50] Nestorius also wrote to the Pope, accusing Cyril of Arianism and Apollinarism.[51]

---

[47] Cyril of Alexandria, Ep. iv (*PG* 77:44–50).

[48] Ep. x (*PG* 77:64ff.).

[49] *PG* 76:1133–1420.

[50] Ep. xi, *Ad Cel.* (*PG* 87:80).

[51] Apollinarism was the usual accusation of Nestorians against their adversaries. Unless you distinguish two persons in Christ, they said, you confuse

Celestine held a synod at Rome (August 430), in which he entirely approved of Cyril's theology, condemned Nestorius, commanded him to receive back into communion the Theotokians he had excommunicated and threatened to excommunicate him unless he drew up a written retractation of his heresy within ten days. The Pope also made Cyril his deputy and legate for the fulfilment of these laws and sent him a copy of the acts of this council.[52] It was on this occasion that Celestine and a Roman deacon, Leo (afterward Pope [Saint] Leo I), persuaded Abbot Cassian to write his treatise *On the Incarnation of the Lord*.[53] Before Nestorius heard of this Roman synod, he wrote again to the Pope describing the whole quarrel as an aggression on

---

his two natures. Just in the same way the Monophysites later accused their opponents of being Nestorians—unless you identify the two natures you separate his person into two.

[52] The acts in Mansi, iv, 1017, 1025, 1035, 1047. The fact that St Cyril was made Papal deputy is important, because it justifies his interference in the affairs of Constantinople. When his uncle Theophilos interfered in St John Chrysostom's affair, it was an unlawful usurpation (above pp. 129–31). But Cyril had delegate authority from the Pope, which makes all the difference. It has been said that the Pope's attitude is simply another instance of the hereditary alliance between Rome and Alexandria as against Constantinople and Antioch. On the other hand, twenty years later, when Alexandria was heretical (Monophysite under Dioskoros), Rome took just as determined a line against her as now against Constantinople. The explanation of the change of ecclesiastical polity is that both times the Roman Church was concerned, not about alliances, but about the Catholic faith.

[53] *De Incarnatione Domini contra Nestorium* (PL 50:9–272). John Cassian (Cassianus) was abbot of a monastery at Massilia (Marseilles). His most famous work is the *Collationes Patrum* (PL 49:477–1328, and in Hurter's *SS. Patrum opuscula selecta*, series altera, iii), twenty-four books of conversations, maxims, and principles of the Fathers of the Egyptian desert, written down for the edification of the monks at Marseilles. But Cassian in the question of Pelagianism conceived a theory of compromise between Pelagius and Augustine, and so became the father of the semi-Pelagian heresy. He died in 435.

Cyril's part and proposing the title *Mother of Christ* (*Christ-otókos*) as a compromise between *Mother of God* (*Theotó-kos*) and *Mother of man* (*Anthropotókos*). He also proposed that a general Council should be summoned to settle the question.[54] Meanwhile his friend, John of Antioch, wrote to warn him not to make a schism and to accept the word *Theotókos*. Obviously the Pope and Cyril would have nothing of his compromise. As a century before, in the case of the semi-Arian *Homoiüsios*, Catholics would accept no half-and-half formula. In Nestorius' answer to John of Antioch, he dilates on the pride and domineering spirit of "that Egyptian", Cyril (this was always his policy, to enlist sympathy at Antioch), and hopes great things from the council for which he is so anxious. Saint Cyril, as soon as he got the Pope's letter and the acts of the Roman synod held a synod himself at Alexandria (November 430), in which he drew up twelve Anathemas against the new heresy: Anathema to those who deny that Emmanuel is truly God, and that therefore his Mother is Mother of God; Anathema to those who deny that the Logos became man as one Christ; Anathema to those who say that Christ is only a man bearing God (Theophóros), and so on.[55] As soon as Nestorius heard of this, not to be outdone, he promptly drew up twelve Anathemas against the Theotoki-ans, which he sent to John of Antioch as his answer to Cyril's synod, adding: "Thou shalt not wonder greatly at this Egyptian's arrogance, because thou knowest of many such examples already." It is still the idea of representing it all as merely one more case of Egyptian pride against

[54] His letter in Garnier, *Præf. histor.* i, 70.
[55] The twelve Anathemas in Mansi, iv, 1082. The decrees of this synod with those of the Roman one were sent by Cyril to Nestorius, John of Antioch and Juvenal of Jerusalem.

Syria and Greece.[56] Other bishops of those parts, Andrew of Samosata and Theodoret of Cyrus, wrote angrily against Cyril, too. Everything was now ready for a general Council to settle the question finally. The emperor (Theodosius II), urged by both sides, especially by Nestorius, in November 430, sent letters to all metropolitans and bishops of the empire, summoning them to a great synod to be held at Ephesus at Whitsuntide 431.

5. The Council of Ephesus (June–July 431)

From Smyrna you may go by the Aidin railway in three hours to the village of Ayasoluk.[57] From here you ride in an hour to the great plain where stand the ruins of Ephesus; they are being very carefully excavated by a commission sent by the Austrian Government. Looking down from the rising ground (*Panayir Dagh*) to the east you see the plain stretch out to the sea between the high mountain (*Bülbül Dagh*—Nightingale hill) and the river Kaystros. A canal brings the water up to the great Ephesian harbour. At your feet lies a glorious and wonderful white Greek city. Standing out from the long grass, the olive trees and the carpet of many-coloured flowers, are the columns of the broad road, the stage of the great library, the curve of the theatre— temples and baths and colonnades, broken and ruined now, but still majestic and splendid in their gleaming white marble and all eloquent of the rich and mighty city that was the capital of Asia. It would be difficult to see without emotion the broad street and the columns under whose shade

[56] Mansi, iv, 754–56.

[57] *Ayasoluk* is a Turkish attempt at ἅγιος θεολόγος. The "holy theologian" is St John the Evangelist, first Bishop of Ephesus. Fine tobacco grows here. [This description dates from the beginning of the twentieth century.—ED.]

Saint Paul rested, the pillars and walls that Saint John knew. Behind, to the right, is the great *Artemision*, the temple of the patron-goddess, sunk in water now and neglected, since no longer great is Diana of the Ephesians. And over in front you may see the ruin of a later building, no less impressive than the others. You will walk across the street and clamber over broken walls and through thick bushes to stand here, too, for this is the double church of Ephesus in which the council was held.

The bishops came in June 431 from all parts of the empire. Nestorius arrived first with sixteen of his followers and with armed retainers, sure of victory because the emperor was on his side. Memnon of Ephesus had forty suffragans. Cyril arrived with fifty Egyptians. Juvenal of Jerusalem and his bishops came late, as did Flavian of Thessalonica with his. Theodosius sent an Imperial commissioner, Candidian, to keep order and to prevent strangers and the great crowd of monks at Ephesus from interfering. And Pope Celestine approved of the summoning of the council and sent his legates, Arcadius and Projectus, both bishops, and a priest Philip, with letters to thank the emperor for having summoned the council. He had already made Cyril his legate for the whole affair: the synod formally recognized Cyril as Papal legate.[58] As legate he presided, and the Latins had received instructions from the Pope to acknowledge him as such and in all things to be on his side. They waited some time for stragglers to come in. John of Antioch still did not appear, and it was supposed that he did not wish to be

[58] The "Alexandrine Cyril, who also holds the place of Celestine, the most holy and most blessed Archbishop of the Roman Church ... being present" (Mansi, iv, 1280). Arcadius and Projectus are also "the most pious and God-beloved bishops and legates", and Philip is "priest and legate of the Apostolic See" (ibid., 1281).

forced to declare himself openly against his old friend Nestorius.[59] At last, on June 22, the synod held its first session in
the double church[60] that it was to make famous throughout the world as the place of the third general Council.
Candidian, who was Nestorius' friend and apparently hoped
that John would come soon and vote for that side, wanted
to wait for him still. But they had already waited a fortnight, so Cyril refused to put off the synod any longer.
There were 198 bishops present. Nestorius seems now to
have foreseen that things would go against him, so he stayed
at home and refused to show himself. In the first session
the Catholic faith was declared, the title *Theotókos* solemnly
recognized, Cyril's twelve Anathemas confirmed. The next
day Nestorius was deposed and excommunicated as contumacious. The second session was held on July 10. The Latin
legates, who had not arrived in time for the first, were present
at this and confirmed what had passed. It was then that
Philip spoke the famous words about the Primacy: "There
is no doubt, indeed it is known to all ages, that the holy
and most blessed Peter, Prince and Chief of the Apostles,
column of the faith and foundation of the Catholic Church,
received the keys of the kingdom, and that the power of
forgiving and retaining sins was given to him, and that he
until the present time, and always, lives and judges in his

[59] Two of his metropolitans (of Apamea and Hierapolis) gave this reason
for his delay. But from the beginning there was something not straight about
John of Antioch. He wrote to Cyril saying that he was on his way, had
already been travelling thirty days and would arrive in five or six more. He
could not possibly have taken really thirty days from Antioch to Ephesus if
he had any sort of idea of the way (you have only to keep due north-west all
the time). In easy horse-stages of 30–40 miles a day he could have got there
in about a fortnight. His letter is in ibid., 1121.

[60] The double church is a building with two churches, one in front of the
other.

successors. Therefore his successor and Viceregent, our holy and most blessed Pope, the Bishop Celestine, has sent us to this synod to take his place." [61] Firmus of Cæsarea in Cappadocia explained that the council had only carried out the Pope's instructions in its first session.

Meanwhile John of Antioch had arrived at Ephesus with his bishops. The council at once sent deputies to him and asked him to come and take his place among the other fathers. But he consulted with Nestorius, and his hatred of "that Egyptian" now conquered his scruples about his friend's orthodoxy; so instead of going to the double church he held a private assembly in his own house. Candidian, who had become more and more sulky with Cyril, went there, too, with a few Nestorian bishops. John, his bishops, and these friends of Nestorius, then proceeded to excommunicate Cyril, Memnon of Ephesus and all the real council as being Arians, Eunomians, and Apollinarists. They deposed Cyril and Memnon and wanted to ordain a new bishop for Ephesus: the Ephesians themselves prevented this. But Candidian sent his account of the matter to his master, so that Theodosius declared himself for John's council and against Cyril's. The fathers of the real council answered the emperor and explained that they had done everything in order and had deposed Nestorius canonically and in accordance with the decision of the Roman Church. The fourth and fifth sessions (July 16 and 17) again invited John of Antioch to come and take his proper place among the fathers, instead of holding a rival sham-synod at home. As he would not do so, his excommunication of Cyril and Memnon was declared null and void, and he and his party were, not excommunicated, but suspended for the present. The sixth

----

[61] Mansi iv, 280.

session (July 22) explained the Nicene creed, and when a member proposed a new semi-Nestorian symbol as a compromise, it forbade anyone to change or alter the old one.[62] The seventh and last session arranged some points of discipline and drew up six canons and an encyclical letter declaring what the council had defined.[63] The people of Ephesus had been on the right side throughout. After the first session, they received the decrees, especially the recognition of our Lady's title, with great joy. They accompanied the fathers back to their lodgings that evening (June 22) with a great torchlight procession. The memory of that procession still clings to the city. The double church was naturally afterward always called the church of the All-Holy Mother of God, the παναγία θεοτόκος. The city, famous already for so many reasons, acquired a new title as the city of the Theotókos. Still the Turkish peasants, who all over the Levant surprise one by their curious memories of local Christian events, have kept a vague consciousness of what was done in the double church,[64] and still as one looks over Ephesus in the evening, one seems to see the gleam of the torches move down the great street among the shadows and the ghosts.

---

[62] This is the decree the Orthodox quote against us, because we have added the *Filioque*. As the council had in view the *original* Nicene creed without the enlargement of Constantinople I, its law would fall with as much force on them as on us, if it meant what they said. They are enormously wrong in the whole question of this decree of Ephesus (*Orth. Eastern Church*, pp. 381–84).

[63] The acts of the council are in Mansi, iv–v; a full history of it in Hefele's *Conziliengeschichte*, 2nd ed., II, 141ff.

[64] The *mukari* who went with me and pretended to talk Greek, but couldn't, when we stood in the double church became tremendously excited, and for the first time said something intelligible: μάλιστα, μάλιστα, παναγία θεοτόκος! All the Turks in Asia Minor call our Lady *Panayia*. But he did not know what θεοτόκος means.

6. After the Council (431–439)

It was some time before the emperor was persuaded to accept the decrees of the real council. Candidian had poisoned his mind against it, and at first he was disposed to take the side of John and Nestorius. Both synods sent deputies to Constantinople, each accusing the other. Theodosius then thought of a master-stroke and meant to satisfy everyone by punishing them all. So he sent his treasurer to Ephesus with a message that he had deposed John and Nestorius, and Cyril and Memnon.[65] Then he found that they were still not satisfied, and he further examined the case, having ordered eight representatives from either council to come to him and explain their views. Eventually he was persuaded that Cyril was right, so he allowed him to go back to Egypt, and he let a new Bishop of Constantinople, Maximian (431–434) be ordained on October 25, 431, in place of the deposed Nestorius. Saint Cyril arrived at Alexandria on October 30, where he was received in triumph as a second Athanasius.

But the bad feeling between Alexandria and Antioch lasted for a long time. John of Antioch had gone home, too, and he was still full of indignation against the Egyptian. In two councils at Tarsus and Antioch, the Syrian bishops declared that Nestorius had been unjustly deposed and that Maximian was a schismatical intruder.[66] It was not till 433 that John accepted the legitimate Council of Ephesus, and Cyril

---

[65] For some time the fathers were kept prisoners at Ephesus.

[66] One expression used by Cyril especially scandalized the Syrians. It was μία φύσις τοῦ θεοῦ σεσαρκωμένη—*one incarnate nature of God*. This seemed to them patently Apollinarist. It had, however, already been used by St Athanasius (cf. Mansi, iv, 689). St Cyril himself explained that by φύσις he meant the same thing as ὑπόστασις (Ep. i, ix, etc.; *PG* 77:232, 241, etc.).

was able to write to the Pope (Sixtus III, 432–440) that peace was restored between them.

But the Nestorians always kept a strong party in Syria. Their leader, Nestorius himself, retired to a monastery, where he died quietly about the year 439.[67] We hear nothing more of him. But the Syrian schools still taught his heresy, defending it as the teaching of their two chief theologians, Diodore of Tarsus and Theodore of Mopsuestia.[68] They translated the works of Diodore and Theodore into Syriac, Persian, and Armenian. These two persons have always been the fathers read and admired by Nestorians.

The centre of Nestorianism was the school of Edessa,[69] under a priest Ibas, who became Bishop of Edessa (435–457). In 489, the emperor Zeno (474–491) closed the school and banished the Nestorians from the empire. They fled across the Persian frontier to Nisibis.[70] Here the bishop, Barsumas (Barsumah, 453–489), became their champion. The

---

[67] A later writer on the subject, J. F. Bethune-Baker (*Nestorius and His Teaching* [Cambridge, 1908]), disputed this and maintained that the heretic lived till the Council of Chalcedon (451) and warmly approved of its teaching. Many modern writers, in Germany especially, deny that Nestorius really meant the heresy of which he was accused.

[68] *Diodore*, Bishop of Tarsus (d. ca. 394), was a leader of the Antiochene school, and a defender of the faith against the Arians. He was a Meletian at the time of that schism and was present at the second general Council. His works in *PG* 33. His pupil *Theodore* (d. ca. 428), a friend of St John Chrysostom, became Bishop of Mopsuestia in Cilicia in 392. Both were representatives of the Antiochene school that undoubtedly paved the way for Nestorianism (see above p. 169). Afterward they were especially attacked by the Monophysites, and for centuries the question of their orthodoxy was the burning one in the east. The condemnation of Theodore was the first of Justinian's *Three Chapters* in 553 (*Orth. Eastern Church*, p. 82). Theodore of Mopsuestia is "the Exegete" to the Syrians. His works in *PG* 66.

[69] Edessa is now *Urfa*, three long days' march north-east of Aleppo. The Moslems say Abraham was born here.

[70] Now Nesibin, five days north-west of Mosul.

Persian king protected them, as being enemies of the Roman Empire, and at Nisibis they spread the Nestorian church that sent missions eastward right across China. Its history forms one of the most curious and romantic, as well as one of the least known, chapters of Church history. There or thereabouts, among the mountains of Kurdistan and in the valley of Urmiah, they still remain, a pitiful remnant,[71] under a katholikos, who bears the title of *Mar Simeon*, calling themselves *Meshihaye* (people of the Messias), or *Syrians* or *Nasrani* (Nazarenes).[72] They remember little of the old heresy that cut them off from the rest of the Christian world,[73] and only as a general inheritance from their fathers do they remember in their liturgy, among the other saints, Saint Diodore, Saint Theodore and Saint Nestorius.

7. The End of Saint Cyril (431–444)

Meanwhile, in the great Catholic Church, that is, the Church of the Roman Empire, Nestorianism soon became a thing of the past. Maximian of Constantinople was recognized by everyone, and he was a determined Theotokian. Our Lady's title was accepted and used triumphantly in every liturgy as a continued protest against the dead heresy, and there is no more trouble about Nestorianism, till the extreme opposite side, the Monophysite party in Egypt, twenty years later remember it as a convenient accusation against their opponents.

[71] There were about seventy thousand in 1833 (Smith and Dwight, *Researches in Armenia* [Boston, 1833]).

[72] They appear to call themselves *Nastoriye* occasionally, too. [The author is writing in the early twentieth century.—ED.]

[73] But they did not quite forget it. In 1247, in answer to one of the many attempts at reunion made by the Pope, they sent a profession of faith to Rome that was quite orthodox, except that they changed the word *Theotókos* into *Christotókos*.

With the triumph of the Council of Ephesus, Saint Cyril's work was done. He lived three more years at Alexandria, the acknowledged hero of the Catholics. He spent those years in removing the last traces of the schism and in gradually pacifying the Syrian bishops who were still sore at what they looked upon as a triumph of Egypt over Syria. One of his last acts was a prudent and charitable one. He stopped an agitation among Catholics to have Theodore of Mopsuestia condemned too. It is true that Theodore had been Nestorius' master and that the root of the heresy can be traced back to him. On the other hand, the cause had triumphed so completely that there was no need further to condemn a dead man, especially as Theodore was so enormously admired by the Syrians that any attack against him would have hurt their feelings very much and would have made their reconciliation and acceptance of the council still more difficult. Saint Cyril died at Alexandria on June 27, 444. He was succeeded by his archdeacon, Dioskoros. Almost at once, the Monophysite troubles began, in which Dioskoros and the Egyptians, pushing the teaching of their hero to an extreme, fell into the opposite heresy.

The Orthodox remember Saint Cyril of Alexandria as the Seal of the Fathers (p. 162). He was the last of the great group that begins with his predecessor, Saint Athanasius; he was also the most systematic and complete in his theology. For he not only wrote against Nestorianism; in all theological questions he for the first time drew up an orderly system of dogma, arranging all the points of the faith logically and tersely in a harmonious whole, so that he disputes with Saint John Damascene the place as systematic theologian among the Greeks that Saint Thomas Aquinas holds among us. The Byzantine Church keeps the memory of "Cyril, Pope of Alexandria",[74] on June 9, and again with the other great Egyptian, Athanasius, on January 18. He is "the defender of the true and unspotted faith",[75] and she remembers him as "a most learned man and splendid fighter for the Catholic faith, whom the Supreme Pontiff, Celestine, thought worthy to take his place as legate at the Council of Ephesus".[76] Before the Byzantine mitre, which is shaped like a crown, was worn by all Byzantine bishops, the Patriarch of Alexandria used it as a special privilege. Greek writers explain this and that patriarch's titles of *Pope* and *Judge of the World* as a legacy from the time when Cyril was legate of the Roman Pope at Ephesus. So Nikephoros Kallistos: "Celestine, the Bishop of Rome, did not himself come to the synod because of the difficulty of the journey. So he wrote to Cyril, telling him to take his place. And it is said that from that time he [Cyril] received the mitre and the titles of Pope and Judge of the whole world, which rights then descended to all the holy bishops who lawfully occupy the throne of Alexandria." [77]

Pope Leo XIII declared Saint Cyril of Alexandria a Doctor of the Church. We keep his feast on February 9,* and he, too, like his namesake of Jerusalem, has a very beautiful collect alluding to the work of his life: "God, who didst make thy holy Confessor and Pontiff, Cyril, a victorious defender of the divine motherhood of the most blessed

---

*After Vatican II his feast was moved to June 27.—ED.

[74] The patriarchs of Alexandria very commonly used the title *Pope* (πάπας) as well as the Roman Pontiffs. Another title, still officially used by them (both Orthodox and Copt), is *Judge of the World*, δικαστὴς τοῦ κόσμου, (cf. *Orth. Eastern Church*, pp. 13, n. 2, and 349, n. 3).

[75] So the Council of Chalcedon (451), Act. 3.

[76] *Menaia* for June 9.

[77] Nikephoros Kallistos, *Hist. Eccl.* xiv, 34 (*PG* 146; cf. Theodore Balsamon in Goar, *Euchologion* [Venice, 1720], p. 259).

Virgin Mary, grant by his prayers that we who believe her to be really Mother of God may be saved by her protection as our mother." And just as the memory of Athanasius lives in our churches each time we say the Nicene creed, so do we echo the voice of Cyril and of the Council of Ephesus every time we sing in the litany, *Sancta Dei genitrix*, and every time we say, "Holy Mary, *Mother of God*, pray for us sinners, now and at the hour of our death."

8. Table of Dates

ca. 380 (?)Cyril born.

    403 Oak-Tree Synod; Cyril present with his uncle, Theophilos.

    412 *Patriarch of Alexandria.*

    415 Hypatia murdered.

    428–431 Nestorius patriarch of Constantinople.

    429 Beginning of Nestorianism at Constantinople.

    429 Cyril's Paschal letter against the heresy.

    430 His dogmatic letter to Nestorius.

    430 Synod of Rome (Aug.); Synod of Alexandria (Nov.).

    431 THIRD GENERAL COUNCIL AT EPHESUS (June–July).

    433 John of Antioch accepts the council.

ca. 439 Death of Nestorius.

    444 *Death of Saint Cyril* (June 27).

    489 Zeno closes the school of Edessa. The Nestorians go to Persia.

9. Works

J. Aubert, a canon of Paris, published the complete text of Cyril of Alexandria in Greek in six folio volumes (Paris, 1638). This is the only complete edition. It is reprinted with a Latin translation in Migne's *Patrologia Græca*, vols. 68–77. Cardinal Mai edited a number of addenda (*Bibl. nova*

Patrum) that are included in Migne. R. P. Smith (*S. Cyr. Alex. arch. commentarii in Lucae evang. quæ supersunt syriace* [Oxford, 1858]), P. E. Pusey (*S.P.N. Cyr. arch. Alex. in XII Prophetas*, 2 vols [Oxford, 1868]; *In D. Joh. Evang. Accedunt fragmenta varia*, 3 vols [Oxford, 1872]; and other works [Oxford, 1877]), and C. J. Neumann (*Cyr. Alex. librorum ctra Julianum fragmenta græca et syriaca*, in *Juliani imp. librorum ctra Christianos quæ supersunt* [Leipzig, 1880]) have collected other works and fragments for a future complete edition.

R. P. Smith translated *A Commentary on the Gospel acc. to St Luke by S. Cyril* (2 vols, octavo [Oxford, 1859]), and W. Wright, *Fragments of the Homilies of Cyril of Alex, on the Gospel of S. Luke, edited from a Nitrian MS.* ([London, 1874], quatro), both from the Syriac. There is an English translation (anonymous) of Cyril's *Commentary on St John* (London, 1880–1886). H. Hurter, S.J., includes the *Encomium in S. Mariam* (the XI homily, fourth preached at Ephesus) in his series, *SS. Patrum opuscula selecta* (vol XII: *De glor. Dei gen. Maria ss. PP. opusc. sel.* [Innsbruck, 1894] pp. 39–52).

POLEMICAL WORKS. Most of these are written against Nestorianism. First come two works on the Holy Trinity against the Arians, *The Book of Treasures about the Holy and Consubstantial Trinity* (ἡ βίβλος τῶν θησαυρῶν περὶ τῆς ἁγίας καὶ ὁμοουσίου τριάδος, *Thesaurus de scta et consubstantiali Trinitate*, PG 75:9–656) in thirty-five discourses (λόγοι), and *Seven Dialogues about the Holy and Consubstantial Trinity* (περὶ ἁγίας τε καὶ ὁμοουσίου τριάδος λόγοι ἑπτά, *De S. et consubst. Trin. dialogi VII*, PG 75:657–1124)—dialogues with his friend Hermias.

The chief anti-Nestorian works are three books addressed to the emperor Theodosius II, to his younger sisters, Arkadia and Marina, to his elder sister, Pulcheria, and wife,

Eudokia—*Defences of the True Faith* (λόγοι προσφωνητικοὶ περὶ τῆς ὀρθῆς πίστεως, *De recta fide*, PG 76:1133–1200, 1201–1336, 1336–1420). Then, *An Answer to the Blasphemies of Nestorius* (κατὰ τῶν Νεστορίου δυσφημιῶν πεντά βιβλος 'αντίρρησις, *Contra blasphemias Nestorii* l.v., PG 76:9–248). He wrote a *Defence of the Twelve Points*[78] to the Eastern Bishops (Ἀπολογητικὸς ὑπὲρ τῶν δώδεκα κεφαλάιων πρὸς τοὺς τῆς ἀνατολῆς ἐπισκόπους, *Apologeticus pro xii capitibus*, PG 76:315–86) and defended them again in his *Letter to Evoptios against the Answer of Theodoret*[79] to the Twelve Points (ἐπιστολὴ πρὸς Εὐόπτιον κ.τ.λ., *Ep. ad Evoptium*, PG 76:385–452) and in a little *Explanation of the Twelve Points* (ἐπίλυσις τῶν δώδεκα κεφαλάιων, *Expositio xii capit.*, PG 76:293–312). After the Council of Ephesus, Cyril wrote an *Apology to the Emperor Theodosius* (λόγος ἀπολογητικός, *Apologia ad Theod. Imp.*, PG 76:453–88), a treatise *On the Incarnation of the Word of God* (περὶ τῆς ἐνανθρωπήσεως τοῦ θεοῦ λόγου, *De incarnatione Verbi divini*, PG 75:1413–20), a work, *That Christ Is One* (ὅτι εἷς ὁ χριστός, *Quod Christus unus sit*, PG 75:1253–1362), a *Conversation against Nestorius* (διάλεξις πρὸς Νεστόριον, *Tract. adv. Nest.*, PG 76:249–56) and a book *Against Those Who Will Not Call the Holy Virgin Mother of God* (κατὰ τῶν μὴ βουλομένων ὁμολογεῖν θεοτόκον τὴν ἁγίαν παρθένον, *Adv. eos qui nolunt vocare s. virginem genitricem Dei*, PG 75:255–92). Lastly, there is an *Apology for the Holy Christian Religion against the Books of the Godless Julian* (ὑπὲρ τῆς τῶν χριστιανῶν

[78] That is, of the twelve Anathemas (see p. 178 above).
[79] Theodoret (386–458) was a disciple of Theodore of Mopsuestia. He became Bishop of Cyrus (κυρός), two days' journey from Antioch, and for a time defended Nestorius. At the Council of Chalcedon, he condemned both Nestorianism and Monophysism and died in communion with the Church. He was one of the most learned men of his time, and a very good and holy bishop. His best known work is a Church history in five books, a continuation of Eusebeios (from 323 to 428).

εὐαγοῦς θρησκείας πρὸς τὰ τοῦ ἐν ἀθέοις Ἰουλιανοῦ, *De scta religione christ. adv. atheum Julianum PG* 76:503–1064), an answer to Julian's three books *Against the Christians*.

EXEGETICAL WORKS. These take up the most place among Cyril's works. He wrote seventeen books *On the Worship and Adoration of God in Spirit and Truth* (περὶ τῆς ἐν πνεύματι καὶ ἀληθείᾳ προσκυνήσεως καὶ λατρείας, *De adoratione Dei in spiritu et veritate, PG* 68:133–1126), in which he explains that, although the letter of the old law is abolished, its spirit remains. Then there are the *Ornaments* (γλαφυρά, *Dicta elegantia, PG* 69:9–678) in thirteen books, a commentary on select texts of the *Pentateuch*, commentaries on *Isaiah* (*PG* 70:9–1450), the *Minor Prophets* (*PG* 71, 72:9–364) and fragments of commentaries on other books of the Old Testament (*PG* 69–70). We have a long commentary on *St John's Gospel* (*PG* 73–74:9–756), parts of that on *St Matthew* (*PG* 72:365–474) and *St Luke* (*PG* 72:475–950) and on *Rom. 1* and *2 Cor.* and *Hebr.* (*PG* 74:773–1006).

HOMILIES. Twenty-nine *Paschal letters* are preserved, sermons preached at the Council of Ephesus, of which the fourth (*PG* 77:991–96) on our Lady's title as *Theotókos* is the most famous, and others preached on various occasions. All are in *PG* 77.

LETTERS. Volume 77 (9–390) of Migne contains eighty-eight letters written by or to Saint Cyril. The three addressed to Nestorius (Nos. 2, 4 and 17) were solemnly approved by the Council of Chalcedon. The thirty-ninth (to John of Antioch), sometimes called the symbol of Ephesus, was approved in the same way.

CHAPTER SEVEN

SAINT JOHN DAMASCENE
(d. ca. 754)

John Damascene, surnamed Chrysorroas,[1] monk and priest near Jerusalem, is in most ways unlike any other Father of the Church. Unless we count Saint Bernard (d 1153) one, John is the last of the Fathers. In any case, he is the last Greek Father, coming long after the others, alone in a very different age. He spent all his life under the government of a Moslem khalifah. His work as a writer was rather to compile and arrange what the older Fathers had said than to add to it. He is the first of the long line of Christian Aristotelians, and one of the two greatest poets of the eastern Church.[2] He was (with Saint Theodore of Studion) the chief defender of images during the Iconoclast troubles, and he is, more than any other author, the theologian studied in

---

[1] Χρυσορρόας, *Gold-flowing*, is the old Greek name of the chief river of Damascus (in Arabic *Nahr barada*); see p. 195 below.

[2] The other poet is Romanos the Singer (ὁ μελῳδός), a deacon of Beirut (d. ca. 565). He wrote one thousand hymns, of which the Byzantine liturgical books have preserved about eighty. Krumbacher (*Gesch. der Byzantinischen Litteratur* [Munich, 1891], pp. 308–9) thinks that some day Romanos will perhaps be counted greatest of all Christian poets. His most famous hymn is one for Christmas, beginning: *Today the Virgin* (ἡ παρθένος σήμερον), which was sung very solemnly while the emperor sat at dinner on Christmas day. The Orthodox (and Melkites) keep the feast of St Romanos the Singer on Oct. 1, on which day the Menologion tells his life.

Orthodox colleges. His treatise *Of the Orthodox Faith* is the standard textbook in their schools still, as Saint Thomas Aquinas' *Summa theologica* is in ours. And he is to them the last court of appeal in theological questions. No Orthodox Christian would dare contradict Saint John Damascene, though occasionally they have to explain what he really meant—as when he writes of the procession of the Holy Spirit from the Father through the Son. We know too little of his life; but to us also he is a very interesting and sympathetic person whose life and times form a singularly picturesque chapter of eastern Church history.

1. The City of Syria

The real eternal city is Damascus, the head of Syria. Centuries before Rome was founded, it was great and flourishing, the greatest city of western Asia. When Solomon reigned at Jerusalem, Razon, his rival, ruled over a great kingdom at Damascus;[3] even then it was an ancient place, beside which Jerusalem was a city of yesterday. Far back in the days when the Chananæan was in the land, Abraham took with him "this Damascene Eliezer".[4] Josephus says Damascus was founded by Uz, the grandson of Shem.[5] Who can say how old it is? Far back as you can trace into the mists that hang over the first age of Syrian history, through them you always see this gleaming white city by the river, at the head of the caravan roads. Tens of centuries ago, Damascus was queen of Asia. Through all the changes since, whatever rulers may reign, whatever religion may be taught, nothing has displaced her. The Egyptian ruled here seventeen

[3] 1 Kings 11:23.
[4] Gen 15:2.
[5] *Ant. Jud.*, 1, 6, 4.

centuries before Christ, the Assyrian came and the Chaldee, the Persian, the Macedonian, the Roman and the Arab, and always Damascus was the head of Syria.

Today still it is the chief town between Constantinople and Cairo in one direction, between Rome and Bombay in the other. For whatever else may change, nothing can affect its superb position. What a great harbour is, at the point where all ships must pass, Damascus at the head of the great roads of western Asia. Still, as for untold centuries, it is from Damascus that the long lines of caravans start. One great route goes across the Syrian desert to Baghdad, another, the Pilgrims' Way, due south through Palestine to Mecca; northward the roads lead to Hama, Aleppo and across Asia Minor to Stambul, north-east to Mosul and on to the Caspian Sea; to the west across the Anti-Lebanon in one day[6] you may reach Beirut and take ship for any part of the world.

At the edge of the great desert, Damascus stands like a heavenly city. Water is the one thing needful in these parts, and Damascus has water in abundance. It is the water and its position that explain how this city must always be the chief place of western Asia. From the Anti-Lebanon, streams flow down to the gardens of Damascus; there is the *Nahr barada* (Cold River), the old Golden Stream (Chrysorroas) of the Greeks, and countless other waters that flow round and through the city in a silver network. One can understand Naaman's indignant question: "Are not Abana and Pharphar, rivers of Damascus, better than all the waters of Israel?" [7] For seven miles, these rivers flow through gardens and orchards around the city. Looking down from the Salihiye height you may see the bright green of the apricot groves (rarest sight in

[6] In nine hours by the railway now [in 1908—ED.].
[7] 2 Kings 5:12.

Syria), a broad girdle around the city whose domes and minarets stand up white and palest gold or flushed with the faint-
est red, all iridescent with subtle suggestion of many colours
in its gleaming whiteness, like a pearl set in emeralds. To come
back to Damascus from the hideous rocks of the Hauran is
like going up to the gates of heaven after hell. After the parched
sand and burning rocks, you walk among green rushes under
showers of apricot blossom and hear the water trickling
beneath the cool damp banks; and all through the shady bazaars
where you look up and see the minarets, pencils of dazzling
white against the blue, you hear the fountains plashing in the
courts of the houses. No wonder that the Bedouin from their
sultry tents look across to the green patch on the horizon and
tell you that there certainly is the most beautiful place on earth;
no wonder that every Arab poet sings of the glories of the
City of Syria; and no wonder that Mohammed the Prophet
when he looked over Damascus said he dared not go down
into it, since a man only once may enter heaven.

Naturally everyone who set out to conquer Syria thought
first of taking the City of Syria.[8] Since the khalifahs reigned
there splendidly in the first and best age of Islam (A.H. 41–137;
A.D. 661–753) people have almost forgotten that Damascus
was for centuries a great Christian town. It was on the way
to Damascus that Saint Paul was converted, and in a house
in the street that is still called Straight at Damascus that he
was baptized.[9] From the time the empire became Christian

---

[8] *Madīnat ash-Shām* (or *Shām* alone) is the name that in Arabic has almost
displaced the old Dimishk (Demeshek). Damascus is called *Shām* (Syria), just
as Cairo is *Misr* (Egypt). To distinguish the city from the land you must say
Madīnat ash-Shām (city of Syria) and *Bilād ash-Shām* (land of Syria).

[9] Acts 9:1–19. The *Sūk at-Tawīle* from the *Bāb Sharkī* (Eastern Gate) by
the Melkite patriarchal church, right through the town (east–west) is still
called *Darb al-Mustakīm* (Straight Street). Carpets and silk are sold here.

to the Arab conquest of Syria, Damascus rivalled with Antioch as the chief town of Christian Syria. It had a great and splendid church, that of Saint John, in which was kept the Baptist's head.[10] This church, built on the site of a heathen temple, is one of the famous basilicas of Justinian (527–565). The Bishop of Damascus took the second place after his patriarch (of Antioch), and the city was an important frontier-fortress of the empire over against the desert. After the battle of Yarmuk (634) at which the Romans lost Syria, 'Omar, the second khalifah (A.H. 11–23; A.D. 632–644) sent Abu-'Ubaida to take Damascus. Since then it has been under Moslem rule. The Crusaders never succeeded in taking it, though in 1126 they came up to its walls.

It was from the time Mu'awiya, the first Ommeyade (A.H. 41–60; A.D. 661–680) set up his capital here till his race was dethroned (A.H. 132; A.D. 750)[11] that Damascus reached its greatest prosperity as centre of the Moslem world. The Ommeyade khalifahs spent enormous sums on adorning the city and building mosques. They were neither unjust nor harsh to their Christian subjects. At first, they allowed them to keep half of the great church, while the other half was made a mosque;[12] and the Christians had fifteen other churches. Although Syria was then full

[10] Now the mosque of the Ommeyades (Jāmi' al-'Umawī). The saint's head is still kept here with great honour, and Damascenes swear by "the head of Yahya", which is what they call St John Baptist.

[11] In 750 Marwan, the last Ommeyade in Syria, was defeated and killed by Abu'l-Abbās, called as-Saffāh, who founded the Abbasside line. As-Saff[-]Jah's brother, Abu-Ja'far, called Al-Mansur, removed his capital to Baghdad in A.H. 150; A.D. 753.

[12] Walid (A.H. 86–96; A.D. 705–715) took away their share from the Christians. Since his time, the whole church has been a mosque.

of Monophysites,[13] the inhabitants of the great cities, who were Greek by blood and spoke Greek, were mostly Orthodox.[14] And we find that the tolerance of these khalifahs, though it did not go as far as putting unbelievers on an equal footing with Moslems, allowed both Christians and Jews to fill important places and often to amass great fortunes. The Rayahs had to pay their poll-tax and to submit to all the other humiliating conditions appointed by Moslem law, of course. But the Commander of the Faithful was glad to make use of their superior skill in most arts, and since his religion taught him perfectly correct principles of justice,[15] if he was an honest and decent person (as many of these Ommeyades certainly were), he paid his servants liberally and allowed them to profit by their service. Jews had a great reputation for medicine, so the khalifah's doctor was nearly always a Jew, and Christians were employed as architects,[16] scribes and administrators. The life of our saint will show us the curious sight of a Christian Father of the Church protected from a Christian emperor and able to attack that emperor's heresy without fear, because he lived under a Moslem khalifah.

2. Before Iconoclasm (ca. 680–726)

At the end of the seventh Christian century, during the years 65–86 of the *hijrah* (A.D. 684–705) Abdul-Malik, son

[13] Since the Council of Chalcedon (451), Monophysism had become a national cause with western Syrians, as was Nestorianism in the eastern part. The real national church of native Syrians is the Jacobite sect.

[14] And, of course, Catholic till the schism of the ninth and eleventh centuries.

[15] It is only fair to remember that the Rayahs were enormously better off than Jews or heretics under mediæval Christian kings....

[16] A great number of "Saracen" buildings in Syria, Egypt and Spain were, as a matter of fact, built by Christian Rayahs.

of Marwan, the fifth prince of the house of 'Ummeyah, reigned at Damascus. He cleared Syria of his domestic enemies, the avengers of Hussain,[17] who still rebelled against the Ommeyades, made himself master of Arabia, Irak, Chaldea and all Northern Africa. At his court was a Christian named John "who kept the flower of piety and the fragrance of Christian knowledge in the midst of thorns".[18] This John is the father of our saint. He held an important place under the Moslem government, being the chief officer in the revenue department. This place seems to have been hereditary in the family. They were all good Christians; "God blessed them as he had blessed Daniel among the Assyrians [he means Chaldeans] because of his piety and Joseph among the Egyptians, although they were captives in a strange and hostile land." [19] The Arabs gave John an Arabic name, *Al-Mansur,*[20] which seems to have become a kind of family surname, since our saint, the son, is commonly called John Mansur too. The father then was an excellent man who spent all his money on redeeming Christian captives and other works of charity. He was very rich and had property all over Judea and Palestine.[21] He was, of course, a Greek by blood, or, at any rate, his family had long been completely Hellenized. Saint John wrote always in Greek.

---

[17] Hussain, the younger son of 'Ali Ibn Abu Tālib and grandson of the Prophet, was barbarously killed (680) at Kerbela, twenty-five miles northwest of Kūfa in Mesopotamia, by command of Yazid I (A.H. 40–64; A.D. 661–683), the second khalifah of the Ommeyade line. The story is well-known from Gibbon, *Decline and Fall*, chap. 1.

[18] Johannis Hieros, *Vita S.P.N. Joh. Damasc.* v (ed. Michael Lequien [Paris, 1712], p. 3). This is the work from which we know the story of St John Damascene. I quote from it throughout.

[19] *Vita Joh.* v (Lequien, p. 4).

[20] Meaning: *He who is helped, Adiutus.*

[21] *Vita Joh.* v (Lequien, p. 4).

The saint was born at Damascus toward the end of the seventh century. We do not know the date of his birth and can only conjecture that it was probably between 680 and 690. He was baptized as a baby[22] and was carefully educated in all suitable knowledge. His biographer gives an amusing description of what he did *not* learn: "His father then took care to teach him, not how to ride horses, not how to wield a spear, not to shoot arrows, not to hunt wild beasts and change his natural mildness into beastly cruelty, as happens to many who commonly lose their tempers (in hunting) and rush about in a furious rage. John, his father, a second Chiron, did not teach him all this, but he sought a tutor learned in all science, skilful in every form of knowledge, who would produce good words from his heart; and he handed over his son to him, to be nourished with this kind of food."[23] Then he was able to procure another teacher for the boy. The Arabs carried on plundering excursions along all the Mediterranean coasts and always came back with a number of prisoners, whom they made slaves. From one of these raids on the coast of Sicily, they brought back a monk named Cosmas.[24] This monk was "beautiful in appearance and more beautiful in his soul".[25] When the Arabs were about to murder some of the captives who were no good as slaves, these martyrs threw themselves at the feet of Cosmas and asked his blessing. The Arabs, seeing this, thought he must be a great prince in his own country and asked him what his rank is. Cosmas answered: "I have no worldly dignity, but only that of a

---

[22] The practice of putting off baptism, of which we have seen many examples, had altogether come to an end by now.

[23] *Vita Joh.* vii (Lequien, p. 5).

[24] He was a Greek, of course. Sicily was still part of Greater Greece.

[25] *Vita Joh.* viii (Lequien, p. 5).

priest.[26] Otherwise I am only a useless monk who has studied philosophy, not only our philosophy which consists in the love of God, but also that which makes men in the world wise." Having said this, his eyes were filled with tears,[27] a natural result under the circumstances.

The author of the life (*Vita Joh.*) tells us great things of Cosmas' learning. He knew grammar and logic, as much arithmetic as Pythagoras and as much geometry as Euclid; and he had studied music and poetry and astronomy. "Such was Cosmas, but I leave others to praise him. My intention here is to tell the fame of John." [28] The father of our saint bought Cosmas for a great price from the government, and from that time the learned monk became his son's tutor and master. They studied all these sciences diligently, but especially theology, with such good result as Saint John's later fame as a theologian shows. While he was learning from the Sicilian monk in his father's house, his studies were shared by a friend who seems to have been an adopted son of the older John and an adopted brother of our saint. This friend was also named Cosmas. He eventually accompanied Saint John to the monastery in which they both became monks and became a saint and a poet—Saint Cosmas the Singer[29]—only less famous than Saint John Damascene.

In spite of his theological training, John did not at first propose for himself any other career than that of his father. This place as minister of the revenue department seems to

[26] The old idea that a monk could not be a priest had disappeared by now, and a certain number of monks were regularly ordained to give sacraments to the others. These are the ἱερομόναχοι, that still form a special class in eastern monasteries.

[27] *Vita Joh.* viii (Lequien, p. 5).

[28] *Vita Joh.* xi (Lequien, pp. 7, 8).

[29] Κοσμᾶς ὁ μελῳδός.

have been hereditary in the family; so when the father died the son took his place and served for a time under the khalifah. In 705 Walid I (A.H. 86–96; A.D. 705–715) succeeded his father, Abdul-Malik. He was the best of the Ommeyade sovereigns, humane, charitable, just and a splendid patron of letters and arts. He built hospitals, schools and granaries; he enlarged and beautified the great mosque at Damascus,[30] the Dome of the Rock[31] at Jerusalem, and the mosque over the Prophet's tomb at Medina. Since he was tolerant and just, there was no special difficulty for a Christian in serving his government, and John already during this first part of his life practised in a Moslem court all the Christian virtues. His biographer tells of his goodness in general and specially praises his humility. Although he was so learned, he was not puffed up, "but just as the branches of a noble tree, when they are laden with precious fruit, bend down toward the ground, so he, bearing a great weight of learning and scholarship, bowed down in meekness."[32] The comparison is a pretty one and suggests the branches heavy with golden apricots that shade the walls of Damascus. It seems that Saint John lived at the capital and filled his post in the government till about the year 730. Then he went to be a monk.[33] But already, before he left the world, he had begun the great work of his life, the refutation of Iconoclasm.

[30] This is the old church of St John, from which he finally expelled the Christians.

[31] *Qubbat as-Sachrah*, the beautiful mosque that stands in the middle of the place of the old temple. Although it is commonly called the mosque of 'Omar, it was built by Abdul-Malik, Walid's father.

[32] *Vita Joh.* xii (Lequien, p. 8).

[33] The khalifahs under whom he served after Walid's death are Sulaimān (715–717), 'Omar II, the Pious (*as-Salah*, 717–720), Yazid II (720–724), Hisham (724–743).

3. The Iconoclasts (726–842)

The Iconoclast heresy was the last of the series of storms that swept over the eastern Church after Arianism. It lasted altogether 116 years, from 726 to 842. Almost immediately after it came the schism of Photius (857) that cut her away from the rest of the Christian world.

Iconoclast means an *image-breaker*.[34] The issue was this. Since the days when they had hidden in catacombs, Christians had painted pictures of their mysteries, of our Lord and of his saints. Everyone who has seen a catacomb has been shown the rude wall-paintings of scenes in our Lord's life, allegorical representations of the holy Eucharist, pictures of the good Shepherd, of the holy Mother with her Child, of the apostles. As soon as the Church was free and more prosperous, naturally these representations became more artistic, richer, more elaborate. It was a difference of taste rather than of principle that led to the greater use of carving and of solid statues in the west, and of flat paintings, mosaics and bas-reliefs in the east. There is no theological difference between a solid representation and a flat one; moreover, the divergence is only a very general one. There were plenty of statues in the east before the Iconoclast troubles.

The Lateran museum contains what is, perhaps, the most beautiful Christian statue ever made, a Good Shepherd of the fourth century.[35] The well-known bronze Saint Peter in his basilica at Rome is of the fifth century. Obviously,

---

[34] εἰκονοκλαστής.

[35] This statue has been often photographed. A print of it may be seen on p. 227 of F. X. Kraus, *Gesch. der christl. Kunst I* (Freiburg: Herder, 1896), and it forms the frontispiece to S. Beissel, S.J., *Altchristl. Kunst u. Liturgic in Italian* (Herder, 1899).

the sign of the cross was from the beginning the Christian standard, long before Constantine put it on his banner.[36] There are numbers of crosses in the catacombs.[37] It was a natural development to add to the cross a figure of our Lord. The mock-crucifix on the Palatine shows that the crucifix was known before Constantine.[38] The first certain evidence we have of a representation of our Lord's death does not occur till some time later. In the time of Justinian (527–565), there was a picture of the crucifixion in a church at Gaza in south Palestine, and Anastasios Sinaitikos (ca. 550) painted one in a book. Venantius Fortunatus (d. 603) saw an embroidered crucifix at Tours and Gregory of Tours (ca. 593) refers to a statue of the crucifix at Narbonne.[39] It is probably merely by chance that we do not find a plain reference to it earlier, though possibly before Constantine the shameful nature of death by crucifixion may have made Christians shy of putting such pictures in public, where pagans could see them. For the same reason, apparently, our Lord was long represented as alive on the cross, not dead, generally fully robed and without any appearance of pain. People insisted more on the triumph of the cross, the idea expressed by the line, *Regnavit a ligno Deus*, than on the pathetic and tragic side of Christ's death. In eastern

[36] Constantine's cross was formed by the monogram of Christ: XP.

[37] See Kraus, *Gesch. der christl. Kunst I*, pp. 130–33.

[38] The mock-crucifix is a caricature of a man worshipping a crucified figure with an ass's head, and the inscription, in Greek: *Alexamenos worships God*. It was scratched by a pagan soldier on the wall in mockery of a Christian comrade. Its date is the beginning of the third century. At one time it was disputed whether the thing was meant for Christianity at all: I believe that practically everyone now admits that it was. See Garrucci, *Il crocifisso graffito* (Rome, 1857), Kraus, *Gesch. der christl. Kunst I*, pp. 172ff., and his *Das Spottcrucifix vom Palatin* (Freiburg im Breisgau, 1872).

[39] Kraus, *Gesch. der christl., Kunst I*, p. 173.

Christendom, a much more popular picture was that of our Lord enthroned in glory, surrounded by his court of saints and accompanied by very beautiful and subtle mystic symbols. So in east and west for centuries, pictures and representations of holy things had formed a normal and prominent part of Christian life.

Naturally these pictures and statues were treated with respect. A sign inevitably shares in the honour of its archetype. No one had ever thought that we adored these things. Every Christian knew the first Commandment quite well, and when we come to the first Christian centuries it is rather late to suppose that anyone really believed he could pray to a painting.[40] On the other hand, paintings and statues form as right and as natural a visible sign of things unseen as motions of our body, kneeling, standing, lifting up hands are of invisible attitudes of mind. And to insult them is to insult the persons they represent, to honour the real thing involves a delegate honour paid to its picture. It was a waste of time in the eighth century, as it would be now, to explain to Catholics that their statues are really only wood or stone, and that they can neither see nor hear nor help us.

However, at this time, suddenly a storm of persecution burst against holy pictures and all who used them; and a succession of emperors suddenly discovered that all such pictures were idolatrous and that the Church must go back to a purer faith and keep the first Commandment. The

---

[40] The pagans did not adore their statues at that time either. It is only in a very low state of civilization that anyone can do so stupid a thing. To suppose that Julian and the Greek philosophers really thought that their statues could hear them is either a ludicrous error or a gross calumny. To them, too, statues were signs and types only. What was wrong with pagans was that their idols were signs of false gods. To honour a statue of your god is perfectly reasonable, but it must not be a statue of Apollo nor Athene.

question at issue then was not in itself an absolutely essential one. Pictures and statues are not essential. But it was naturally one that made more disturbance than would a greater, but less obvious, controversy. Simple people might spend their lives in peace and go to church regularly without ever understanding much about the mysteries of nature and person in Christ; but the poorest peasant understood what was happening when the government sent soldiers to tear down and break up the holy pictures. And all Catholics, not only the simple people but theologians, and philosophers, monks, bishops, patriarchs and popes, stood out to the end for the pictures, and martyrs shed their blood for them. They could not let a venerable and ancient practice go at the command of a secular tyrant, they could not admit that the whole Church had practised idolatry till now, nor even seem to acknowledge the heretical confusion and calumny that was the argument against the holy *icons*.[41] Iconoclasm was a heresy because it involved a heretical argument; and any point of Church discipline is worth dying for, if it is attacked by a government that claims the right to make laws for the Church.

The movement against the icons seems to have begun through Moslem influence. No Moslem will ever have a picture of any living thing; that is a fundamental point of his law.[42] The khalifahs Yazid I (680–683) and Yazid II

---

[41] *Eikon* (εἰκών) is Greek for an image. It is a convenient word, first because it became a kind of technical name used in Latin too (icon), and also because it covers both pictures and statues. [We will use the more familiar Latin spelling hereafter.—ED.]

[42] The Shiahs have modified this, and the Shah of Persia puts an image of his head on stamps [in 1908—ED.]. But any sort of picture of a man is still an abomination to the Sunni. In Turkey the Sultan's autograph takes the place of his portrait on coins or stamps; it is treason to have a picture of him. He is the only sovereign who has never been photographed, or, at least,

(720–724) made a crusade against pictures, considering them to be idols. It seems strange that Christians should have followed enemies of their faith in such a matter as this; but there were some who did so. A Nestorian bishop, Xenaias of Hierapolis (Ba'albek in Syria), took up the idea,[43] and gradually a party was formed of people who wanted to do away with all holy pictures. Their arguments were, first that such pictures are idolatrous and forbidden by the first Commandment, and secondly that they scandalize and frighten away Jews and Moslems from Christianity. Then the government took up the cause of these people, and the Iconoclast persecutions began.

"At that time Leo the Isaurian ruled the Roman empire, who raged like a furious lion against the venerable icons and against the orthodox congregation of the Church."[44] Leo III, the Isaurian[45] (717–741), who is remembered in Church history as the Iconoclast persecutor, was, in spite of that, a very valiant and heroic prince. In his reign for the first time the Moslems came to the gates of Constantinople (717), and Leo drove them back and then carried on a victorious war against the enemies of Christendom, till he utterly routed them at Akroinos in 740. But he was tyrannical to his own subjects. In 722, he wanted to force all Jews in the

---

whose photograph no one has ever seen. This hatred of pictures has produced one good effect among Moslems. Since they have strong natural artistic feeling they express it in the only way they may, by writing texts. Most mosques are adorned with superbly beautiful inscriptions, and the artist in Islam is the scribe. So they have always taken that art very seriously and have kept a tradition of beauty in writing that no one else has. The Arab is the only man who can write really beautifully.

[43] Hardouin, *Concil. Coll.* iv, 306.

[44] *Vita Joh.* xiv (Lequien, p. 9).

[45] Isauria, his birthplace, is in the south of Asia Minor.

empire to be baptized, and he cruelly persecuted the remnant of the old Montanist heresy. It is said that the khalifah 'Omar II (717–720) tried to convert him to Islam. He succeeded only up to the point of persuading Leo to abhor icons. In 726, the emperor made his first proclamation, forbidding anyone to keep or honour an icon and ordering those in all churches to be destroyed. Outside his palace was a famous miraculous picture of Christ called the "Answering Christ" (Χριστὸς ἀντιφωνητής). This was removed in spite of the open indignation of the people. Germanos I, Patriarch of Constantinople (715–730), steadfastly withstood the tyrant and defended the icons. He was made to resign and died soon after. Then the emperor wrote to Pope Gregory II (715–731), telling him to destroy all his images; otherwise, said Leo, "I will send an army to break your idols and to take you prisoner." Gregory answered sternly, reproaching the emperor for his new law and expressing his astonishment that the ruler of the Roman world does not yet know the difference between a statue and an idol. In 730, a new edict against icons appeared and new laws were made against "image-worshippers".[46] Gregory III (731–741) excommunicated the emperor in 732.

Constantine V (Kopronymos, 741–775), who succeeded his father Leo, carried on the war. The monks were specially devoted to the holy icons, so they were most perse-

---

[46] *Worship*, of course, here did not mean the adoration paid to God, nor even necessarily the honour paid to saints. It was a general word for reverence of any kind ("with my body I thee worship", in the marriage-service; magistrates and such people are "worshipful"). As long as its broader meaning was understood *worship* was an accurate rendering of προσκύησις, and *image-worshipper* is the natural opposite of *image-breaker*. [However, since *worship* now is more commonly used for adoration toward God, it should be understood that what was meant was honor given to something sacred.—ED.]

cuted. Their monasteries were burnt down, and numbers of them were martyred. John of Monagria and Abbot Stephen are the most famous of these martyrs. In 754, Constantine summoned a pretended œcumenical synod at Constantinople that forbade the use of images. The patriarchs of Rome, Alexandria, Antioch, and Jerusalem refused to send legates to it. The great church of the blessed Virgin at Constantinople was stripped of its icons and painted in a new style, which people said made it look like a bird-cage and a fruit shop. Pope Stephen III (768–772) held a synod at the Lateran in 769 and excommunicated the image-breakers. Under the emperor Leo IV (775–780) the persecution was less sharp; when he died his wife Irene, who became regent for her son Constantine VI (Porphyrogennetos, 780–797), arranged with the patriarch Tarasios of Constantinople (784–806) for the restoration of the icons.

In 787, the second Council of Nicæa (the seventh general Council) met. Pope Adrian I (772–795) and the other patriarchs sent their legates.[47] About three hundred bishops were present. They declared accurately the difference between the honour paid to images (προσκύνησις) and adoration (λατρεία), commanded all icons to be restored and honoured, and they drew up twenty-two canons in defence of them, as well as to arrange other points of discipline.[48] The last session was held at Constantinople in the presence of the empress and her son with great pomp; it seemed as if the whole trouble had passed over. It broke out again later,

---

[47] The Pope sent an Archpriest Peter and an Abbot Peter of St Sabas' monastery at Rome; Politianos of Alexandria, Theodoretos of Antioch and Elias of Jerusalem were represented by monks.

[48] The Acts of Nicæa II in Mansi, xiii, 442–58. See also Hefele, *Conziliengeschichte*, 2nd ed., III, 460ff.

however, under the emperor Leo V (the Armenian, 813–820), who renewed the old laws against the icons. Saint Theodore, Abbot of the Studion monastery at Constantinople (d. 826), was a great defender of the Catholic practice at this time. Michael II (the Stammerer, 820–829) recalled the banished image-worshippers and wanted to make peace. But his son Theophilos (829–842) began the persecution again and ordered fearful punishments against everyone who painted an icon.

At last the final peace was restored to the Church after the death of Theophilos by his widow Theodora, regent during the minority of her son Michael III (the Drunkard, 842–867).[49] This lady annulled all the Iconoclast laws and declared her acceptance of the second Council of Nicæa. On February 19, 842, the holy icons were brought back in solemn procession through the streets of Constantinople and set up again in the Hagia Sophia, the great church of the Holy Wisdom. It was the first Sunday of Lent. The Byzantine Church still remembers that final triumph and peace after the long storm; every year on the first Sunday of Lent she keeps the *feast of Orthodoxy* on which the icons are carried in procession round the churches and a hymn (ascribed to Saint Theodore of Studion) in their honour is sung.[50]

---

[49] The end of the Iconoclast trouble brings us to the eve of the great schism. It was this Michael III, the Drunkard, who intruded Photius at Constantinople in 857.

[50] κυριακὴ τῆς ὀρθοδοξίας, ἤγουν ἀναστηλώσεως τῶν ἁγίων εἰκόνων. *The Sunday of Orthodoxy, that is, of the restitution of the holy icons.* Both Orthodox and Melkites keep this feast. Because of the name *Orthodoxy*, which originally referred only to this question (against Iconoclasm), they have gradually made the feast apply to true belief in general, and on it they read a long *Synodikon* containing Anathemas against a most varied collection of heretics (in Russia they add curses against revolutionaries) and blessings on defenders of the faith, from Constantine and Helen to Photius and Cerularius. The

4. Revenue-Officer and Theologian (726–730)

Saint John did not live to see that feast of Orthodoxy, but from the beginning of the trouble till his death (ca. 754) he was the chief defender of the faith against the image-breakers. No one will dispute that he and Theodore of Studion were the leaders of the Catholics in their writings, and John was the greater of the two. So in this case again we have a Father of the Church whose great title to fame is his opposition to a contemporary heresy; the name of John Damascene is always bound up with the story of Iconoclasm. He did not suffer for the faith. All the time he was safe from the emperor's vengeance under the protection of the khalifah; but from this shelter he wrote the works that became at once what they are still, the classical apology for the use and worship of holy images. As soon as Leo the Isaurian published his first edict against the icons (726),

---

names of heretics are read out, and to each the choir answers "thrice accursed"; to the names of Orthodox heroes the answer is "thrice eternal memory". The latest development is that Sunday of Orthodoxy has become the great day for declaring their hatred of Latin heresies. This is very far from the original idea of keeping the memory of the triumph of the icons, which triumph was almost entirely the Pope's work against the Byzantine court. In Iconoclast days, as so often before, Rome never swerved, and all the image-worshippers looked to the Pope as their leader (Theodore of Studion especially), while the Patriarchs of Constantinople wavered backward and forward at the emperor's command. The Melkite *Synodikon* naturally only condemns people that Catholics consider heretics, and the list of heroes has been purified. The *Canon* (wrongly) ascribed to St Theodore is a very splendid poem. It begins: "Let us sing a hymn of thanksgiving to God the giver of all blessing, who has raised up to us a horn of salvation defending the orthodox faith." A version in English rhymes by Dr J. M. Neale is in his *Hymns of the Eastern Church*, no. 40, ed. Hatherly, J. T. Hayes (1882), p. 102–3. For Sunday of Orthodoxy and its *Synodikon*, see Nicolaus Nilles, *Kalendarium Manuale*, 2nd ed. (Innsbruck, 1896), pp. 103–18, and Prince Max of Saxony, *Prælectiones de Liturgiis orientalibus*, i (Freiburg: Herder, 1908), pp. 91–100.

Saint John answered it with his first treatise *Against the Destroyers of Holy Icons* (see p. 237 below); he was probably still at Damascus when he wrote the second treatise.

A story is told by his biographer that forms the fourth lesson of the [pre-Vatican II] Roman breviary on his feast. The emperor Leo is said to have tried to punish his opponent by guile, since he could not seize him himself. So he, Leo, forged a letter purporting to be addressed to himself by John, in which the saint tells him that Damascus is ill-defended and that the Romans can easily come and take it, and that the writer is willing to help this invasion by treachery. The emperor then sent this forgery to his enemy the khalifah, adding a note of his own, to the effect that he hates treachery and could not think of breaking the peace he had concluded with the Moslems; so he thinks it best to let his noble ally know how his revenue-officer is behaving. It was, indeed, as the *Vita Joh.* says, "a snake-like wile". The khalifah reads Leo's note and the enclosure, and is, of course, furious. He sends for John Mansur, will listen to no denial and has his right hand cut off as a punishment for such treason. One wonders why he did not have him put to death. So Saint John is crippled, and "the hand that was generally stained with ink as it wrote defences of the holy icons was now stained with blood." [51] John goes home and then sends a message to the khalifah imploring him not to leave his hand "hung up in the market-place", but to send it to its original owner. The khalifah sees no harm in this, the hand was not much use now, but John may keep it if he likes. The saint receives it and carries it into his private chapel, where he has a picture of the holy Theotókos, prostrates himself and says this prayer in hexametres: "Lady

---

[51] *Vita Joh.* xvii (Lequien, p. 11).

and purest mother, who didst give birth to my God, because of the holy icons my right hand is cut off. Thou knowest well the cause, that Leo the emperor rages; so help me at once and heal my hand by the power of the Most High, who became man from thee, who works many wonders by thy prayers. May he now heal this hand through thy intercession, and it shall in future always write poetry in thy honour, O Theotókos, and in honour of thy Son made man in thee and for the true faith. Be my advocate, for thou canst do anything, being Mother of God." [52] Such was the prayer and the poem that our Lady could not resist. At once his hand was joined again to the arm; he used it first to write a thanksgiving. And "all the barbarians admitted the miracle and were convinced of his innocence", though they do not seem to have been converted to John's religion. [53]

The next step in our saint's life was that he and his foster-brother Cosmas left the radiant city of Syria to be monks in a horrible wilderness near Jerusalem. The khalifah let them go, after a struggle, for he valued his revenue-officer. John gave all his goods to the poor and set out for the monastery of Saint Sabas.

5. Monk at Mar Saba (ca. 730–ca. 734)

Saint Sabas (*Mar Saba*) was then, as now, the chief monastery in Palestine. It had been founded by Saint Euthymios

---

[52] *Vita Joh.* xviii (Lequien, p. 12).

[53] The whole story in the *Vita Joh.* xv–xx (Lequien, pp. 10–13). Both the Latin religious houses at Damascus are on the sites of great events. The Franciscans near the *Bāb Tumā*, who were there first, show the place where St Paul was baptized in Ananias' house. The Jesuits across the road have the next best thing, St John Damascene's house, where this miracle happened. You may see a picture of it in their church; but they represent St John kneeling before a statue, whereas it was certainly a flat picture.

in the fifth century. His more famous disciple, Saint Sabas, a Cappadocian and a defender of the faith against the Mono-physites (d. 531) had left his name to the great laura. His tomb[54] and that of Saint John Damascene are still its chief treasures.

From Jerusalem, you cross the valley of the Cedron and take the road toward the Dead Sea. In about three hours, you will have left the green valley and will come out into the burning desert whose barren rocks slope down toward Jericho. And here you find one of the most wonderful sights of Palestine, Mar Saba. The monastery is not well seen from the road, only a great tower and a wall appear. One must go in at the gate, through the court past Saint Sabas' mirac-ulous palm-tree, down into the *wadi* and along the bed of the dried-up torrent. Here you pick your way among burn-ing rocks and climb up the other side. It is from here that, looking back, you may see the strange and wild beauty of Mar Saba.

Against a sky that is at once deep blue and yet glowing with hot light[55] every tint of white and yellow, from daz-zling dead white through pearl grey to warm brown, is piled up in a savage kind of order. Rocks, sand, white earth and cliffs are heaped together like a gigantic fortress. And climb-ing up the side of the *wadi* is the fortress-monastery. Its walls rise out of the rocks so naturally that you cannot see where they really begin, its terraces are hewn out of the

[54] Now empty. The Venetians stole his relics, as they stole St Mark from Alexandria.

[55] The sky is generally the most wonderful part of any Syrian landscape. In summer it is often almost indigo, deeper in tone than the shadows, so that everything stands out against a dark background; and yet those dark skies give one an impression of glowing heat that is even greater than that of the dazzling whites and yellows of the earth.

cliff and its towers mount buttressed in tiers up into the sky. Its balconies are bridged over frightful chasms, and its walls lie in winding curves up and down the ground like monstrous snakes. The whole makes the most incredibly picturesque group of buildings that one could conceive, all carved and fretted in dazzling white and shining gold as the heart of a superb and awe-inspiring scene. Two notes of green alone relieve the barren splendour, the miraculous palm-tree planted by Saint Sabas, whose dates have no stones, and the bright green copper dome of the church. It is now [1908] a place of punishment for refractory monks of the Orthodox Church. They feed doves and tame jackals in their courtyard and throw bread from the strong ramparts to the Bedouin who ride up and demand it with awful threats. All night the wolves howl and the jackals bark outside; and the wailing chant of the *kalogeroi*, the "good old men", comes from the beautiful church, where they stand under stern Byzantine frescoes and sing their hours. And when they do the honours of their laura they take you to make the great salam before the now empty tomb of our Father among the Saints, John Mansur, called Chrysorroas.

It was soon after the year 730 that John and Cosmas[56] came to this monastery. As monks they went on writing pious books, and especially hymns. But the community, true to the ideas that still rule every eastern monastery, did not approve of this at all. These newcomers, instead of fleeing the world and accepting the proper ideal of the angelic life— namely, to fast, pray, and do nothing else at all—were introducing disturbing elements into the monastery. To write

---

[56] Cosmas the Singer, John's foster-brother. The [pre-Vatican II] Roman breviary confuses him with Cosmas, the old Sicilian monk, who had been John's master (S. Joh. Dam. 27 martii, lect. iv).

books was bad, to sing hymns or compose verses was very much worse. Monks—it is the unchanging idea in the east—must not do anything at all. So there was great discontent. Things came to a climax when Saint John wrote a poem about death, though one would think that, at any rate, this subject would not seem too worldly. One of the monks died, and his brother, very much distressed at his loss, came to John, who was already a famous poet, and asked him to compose a canon that could be sung by the mourner to comfort his soul. John said he would do so and wrote the verses that are still famous:

> All human things are foolish,
> For death destroys them all.
> We keep no wealth nor glory
> That death shall not recall.
>
> So we in Christ confiding,
> Our one immortal King,
> Pray that he grant us mercy,
> Who takes from death its sting.
>
> And when the hour determined
> Shall bring us to the grave,
> May he in heaven receive us,
> Who died our souls to save.[57]

The Latin reader will not consider the composition of this hymn scandalous for a monk. He does not know the good old men. It is scandalous to do anything at all in a Byzan-

---

[57] This is the hymn: Πάντα ματαιότης τὰ ἀνθρώπινα, composed by St John on this occasion. It does not, I believe, occur in any part of the Byzantine liturgical office, but it is still a well-known hymn among Greeks. The Greek text is printed by Lequien (p. 16) in a note to the *Vita Joh.* xxvii.

tine laura. John, having written his hymn, proceeded to compose a tune for it, and he sang it "with a sweet sound" [58] in his cell. An old monk who was passing heard him and was perfectly furious. "Is this the way you forget your vows," he said, "and instead of mourning and weeping, you sit in joy and give yourself delight by singing?" [59] This old monk was John's "master", that is, the person whose cell he shared and from whose teaching and example he was to learn the angelic life.[60] The master then, having reproached him, turned him out of the cell and refused to allow him back. After some days, he relented and said he would forgive all, on condition that John went round the whole laura and cleared up all the filth with his own hands. Of course John did so at once, "and he did not hesitate to stain that very right hand that Christ had healed." [61] The end of the story is that the all-holy Lady appeared to this old monk and told him to let his disciple write books and poetry as much as he liked. So from this time the saint spent time in study and writing—an almost unique case in the long history of eastern monasticism. We hear of him being sent to Damascus to sell baskets, too; his biographer is duly impressed by the fact that he was not ashamed to do so in the very city in which he had once held so great a place.[62] His chief works, the *Logic*, the *Fount of Knowledge*, etc., and most of his poems were written at this time. Saint Cosmas, too, was writing his odes. And then a great change came for both of them.

[58] *Vita Joh.* xxviii (Lequien, p. 17).

[59] Ibid.

[60] This was the regular system. Each new arriver put himself under obedience to an old and experienced monk who became what we should call his novice master.

[61] *Vita Joh.* xxx (Lequien, p. 17).

[62] *Vita Joh.* xxvi (Lequien, p. 15).

6. Saint John Ordained Priest (ca. 734)

The Patriarch of Jerusalem, John V (d. 735), had heard of
the fame of these two friends, and he thought he would
like to have them among his clergy instead of at Mar Saba.
First he took Cosmas and ordained him Bishop of Maiumas, the port of Gaza in southern Palestine, on the road to
Egypt. We are told that Cosmas gave way and was ordained,
"not freely but by force".[63] However, once he was ordained,
he became a very good bishop, "ruled his flock admirably,
as is pleasing to God, and in a good old age went to rest
with his fathers, or rather went to God."[64] Saint Cosmas
the Singer apparently outlived his friend. The date of his
death is not known.

The same patriarch ordained John priest and brought him
to Jerusalem, that he might fill some place in that church.
But the saint did not stay long in the world; he went back
almost at once to his monastery, "this eagle flying away sought
his old nest."[65] The only difference in his position now
was that he had become a *hieromonachos*, a priest-monk. The
old idea that a monk could not be a priest[66] had quite died
out by now, and there were, as a matter of course, a certain
number of priest-monks in each laura who celebrated the
holy Liturgy and administered sacraments to the others. On
the other hand, our western principle that every choir-
monk should be a priest was unknown to this day in the

---

[63] *Vita Joh.* xxxiv (Lequien, p. 20). This fear of ordination is the com-
monest feature among holy men in the eastern Church at all times (see above,
pp. 89–90, 92–93, passim). It seems to be part of the normal programme that
they should resist and be compelled to be ordained.

[64] Ibid.

[65] *Vita Joh.* xxxv (Lequien, p. 21).

[66] See p. 53.

east.[67] Saint John as a hieromonachos thought that "priests must practise double humility and must do all their religious duties with double zeal."[68] He revised all his writings carefully, "and wherever they flourished with blossoms of rhetoric or seemed superfluous in style he prudently reduced them to a sterner gravity, lest they should have any vice of display or levity or want of dignity."[69] By this time his works in defence of the icons were known and read everywhere; the faithful Catholics in the empire found in them comfort and arguments against the image-breakers. So naturally the persecuting emperors hated John Mansur. Leo III's attempt to have him killed by the khalifah had failed; he never put himself in the power of the Roman government by crossing the frontier of the empire, so they could not really hurt him. However, they showed their hatred by cursing him copiously. It was an age of playful nicknames. Constantine V (741–775) was called *Kopronymos* because of an accident at his baptism,[70] and he shared the general taste. So he changed John's name from Mansur and called him *Manzeros*, which is a very bad attempt at the Hebrew for bastard.[71] It was a little far-fetched, perhaps, but (when explained) agreeably offensive.

---

[67] When a *kalogeros* tells you he is a monk, he is not a priest; if he were, he would describe himself as a *hieromonachos*. You should say πάτερ μου to a monk, αἰδεσιμώτατε πάτερ to a priest-monk, and σεβασμιώτατε πάτερ to the hegumenos. In Arabic (they speak both at Mar Saba), *abūna* will do for anyone.

[68] *Vita Joh.* xxxv (Lequien, p. 21).

[69] *Vita Joh.* xxxvi (Lequien, p. 22).

[70] Κοπρόνυμος, *Dirt-named*. When he was baptized as a baby, he had dirtied the font.

[71] *Mamzer*. One wonders how many Greeks would have even seen the joke.

7. Saint John's Philosophy and Theology

Our saint, the last of the Greek Fathers, had the mission of collecting and classifying what had been said by the others. He is the most systematic of all. His only original contribution to theology was his defence of holy images, and that defence is, perhaps, his chief title to fame. But it is not his only one. He was a poet of very rare merit, an ardent Aristotelian philosopher and a theologian who wrote of every question of theology that had been raised before his time. Since his works contain very complete courses of philosophy and dogmatics it is easy to understand his view on each point. In philosophy, he is entirely a disciple of Aristotle (d. B.C. 322). He wrote a treatise of logic (see p. 235 below), which in his time included a great deal of metaphysics and psychology. He has an unbounded respect for science and no sympathy with people who despise it in the name of faith and Christian simplicity. "Science is the light of the reasonable soul as ignorance is its darkness." "Nothing is better than knowledge." [72] "Philosophy is the science of beings, inasmuch as they are beings, that is, of their nature." [73] But since we live not only in our soul, but also in a body, we have no philosophy from ourselves, so we need a master. The master is infallible Truth, Christ himself, who is subsistent wisdom and truth, in whom are hidden all treasures of knowledge. [74]

Although John is peripatetic, he proposes to take what is good from all Greek philosophers, [75] and he "will say nothing of his own but only gather up what has already been

---

[72] *Dialectica* (the first part of his *Fount of Knowledge*) i (*PG* 94:529).
[73] *Dialectica* lxix (*PG* 94:669).
[74] *Dialectica* i (*PG* 94:529).
[75] Introd. to the *Fount* (*PG* 94:524).

said by approved teachers".[76] That is an exact account of his method in general. He distinguishes four kinds of logic— division (διαιρετική), definition (ὁριστική), analysis (ἀναλυτική) and demonstration (ἀποδεικτική).[77] In metaphysics, the root of his system is Aristotle's distinction of *actus* (ἐνέργεια) and *potentia* (δύναμις), with which Saint Thomas Aquinas has made us familiar. *Essence* (οὐσία) does not exist in itself but in a hypostasis (our *subiectum*).[78] *Nature* (φύσις) is the principle of movement and rest.[79] *Form* (μορφή, *forma substantialis*) gives to each being its specific nature, the being then is an *informed essence* (οὐσία μεμορφωμένη).[80] Essence, nature and ultimate actual species are the same thing.[81] Evil is nothing but the privation of Good.[82] Real being is either *substance* (σύστασις) or *accident* (συμβεβηκός).[83] He distinguishes these two exactly according to Aristotle.[84] *Hypostasis, person* (πρόσωπον) and *individual* (ἄτομον) are the same thing.[85]

In psychology, he distinguishes four internal faculties— *imagination* (φανταστικόν), *memory* (μνημονευτικόν), *reason* (διανοητικόν) and *will* (θέλημα). The reason generates a *word* (λόγος, our *verbum mentale*).[86] Like all Greeks, John Damascene insists very much on *free will*: man is free because he is reasonable; all actions that depend on us are free.[87] It is also

---

[76] *Dialectic* (PG 94:525).
[77] *Dialectic* lxviii (PG 94:672).
[78] *De fide orth.* iii, 6 (PG 94:1004).
[79] *Dialectic* xl (PG 94:605).
[80] *Dialectic* xli (PG 94:608).
[81] Ibid.
[82] *Contra manich.* xiii (PG 94:1517).
[83] *Dialectic* xxxix (PG 94:605).
[84] *Dialectic* xlvii (PG 94:621).
[85] *Dialectic* xliii (PG 94:613).
[86] *De fide orth.* ii, 17–20 (PG 94:933–40).
[87] *De fide orth.* ii, 26–27 (PG 94:957–60).

characteristic of his nation that John is little concerned about the mysteries of God's co-operation (in philosophy) and predestination (in theology). In all his philosophy, then, we see a faithful reflection of Aristotle, who has become through him the "master of them that know",[88] to Greeks and the Orthodox Church as much as he has to Latins and Catholics through Saint Thomas.

In Saint John's theology we find that he produces three of the five scholastic arguments for the existence of God, namely, those from motion, from the conservation of the world and from the order of nature.[89] The attributes of God, his unity, simplicity, perfection, immensity, etc., are demonstrated as in our schools.[90] God can be known, but not comprehended by us.[91]

The Arian and Pneumatomachian controversies had left a very clear consciousness of their faith in the Holy Trinity to Greeks as to Latins: "I believe in the Father, the Son and the Holy Spirit, one consubstantial Trinity and Unity in three Persons, one principle, having no principle, one will, one action, one power, one royalty, three hypostases (persons) having no difference except that one is unborn (ἀγέννητος), one born and one proceeding."[92] The Incarnation was the redemption of man from sin, especially from original sin.[93] Here, too, one sees that Saint John knew about the Pelagian heresy and definitely defended the faith against it. It is because his date is so late and because all the great controversies had already taken place that he is able to

---

[88] Dante, *Inferno* iv, 131.

[89] *De fide orth.* i, 3 (*PG* 94:796–97).

[90] *De fide orth.* i, 1–5 (*PG* 94:789–801).

[91] *De fide orth.* i, 1 (*PG* 94:789).

[92] *Libellus de recta sent.* i (*PG* 94:1421).

[93] *De fide orth.* iv, 13 (*PG* 94:1137).

write so clearly and systematically on each point. He argues at length against the Christological heresies. He defends the word *Theotókos* against Nestorians, the blessed Virgin is "truly Mother of God, because she gave birth to the true God made flesh from her";[94] he wrote a whole treatise against that heresy.[95] He also wrote a book against the Monophysites[96] and another against the Monotheletes.[97] It is, therefore, hardly necessary to insist on his orthodoxy on these points.

He has very little, hardly anything, to say about the Church, an omission that can only be an accident in the eighth century, but he writes at length on baptism,[98] speaks in passing of confirmation with chrism,[99] and has much to say about the holy Eucharist:[100] "the bread and the wine are not figures of the Body and Blood of Christ, God forbid, but the divine Body of the Lord, for he said: This is—not the figure of my Body but—my Body, and—not the figure of my Blood, but—my Blood."[101] And he teaches Transubstantiation: "We may say that just as bread and wine are changed by digestion into the body and blood of him who eats and drinks them, and they become, not a different body but his very body, so the bread, the wine and the water of the oblation by the invocation and power of the Holy Spirit are changed supernaturally into the Body and Blood of Christ; and they are not a different thing, but one and the same thing."[102] The honour we pay to

---

[94] *De fide orth*. iii, 12 (*PG* 94:1028–32).

[95] *Against the Heresy of the Nestorians* (see p. 237 below).

[96] *Letter to a Jacobite Bishop* (see p. 237 below).

[97] *Of the Two Wills in Christ* (see p. 237 below).

[98] *De fide orth*. iv, 9 (*PG* 94:1117–21).

[99] *De fide orth*. iv, 9 (*PG* 94:1125).

[100] *De fide orth*. iv, 13 (*PG* 94:1137–49).

[101] *De fide orth*. iv, 13 (*PG* 94:1148).

[102] *De fide orth*. iv, 13 (*PG* 94:1144).

saints is part of the theology of the holy icons of which
Saint John was the chief defender, so naturally he explains
and proves the rightness of this at great length,[103] as also
the use of relics.[104]

He is always very uncompromising in his resistance to the
interference of the secular government in affairs of the Church.
One of the worst features of the Iconoclast persecution was
that it was a shameless attempt of the emperors to dictate to
the Church. "The emperors have no power to make laws for
the Church. Listen to what the Apostle says: God placed
in the Church, first apostles, then prophets, thirdly shepherds
and teachers to make the Church perfect. He does not say
emperors. . . . We will obey you, O emperor, in the things of
this world, in paying taxes and duty-money, in accepting your
office and in those things in which our affairs are committed
to you; but for the things of the Church we have shepherds
who speak the word and give us ecclesiastical laws." [105]

Two points, lastly, that will interest Catholics are his attitude toward the Roman Primacy and about the Procession
of the Holy Spirit. Concerning the *Primacy*, he says practically nothing. The omission is less to be regretted since
he lived in an age when no one disputed that it was acknowledged by all the Orthodox in the east, and since he was a
leader of those image-worshippers who looked up to the
Pope with special reverence as their head and champion
against the Iconoclasts.[106] There is, however, one place in

[103] *De fide orth.* iv, 15 (*PG* 94:1164–65); *De Imaginibus, Oratio* iii, 33 (*PG* 94:1352–53).

[104] *De fide orth.* iv, 15 (*PG* 94:1165).

[105] See the whole passage, *De S. Imag.* ii, 12 (*PG* 94:1295–98).

[106] On the other hand, his fellow defender of the icons, St Theodore of
Studion, has the plainest things to say about the Pope's authority and primacy
(cf. *Orth. Eastern Church* [London: Catholic Truth Society, 1907], pp. 65–66)

which he speaks plainly of the Primacy of Saint Peter.[107]
About the *Procession of the Holy Spirit* he repeats what he
has learned from Saint Basil and other Greek Fathers, and
so sums up the attitude that was characteristic of the Byzantine Church before the schism, which the Council of
Florence (1439) accepted as correct and Catholic.[108] Namely,
God the Father is the *cause* (αἰτία) of the other Persons, and
the Holy Spirit proceeds *from* the Father, *through* the Son.[109]
Saint John Damascene explains many other points of philosophy and theology at length, giving for each the arguments he has learned from Aristotle and the Fathers. There
is not space to quote more here, but a glance at his works,
especially the *Fount of Knowledge* and quite especially its third
part, *On the Orthodox Faith*, will show that his people have
done well in taking them as the standard work of theology,
and that it is by a very right comparison that he is called
the Aquinas or the Peter Lombard of the eastern Church.

8. Saint John's Poetry

Our saint has a further title to fame as a poet. Both he and
his friend Saint Cosmas wrote a great quantity of poetry,
and that of John is certainly the better of the two. He uses
sometimes the old measure of quantity, as in his poems for
Christmas, the Epiphany and Whitsunday,[110] and sometimes the new rhythm of stress-accent. Nearly all his poems

---

and the Council of Nicæa in 787 that was the triumph of St John's side and
declared his orthodoxy (see below p. 231) also declared its belief that "The
see of Peter shines as holding the primacy over the whole world and stands
as head of all the Churches of God" (ibid., p. 81).

[107] *Sacra parall.* (but see below p. 238, about this work), iii (150).

[108] *Orth. Eastern Church*, pp. 379–80.

[109] Ἐκ πατρὸς μὲν δὶ υἱοῦ ἐκπορεύεται. *De fide orth.* i, 12 (*PG* 94:849).

[110] They are in iambic trimetres.

are hymns in honour of feasts of the Church or about points of the Christian faith. He wrote, besides poems strictly so called, a great number of canons, that is, pieces in rhythmical prose to be sung in the Byzantine office. The Orthodox ascribe the whole of the canons in their Oktoechos[111] to him.

Doctor J. M. Neale, in his *Hymns of the Eastern Church*,[112] has translated twelve odes, a sticheron, and an idiomelon of Saint John.[113] Doctor Neale is less happy as a translator of Greek than of Latin poems. The task in the case of Greek chants is also very considerably more difficult. In order to make them acceptable and fit for singing in English, he turned their prose into English metres with rhymes. His metres when compared with the originals seem, as a rule, undignified; and his versions are so free that in many cases he has practically written a new poem on the same subject. For people who wish to see his translations the book is easily accessible. I will give a more exact idea of one or two of Saint John's most famous odes by translating them into the same sort of rhythmical prose as the originals.

The most famous of all are those of his *Golden Canon* (for Easter day). During the holy night, between Easter eve

---

[111] The *Oktoechos* is the book that contains the offices for the Sundays from All Saints' Sunday (first after Pentecost) to the tenth before Easter, arranged according to the eight modes (ὀκτὼ ἤχοι).

[112] First edition, 1862, and often reprinted. I have the fourth edition with music by S. G. Hatherly (London: J. T. Hayes, 1882).

[113] A *canon* is divided into nine *odes* (of which the second is left out except on Tuesdays in Lent), the odes into *troparia*. A troparion (τροπάριον) is a short verse. The first is called *heirmos* (εἱρμός) because it fixes the mode and drags the others after it. A *sticheron* (στιχηρόν) is a longer poem modelled on a verse (στίχος) of a Psalm. An *idiomelon* (ἰδιόμελον) does not follow a heirmos, but has its own melody. All are composed in rhythmic prose.

and Easter day, the clergy of the Byzantine Church assemble with their people and wait with unlit candles for midnight. As soon as midnight strikes, the metropolitan or chief priest lifts up a cross and cries out: *Christ has risen* (Χριστὸς ἀνέστι), the cry is taken up by everyone, the candles are lit, and a sea of fire spreads over the crowd. Then Saint John Damascene's Paschal ode is sung, announcing the feast of feasts, as the three Alleluias on Holy Saturday do to us. It is the dramatic moment of the year in the Byzantine Church, the sudden glare of the candles, the shout of *Christos anesti*, and then the rolling chant of this glorious canon[114] make an impression as great as that of our Gloria and bells and organ at the first Easter Mass. The first ode is:

> The day of Resurrection,
> Let us make glorious the Pasch, the Pasch of the Lord.
> From death to life, from earth to heaven Christ our
>   God has led us,
> As we sing his victory.
>
> Let us cleanse our senses,
> And we shall see Christ radiant in the glorious light of
>   his Resurrection,
> And we shall hear him greet us clearly,
> As we sing his victory.

---

[114] The first Easter hymn at midnight is, however, not this canon (which is sung rather later) but the short verse, repeated continually throughout the feast:

> Christ has risen from the dead;
> By death he trampled on death
> And to those who are in the tomb
> He gives back life.

The heavens rejoice and the earth is glad,
All the world both seen and unseen keeps this feast,
For Christ who is our everlasting joy
Has come back to life.[115]

There follow then the other odes, from III to IX (no. II being left out). It would be too long to quote all. The ninth is:

Be enlightened, new Jerusalem, be enlightened, for the
glory of the Lord has risen in thee.
Sion, leap and rejoice,
And do thou exult, all holy Theotókos,
For thy Child has risen again.

Oh blessed, holy and most sweet promise,
That thou wilt be with us all days to the end,
These are thy words, Christ, who canst not deceive,
And we, trusting to them, with firm hope rejoice.

Oh, great and most sacred Pasch of Christ,
Do thou, Wisdom, Power and Word of God,
Grant that we may see thy presence in thy kingdom,
In that day that has no evening.[116]

---

[115] These irregular lines give, I think, very nearly the effect of the original. For instance, the first troparion is:

Ἀναστάσεως ἡμέρα,
λαμπρυνθῶμεν λαοὶ πασχα κυρίου, πάσχα,
ἐκ γὰρ θανάτου πρὸς ζωὴν καὶ ἐκ γῆς πρὸς οὐρανὸν Χριστὸς ὁ θεὸς ἡμᾶς
διεβίβασεν
ἐπινίκιον ᾄδοντας.

[116] The whole *Golden Canon* will be found among St John's works. In Lequien's edition (Venice, 1748), it comes in vol. I, pp. 685–86.

There is a beautiful canon for Lady-day, of which the first troparia end with the first line of the Benedicite, and the last with Saint Gabriel's greeting:

> Listen, maiden, purest Virgin, Gabriel tells of God's
>   high counsel,
> And thou art ready to receive thy Lord,
> Through thee the Almighty comes down to mortal
>   men,
> Wherefore I sing: Bless the Lord, all ye his works!

And further down (trop. VII):

> Living Ark that shelters God,
> No impure hand shall dare to touch thee,[117]
> But the lips of the servants of the Theotókos always
>   sing the Angel's words,
> Hail, full of grace, the Lord is with thee.

A number of these canons and poems are acrostics, so arranged that the initial letters of each line, if read downward, make a verse. Thus the poem for Christmas mentioned above (p. 225) begins:

> The Lord has saved his people; God's own Son,
> Who dried for them long years ago the sea.
> Born of a Virgin greater things has done
> Who coming down to earth has set us free.

---

[117] A reference, of course, to Uzzah, who touched the Ark of the Covenant and was struck dead (2 Kings [= 2 Sam in RSV], 6:6–7). Their canons are full of such allusions to the Old Testament, as types (many of them being very far-fetched).

And the first letters of the lines make this verse:

> With joyful sound this canon tells the birth
> Of Christ the Son of God, who came to bring
> Salvation to his people here on earth;
> And may he bless us while we gladly sing.

As a last specimen of Saint John's poetry, this is a long rhyme
in short anacreontic verse, expressing contrition, shame for
sin and hope of forgiveness:

> Christ, from a wicked tongue,
> From a heart that yet may dare
> With shame and sorrow wrung
> To turn to thee in prayer,
> Receive my humble cry,
> Nor turn away thy face,
> And when I mourn and sigh
> Refuse me not thy grace.
> My soul with sin is black,
> I have no right to plead,
> Yet, Saviour, take me back
> And pity my great need.
> For lowly, poor and meek,
> I come to thee in fear;
> Teach me then how to speak
> So that thou mayest hear.
> Let me thy mercy feel
> When I come to entreat
> Before thy throne to kneel
> And kiss thy sacred feet.[118]

[118] There are over one hundred lines altogether. In Lequien's edition, vol. 1,
pp. 691–93.

9. Saint John's Death (ca. 754)

There is nothing more to say of our saint's life. He spent the rest of it in his monastery, writing theology and poetry. Here at Mar Saba he died, sometime not long before the year 754, and here he was buried. His relics were taken to Constantinople in the fourteenth century; but the tomb, though now empty, that once held them is still the chief treasure of the laura. He had been the great defender of the holy icons, so it was natural that the icon-breakers should hate and revile his memory. The Iconoclast Synod of Constantinople in 754 (p. 209) curses him at great length. It remembers three defenders of the images specially, the Patriarch Germanos of Constantinople (p. 208), a certain George of Cyprus and John Mansur of Damascus; and it declares that "the Trinity destroyed these three." [119] Our saint receives a special series of curses: "To Mansur of evil name, Saracen at heart, [120] Anathema. To Mansur, the image-worshipper and writer of falsehoods, Anathema. To Mansur, who denied Christ and betrayed his sovereign, Anathema. To Mansur, the teacher of impious doctrine and the perverter of holy Scripture, Anathema." [121] It is equally natural that all image-worshippers should look upon John of Damascus as their great hero. The seventh general Council, [122] that restored the honour of the icons, was also concerned to restore his honour. The Fathers expressly repudiated the Anathemas of the Iconoclast synod, declaring in opposition that "the

[119] ἡ Τριὰς τοὺς τρεῖς καθεῖλεν (quoted by the second Synod of Nicæa, Act. 6; Mansi xiii, 356).

[120] This is preposterous. It was the Iconoclasts who got their ideas from the Saracens.

[121] Mansi, xiii, 356.

[122] Nicæa II, in 787; see above p. 209.

Trinity made these three glorious" [123] and proclaiming that "John, who has been called Mansur in scorn,[124] imitating Matthew the Evangelist, left all and followed Christ, counting the reproach of Christ as better than all the treasures of Arabia, choosing rather to suffer with the people of God than to enjoy worldly pleasure." [125]

And since the image-breakers disappeared, together with the triumph of his cause, the honour of his name has spread throughout Christendom. Theophanes[126] says that John is rightly surnamed *Chrysorroas*, after the chief river of his city, "because in his life and in his teaching goldgleaming spiritual graces shine".[127] This name, however, has not become the common one. It is rather as John Damascene (δαμασκηνός, *damascenus*) that he is known and honoured in east and west. We have seen how important his writings are in eastern theology. His own people keep his feast on December 4;[128] on that day they sing: "Let us, O faithful people, praise the venerable John, the hymnwriter, teacher and light of the Church, our defender against enemies; for lifting up the cross of Christ with this weapon he defeated all wiles of heresy, and now as a true intercessor with God he obtains forgiveness for all our sins." [129] Saint John is remembered in the Roman Martyrology on May 6:[130] "At Damascus the birth of blessed John

---

[123] ἡ Τριὰς τοὺς τρεῖς ἐδόξασεν (Mansi, xiii, p. 400).

[124] This is a mistake; it was an honourable name inherited from his father. Possibly the council has Constantine V's nickname in mind (above, p. 219).

[125] Mansi, xiii, p. 400.

[126] Theophanes, surnamed *the Confessor*, was a chronicler who died about 817 (Krumbacher, *Gesch. der Byzatinischen Litteratur* [1891], pp. 120–24).

[127] *Chronogr.* ad ann. 734.

[128] With St Barbara, the Megalomartyr.

[129] In the *Horologion* for Dec. 4, Kontakion to the fourth authentic tone.

[130] It is the feast of St John (the Evangelist) before the Latin Gate.

Damascene, famous for his piety and learning, who valiantly strove against Leo the Isaurian by word and writing for the worship [honor paid toward] (cultus) of holy images, who, when his right hand had been cut off by this man's order, praying for himself before the image of the blessed Virgin Mary which he had defended, straightway received it back cured and whole." [131]

Pope Leo XIII declared Saint John Damascene a Doctor of the Church and appointed March 27 as his feast [now it is December 4.—ED.]. The Gospel (in allusion to the story of the saint's right hand) is Luke 6:6–11, about the healing of the man whose hand was withered; and the collect is: "Almighty and eternal God, who didst give to blessed John heavenly knowledge and admirable strength of mind to defend the worship of holy images; grant by his prayers and example that we may copy the virtues and enjoy the protection of those whose pictures we honour."

10. Table of Dates

661 The Ommeyade khalifahs set up their throne at Damascus.

680–690(?) Saint John Damascene born. Cosmas the Monk from Sicily his teacher. Cosmas the Singer his foster-brother.

[By or before 715]: *John revenue-officer at Damascus.*

717–741 Leo III the Isaurian.

726 *Leo III's first edict against* icons. Saint John's first treatise against the Iconoclasts.

730 Leo's second edict. The story of John's right hand. *He and Cosmas the Singer go to Mar Saba.*

[131] *Martyr. Rom.* ad 6 Maii.

732 Leo III excommunicated by Pope Gregory III. Saint John ordained priest.

741–775 Constantine V, Kopronymos.

ca. 754 *Death of Saint John.*

754 Iconoclast synod at Constantinople.

769 Roman synod against Iconoclasm under Stephen III.

775–780 Leo IV emperor.

780–797 Constantine VI, Porphyrogennetos. Irene regent.

787 SEVENTH GENERAL COUNCIL (NICÆA II).

813–820 Leo V, the Armenian. Second Iconoclast persecution.

842–867 Michael III, the Drunkard. Theodora regent.

842 (Feb. 19) First Sunday of Lent, *Feast of Orthodoxy.*

11. Works

The first complete edition of Saint John Damascene was made by the learned Dominican, Michael Lequien,[132] in two folio volumes (Paris, 1712), with a parallel Latin version (reprinted at Venice, 1748). Migne reprints this in his *Patrologia Græca*, 94–96 (Paris, 1864), with a supplement containing additions since discovered, most of which are spurious or at least doubtful. H. Hurter, S.J., has published the *De fide orthodoxa* in his *SS Patrum opuscula selecta*, vol. XLI (Innsbruck, 1880) and seven sermons about the blessed Virgin in the same series, vol. XXXIV (pp. 4–156).

DOGMATIC WORKS. The great compendium of Saint John Damascene (the summa theologica, and philosophica too, of the Byzantine Church) is his *Fount of Knowledge* (πηγὴ γνώσεως, *Fons scientiæ*, PG 94:517–1228), dedicated to his

---

[132] Lequien is the author of the great *Oriens Christianus*, 3 vols. (Paris, 1740).

friend, Cosmas the Singer, Bishop of Maiumas. It has three parts. The first is entitled *Chapters of Philosophy* (κεφάλαια φιλοσοφικά, *Capita philosophica*), but is generally known as the *Logic* (διαλεκτική, *Dialectica*). This part contains, not only what we call logic, but a complete course of Aristotelian ontology as well. The second part is *A Compendium about Heresies* (περὶ αἱρέσεων ἐν συντονίᾳ, *De hæresibus compendium*), arranged under their names, giving in each case an account of their teaching. Most of this part is only a new edition of the *Panarion* (πανάριον, *Hæreses*) of Epiphanios (d. 403), but at the end, Saint John adds paragraphs about Moslems, Iconoclasts and other later heretics. The third part is the most important; it is his great work *On the Orthodox Faith* (ἔκδοσις ἀκριβὴς τῆς ὀρθοδόξου πίστεως, *Expositio accurata fidei orthodoxæ*, quoted always as *De fide orthodoxa*). This is the classical compendium of theology in Greek. The Latins have divided it into four books, in imitation of Peter Lombard's four books of sentences.[133]

The first book (nineteen chapters) treats of God; the second (thirty chapters) of creation, angels and demons, nature, man and Providence; the third (twenty-nine chapters) of the Incarnation and its consequences (against Nestorians, Monophysites, etc.); and the fourth (twenty-seven chapters) of various other questions in no very definite order, namely, of the glory of God the Son, of sacraments, saints, relics and images, of the canon of holy Scripture, of the problem of evil, of the last things. The *Fount of Knowledge* was written toward the end of Saint John's life. It is, as he declares (*Prolog.*), a gathering up of tradition on these subjects. Earlier and shorter dogmatic works are *A Treatise about*

---

[133] Peter Lombard (d. 1164) knew the *De fide orth.* in a Latin version made by Burgundio of Pisa (d. 1194); he used it as his model for the *Sententiæ*.

Right Opinion (λίβελλος περὶ ὀρθοῦ φρονήματος, *Libellus de recta sententia*, PG 94:1421–32), which is a short profession of faith, an *Elementary Introduction to Dogmas* (εἰσαγωγὴ δογμάτων στοιχειώδης, *Institutio elementaris ad dogmata*, PG 95:99–112) addressed to John, Bishop of Laodicea in Syria. It is another work on logic and metaphysics, covering the same ground as Part I of the *Fount of Knowledge*. Three more dogmatic works should be mentioned: *Of the Holy Trinity* (περὶ τῆς ἁγίας Τριάδος, *De S. Trinitate*, PG 95:9–18) in the form of a dialogue; a *Treatise on the Trisagion* (Περὶ τοῦ τρισαγίου ὕμνου, *De hymno Trisagio*, PG 95:21–62), in the form of a letter to an Archimandrite Jordanes, in which he declares that the trisagion is sung of the holy Trinity and not of the second Person only; wherefore the Jacobite addition about the crucifixion should not be made;[134] and lastly, there is a short treatise *On Confession* (περὶ ἐξομολογήσεως, *De confessione*, PG 95:283–304), of doubtful authenticity, written to defend the practice (that occurred intermittently in both east and west for a long time) of confessing one's sins to a holy man (generally a monk),[135] who was not a priest and therefore could not absolve.

---

[134] The *trisagion* is the verse: "Holy God, Holy Strong One, Holy Immortal One, have mercy on us." We sing it in Latin and Greek on Good Friday; it occurs often in the Byzantine rite. Peter the Dyer of Antioch, a Monophysite (470–488), had added to the form the words "who wast crucified for us". This addition was considered unsound, if not heretical, as implying that the Divinity itself was crucified. It was very much discussed during the Monophysite controversy and is still a speciality of the rite used by the Jacobite sect in Syria.

[135] In the west, confession to a deacon was a not uncommon practice at one time, especially in England. It is referred to in synods at York in 1195, London 1200, Rouen 1231 and Canterbury 1236. There does not seem to be any mistake as to the power of absolving. It was merely an act of humility and protest of contrition. The deacon then prayed for the penitent's forgive-

POLEMICAL WORKS. The most important of these are the three treatises *Against Those Who Destroy Holy Icons* (λόγοι ἀπολογητικὸι πρὸς τοὺς διαβάλλοντας τὰς ἁγίας εἰκόνας, *Orationes apologeticæ adv. eos qui sacras imagines abiiciunt*, PG 94:1231–1420, generally quoted as *Pro sacris Imaginibus*). The first was written in 726 before Saint John became a monk, the second about 730, the third a few years later. They are the classical apology for the use of images and for reverence paid to them, with a clear distinction between the adoration due only to God (λατρεία) and honor or reverence in the sense of *cultus* (προσκύνησις). Other polemical works are a *Dialogue against the Manichæans* (κατὰ μανιχαίων διάλογος, *Contra manichæos dialogus*, PG 94:1505–84), the *Argument of John the Orthodox against a Manichæan* (διάλεξις Ἰωάννου ὀρθοδόξου πρὸς Μανιχαῖον, *Disquisitio Joh. orthod. adv. Manichæum*, PG 96:1319–36); a *Disputation between a Saracen and a Christian* (διάλεξις σαρακηνοῦ καὶ χριστιανοῦ, *Disceptatio Saraceni et Christiani*, PG 94:1585–98, another text in PG 96:1335–48); two treatises *Against the Nestorians* (κατὰ τῆς αἱρέσεως τῶν νεστοριανῶν, *Adv. hær. Nest.*, PG 95:187–224, and περὶ συνθέτου φύσεως, *De natura composita*, PG 95:111–26); a *Letter to a Jacobite Bishop* (πρὸς τὸν ἐπίσκοπον δῆθεν Τουδαρίας τὸν Ἰακωβίτην, *Ad episcopum Tudariæ jacobitam*, PG 94:1435–1502); *Of the Two Wills in Christ* (περὶ τῶν ἐν τῷ Χριστῷ δύο θελημάτων, *De II voluntatibus Christi*, PG 95:127–86); and a curious fragment *On Dragons and Witches* (περὶ δρακόντων καὶ στρυγγῶν, *De draconibus et strygibus*, PG 94:1599–1604), which contains a great deal of information as to the habits of these little understood creatures.[136]

---

ness without any idea of conferring a sacrament (cf. J. N. Seidel, *Der Diakonat*, §32, *Bei der Bussdisciplin* [Regensburg, 1884], pp. 141–44).

[136] He says that dragons never turn into men, they have no poison and are not liable to be killed by lightning. Witches cannot go through closed doors

EXEGETICAL WORKS. Saint John wrote a *Commentary on St Paul's Epistles*, which is a compilation from Theodoret of Cyrus, Saint Cyril of Alexandria and especially Saint John Chrysostom (*PG* 95:441–1034).

ASCETIC WORKS. The *Sacred Parallels* (τὰ ἱερά παράλληλα, *Sacra parallela*, *PG* 95:1039; *PG* 96:442) is a long collection of texts and quotations from the Bible, the Fathers and even heathen philosophers, arranged to illustrate various points of faith and morals. The collection was made before the time of our saint; there are many editions of it, of which he made the one included among his works. He wrote treatises *On Fasting* (περὶ τῶν ἁγίων νηστειῶν, *De s. jeiuniis*, *PG* 95:63–78), *On the Eight Evil Spirits* (περὶ τῶν ὀκτὼ τῆς πονηρίας πνευμάτων, *De VIII spiritibus nequitiæ*, *PG* 95:79–86), and *On Virtues and Vices* (περὶ ἀρετῶν καὶ κακιῶν, *De virtutibus et vitiis*, *PG* 95:85–98).

HOMILIES. Thirteen sermons of John Damascene are preserved, of which three are about the *Falling Asleep of the Holy Theotókos* (εἰς τὴν κοίμησιν τῆς ἁγίας θεοτόκου, *De dormitione S. Dei genitricis*, *PG* 96:699–762), all preached on one day. There are others on her *Birth* (*PG* 96:661–98) and *Annunciation* (*PG* 96:643–62).

HYMNS AND CANONS. We have already seen specimens of these; they are collected in *PG* 96:817–56, 1363–1408. Some of them are of doubtful authenticity.

The *Life of Barlaam and Joasaph*, in which J. Robinson discovered the lost Apology of Aristides (in the second cen-

---

nor fly about in the air, nor do they eat babies. On the whole, both dragons and witches turn out to be much less harmful than one had thought.

tury), is included (in one version) among Saint John
Damascene's works (*PG* 96:859–1240). It was not composed by him, but by another monk of Mar Saba, also named
John. It is a novel about the conversion of an Indian prince,
named Joasaph, through the discourses of a hermit, Barlaam, that had a very great vogue in the middle ages, and it
is a most curious and valuable example of a legend that has
travelled all over the world. The original story was an Indian
legend about Buddha; it was altered and reedited to form a
Christian one.

CONCLUSION

This brings us to the end of the great Greek Fathers. The line that began in Greek Egypt with the mighty Athanasius and the thunder of the Arian storm led us for two centuries through Asia Minor, Constantinople and Palestine through the chain of heresies that rent the eastern Church. Now, after a break, we leave it at the close of the last of those heresies in Moslem Syria.

The age of the Fathers is over. The khalifah sits at Damascus; a new line of emperors will begin at once in the west; Photius is a promising cavalry officer with a grudge against Ignatius; the long ships of the Northmen have begun to be a terror to all the coasts of Europe; people are just discovering that what they speak is no longer Latin—we have reached the great turning point. The old world is dead and the middle ages have begun.

INDEX